W0037743

The Bible and Cultural Studies

Series Editors
Hal Taussig
Union Theological Seminary
New York, NY, USA

Maia Kotrosits
Religion Department
Denison University
Granville, OH, USA

The Bible and Cultural Studies series highlights the work of established and emerging scholars working at the intersection of the fields of biblical studies and cultural studies. It emphasizes the importance of the Bible in the building of cultural narratives—and thus the need to intervene in those narratives through interpretation—as well as the importance of situating biblical texts within originating cultural contexts. It approaches scripture not as a self-evident category, but as the product of a larger set of cultural processes, and offers scholarship that does not simply "use" or "borrow" from the field of cultural studies, but actively participates in its conversations.

More information about this series at
http://www.springer.com/series/14449

Deborah Niederer Saxon

The Care of the Self in Early Christian Texts

palgrave
macmillan

Deborah Niederer Saxon
Butler University
Indianapolis, IN, USA

The Bible and Cultural Studies
ISBN 978-3-319-87861-4   ISBN 978-3-319-64750-0   (eBook)
DOI 10.1007/978-3-319-64750-0

Cover illustration: "Strigilate sarcophagus with the deceased woman and two shepherds," 300–325 A.D., Pio Cristiano Museum

Printed on acid-free paper

This Palgrave Macmillan imprint is published by Springer Nature
The registered company is Springer International Publishing AG
The registered company address is: Gewerbestrasse 11, 6330 Cham, Switzerland

To my parents, Ray and Ann Niederer, who started me on the path through life and my husband, John, who continues to walk it with me.

Acknowledgements

First, I want to thank my parents, Ray and Ann Niederer for their unwavering support. It was their love of education and my dad's fascination with Christian history as well as my parents' openness to others that has inspired my own study and research. They taught me that each idea or person I encounter has something to offer that will enrich my own journey and have thus shaped my own desire to engage with ideas or people who are easily dismissed. I also offer my deepest gratitude to my husband, John, who shares my own sense of curiosity and enthusiasm for the care of the self/soul and has walked every step of the process of birthing this book with me as well as the journey of life itself. Not only has he provided unfailing moral support and encouragement especially when the task seemed overwhelming, he has engaged in countless conversations, reading every bit of this book several times over and serving as my first and best editor.

In addition, I deeply appreciate the members of my dissertation committee who helped me complete what served as the basis for this book. I am grateful for the support of Albert Hernández who helped me to understand the importance of historiography and cultural theory for my work, and I am likewise very thankful to Frank Seeburger who helped me understand the significance of Foucault for this topic specifically. Most especially, this book would not have come into being without the support of Ann Graham Brock. It was Ann's enthusiasm for extracanonical texts that allowed me to see the way that they complement those of the New Testament. In fact, I would not even have thought seriously about taking a class in religion without her captivating description of a course that promised to introduce us to lost voices, particularly those of women, in extracanonical, Christian writings. Ann has been a mentor ever since. While writing my dissertation, she really went the extra mile at each stage of formulating ideas, getting them on paper, and editing multiple drafts, even mailing me a Coptic dictionary when I was finishing up my project in Tokyo!

The coeditors of the Series for Biblical Studies and Cultural Theory, Hal Taussig and Maia Kotrosits, have also been extremely helpful. Maia's own work has opened my eyes to new conceptual possibilities regarding identity, and Hal came into the picture when I saw the flyers for *A New New Testament* in the SBL/AAR annual meeting bags just after its publication. I immediately bought a copy and started using it with various groups I was teaching. When I had an opportunity to meet Hal in person, he graciously offered to read my initial work on the care of the self/soul. He has believed in its potential and has supported me in specific, innumerable ways throughout the process of writing this book, carefully listening as new ideas coalesced in my mind and helping me frame the content and articulate its significance in substantive ways all while introducing me to new perspectives that have pushed my work further along.

In addition, I have been able to articulate the ideas that I discuss in this book with wonderful conversation partners and colleagues over the past years, especially Lisa Schrader who has provided many opportunities to copresent and try out this material with public audiences. In addition, colleagues Ally Kateusz, Jan Duce, Karen Dumford, Gail Finlay, Sue Humble, Iwona Jezierska, Sharon Littrell, Lucy McGuffey, Shirley Paulson, Polly Strovink, Lisa and John Vincent-Morrison, Sherry Walker, Jana Watt, and Stephanie Yuhas have all helped me work through and articulate my ideas in significant ways. When I was starting my dissertation, Lucy was the one who first suggested I look at Foucault's later work and then helped me think through the *Hermeneutics of the Self* on a sunny park bench. As that project has become this book, Ally has read each chapter and given invaluable assistance in helping me edit the final draft, supporting me through the last steps of a long process. There are others whom I want to mention as well. Karen Smith has helped me throughout the process in invaluable ways particularly with grasping the nuances of materials in French. Brian Hartman and James White also read and suggested improvements for significant portions of this book. At the University of Denver/Iliff School of Theology, coordinators Meghan Laurvick and Arianna Nowalkowski helped with many details involved in bringing the initial version of this work to fruition as did librarians Katie Cook, Laura Harris, Alice Runis, Douglas Brown, Donna Groben, and Michelle Kyner.

In addition, former professors, Glen Hilburn, Julio Jiménez, Alan Robb, and Anabel Newman planted the seeds for this book many years ago and have continued to discuss my research. Other conversation partners in my communities of faith and contexts of broader learning have also eagerly engaged in conversation about this topic and sustained me in continuing to articulate its importance. I would especially like to thank the OCWM (Our Church's Wider Mission) Committee of First Congregational UCC-Colorado Springs for funding as well as the members of Christ's Episcopal Church, Castle Rock, particularly those who participated in our weekly service at 6 a.m. and listened to my latest developments over coffee. The same goes for the group of women who met with me monthly in Colorado Springs to discuss *A New New Testament* and furthered my own thinking. I will never forget the joy of hearing the sounds of a window harp from the breeze coming through the window of Siri Everett's home as we read lines from the *Odes of Solomon* that discuss the Spirit of the Lord speaking through one's own being just as "the wind passes through the lyre" (6.1). There are so many others who listened hard and carefully as well, and I am so grateful for your support.

My own family and close friends have also been a tremendous source of strength: my brother David and his family, Shannon Black, Darryl and Dorothy DeBorde, and especially my parents-in-law—George and Dottie Saxon, brother-in-law Rob and family, Jerry and Frances Bray, David Brock, Mary Kay Carlson, Dick and Chris Hall, the Hay family, and many others. All of these friends and family members have discussed versions of the topics in this book while plying me with food, coffee, or sustenance and support in various forms. In moving to Indiana, I have had many good new conversation partners regarding this book. I have also had many opportunities to speak about the topics in these books through my participation in CFT (Christian Feminism Today), the Tanho Center, and the Westar Institute, and I want to thank Marg Herder, Mark Mattison, and Martha Vaught of CFT; Celine Lilly, Natalie Perkins, and John Rogers at Tanho, and Cassandra Farrin, David Galston, and Perry Kea of Westar as well as Ann Kish, Leah Rumsay, Sarah Lund, A.B. and Mary Rudy, and Diane and Jerry Zehr for listening and helping me flesh out ideas in this book.

Lastly, Phil Getz and Amy Invernizzi, my editors at Palgrave Macmillan, have provided wonderful support as has Subasree Sairam, the project manager. There are also many omissions as so many people spurred my thinking and helped in ways too numerous to list, but I offer my deepest thanks and appreciation to each person who has played a role in bringing this book into being. However, in the end, I also acknowledge that any problems or flaws with the final product are solely my responsibility.

CONTENTS

AUTHORS NOTE

The image of the deceased woman on the front cover is carved into a sarcophagus that dates to 300–325 C.E. It was found near a crypt filled with Christian iconography, the Coronation Crypt of the *Pretestato* Catacomb—a catacomb on the via Appia circling ancient Rome. Do you see the scroll that she holds in her left hand? A dove sits at her feet, and on the other side is a small coffer for storing scrolls. The inscription at the Pio Cristiano Museum in the Vatican where the sarcophagus now rests states that the woman is posed "in a philosophical stance." Her image serves to provide one more example of "the care of the self" and "philosophy as a way of life" among ancient women, including those belonging to early Christ movements.

CHAPTER 1

Introduction

While walking past the front desk at a seminary a few months ago, I asked the student receptionist for some scratch paper to jot down a few notes. After a moment of rummaging around, she pulled out some yellow-lined notebook paper with scribbled class notes on the back. "Here," she said, "I'm sure I'll never need these again." The notes turned out to be from her previous semester's Christian history course.

As a professor myself, I could not help being amused and wondering whether my own students' class notes would ultimately meet a similar fate. Diverted from my original purpose, I started to examine what she had written. I was particularly taken by the long list of figures and groups that various "church fathers" had deemed as "heretics" or "Gnostics."

© The Author(s) 2017
D. Niederer Saxon, *The Care of the Self in Early Christian Texts*,
The Bible and Cultural Studies, DOI 10.1007/978-3-319-64750-0_1

Her professor had described Christian history as a litany of doctrinal disputes in which heresies splintered off from a supposed original orthodoxy at a rather alarming rate.[1]

In a manner both wonderfully mundane and powerfully haunting, this anecdote unveils one of the major difficulties involved in encountering the unexamined master narrative of early Christianity. Many contemporary historians continue to write a caricatured version of the emergence of Christianity in the first three centuries C.E., drawing only upon texts that provide information from the eventual winners of struggles that erases or distorts the complex diversity within and among early Christ movements. Such histories continue to successfully eliminate most public consciousness of significant parts of the New Testament, wide swaths of recently discovered writings of early Christ movements, and thick layers of early church leaders' narratives and poetry.

It is a privilege to write this book in a moment of scholarly upheaval, rethinking, and creative counterproposal, a time when it is possible to challenge the master narrative and articulate its contradictions. Yet, in wrestling with the troubling theologies of exclusion against "heretics" and

---

[1]The term "Christian" is problematic with regard to the period preceding Constantine. It is used only three times in the entire New Testament (Acts 11:26, Acts 26:28, and I Peter 4:16). Neither Paul nor any follower of Christ actually refer to themselves as "Christian." See Taussig, "Preface," xvi–xix. During this period, small groups of people identifying with Christ were widely dispersed across the Roman Empire. Maia Kotrosits, for example, beautifully captures what a more meaningful interpretation of works utilizing Christ imagery in the early centuries could look like when she poignantly wonders "what it would mean to read 'early Christian' literature not as the core beliefs of a religious movement, but as a set of responses to social brokenness. I want to suggest that, rather than static truths about Jesus or God, early Christian texts represent a number of creative and improvised ways of trying to make sense of who one is, where one belongs, and what God means in the face of loss." See Maia Kotrosits, "Rethinking the Beginnings of Christianity," in *The Fourth R* 28.4 (2015): 3–5, 23. Her book, *Rethinking Early Christian Identity: Affect, Violence, and Belonging* (Minneapolis: Augsburg Fortress Publishers, 2015) expands this argument. In addition, the term "heresy" did not originally hold a pejorative connotation. In ancient Greek, it simply meant "choice." There were various philosophies and ways of living; i.e., "choices." However, Bishop Irenaeus, the author of the influential multivolume *Against Heresies* written around 180 C.E. clearly disapproved of many other choices. The full text of this work is found in Roberts, *Ante-Nicene Fathers*.

"heresies," I find myself less interested in critiquing them than in replacing those caricatures by reframing ways of reading, understanding, and interpreting the literature of these periods.

This book, therefore, takes a different tack than the tired notes from the seminary student who so readily turned her course notes into scrap paper. Here, I reconceptualize the brittle, overblown, hyper-doctrinalized, and under-researched history of early Christ movements in the second and third centuries C.E. My project avoids the flat cartoons of the heresy-orthodoxy debates by focusing on *practices* as ways of understanding character, meaning, and identity.

This is a departure from the normative procedure of presenting history by discussing doctrines and beliefs that became "standard" only in later eras. Often historians present these doctrines and associated doctrinal disputes as if they were part of a coherent and preordained divine preference from the beginning. In fact, scholars tend to ignore the major differences between the meaning of "belief" itself in the first centuries of the Common Era and later apologetic and "official" creedal statements. The word that has often been translated as "belief," or "faith," is simply a translation of the Greek word, *pistis*. Today many scholars recognize that it is often more accurate to translate *pistis* as "trust," "confidence," or "loyalty" instead.

There are several key thinkers on whose work I build. First and foremost is Michel Foucault. His insights are helpful in two main ways. First, he has illuminated the power of "discourse" and the role it plays in shaping the very categories in which we think. For Foucault, "discourse" is the language of "texts" (oral or written) that produce certain kinds of knowledge and shared meanings in those who hear or read them—those statements that provide a language in which we can converse about a specific topic at a particular moment in history.

These discourses have real consequences. Foucault saw that, under the unconscious influence of discourses, we begin to think in certain kinds of ways rather than others, especially with respect to those categories that shape how we identify and describe ourselves and others. Simply the way particular topics are talked about can prohibit certain perspectives from being discussed or even thought about.[2] Foucault's work is especially insightful with regard to discourses that rely on binary oppositions, such as

---

[2]For a good introduction to Foucault's concept of discourse, see Hall, ed., *Representation*, 42–45.

"sane/insane," and conflate a spectrum of possibilities into only two options. Though these reductions may not be "real," the effects and consequences of thinking in these terms are very real indeed.

The discourse of "heresy"/orthodoxy" is one such false binary opposition. Although today many think of this division as natural, as the way things really are, in the second and third century C.E., "orthodoxy" and "heresy" were not binary oppositions based on doctrinal differences nor were they defined in terms of essential characteristics. When we read works newly discovered in the last two centuries alongside those of the New Testament, the "church fathers," and martyrdom accounts, it is clear that the ancient heresiologists who denounced others as "heretics" indulged in discursive differentiation, that is, rhetorically-charged exaggeration and distortion. Often, they lumped those groups with whom they disagreed—groups actually differing from each other—together as "Gnostics."[3] Such labeling served to define "orthodox" Christianity in terms of what it was not. Moreover, the discursive strategies of the ancient heresiologists so successfully convinced later eighteenth- and nineteenth-century historians and theologians that these later scholars coined their own "ism" for these groups—"Gnosticism"—a word that did not exist in the ancient world.[4] As Karen King has explained, "There was and is no such thing as Gnosticism, if we mean by that some kind of ancient religious entity with a single origin and a distinct set of characteristics. Gnosticism is, rather, a term invented in the early modern period to aid in defining the boundaries of normative Christianity."[5]

---

[3]Michael Williams has argued this persuasively in Williams, "*Rethinking Gnosticism*," see especially his summary on page 28.

[4]The term was first used in 1669 in the context of Catholic-Protestant polemics. See Layton, "Prolegomena to the Study of Ancient Gnosticism," 348–349.

[5]King, *What is Gnosticism?*, 2–3. See also King, "Origins of Gnosticism and the Identity of Christianity," 103–120. I find Williams's and King's arguments very persuasive, but the issues for jettisoning, retaining, or modifying the term are explored thoroughly in the essays in Marjanen, ed. *Was There a Gnostic Religion?*. Scholars such as Ismo Dunderberg prefer to use terms that delineate a specific group (such as Valentinian). See Dunderberg, *Beyond Gnosticism*. David Brakke has argued for using the term "Gnostic" but only for those works that contain a certain kind of creation myth usually termed Sethian. In supporting this thesis, he provides an excellent overview of this issue in Brakke, *Gnostics*. For arguments in favor of retaining "Gnosticism," see Burns, "Providence," 55–79; De Conick, *Gnostic New*

Foucault's second main insight for me is his later work in recovering the importance of a *practice*—the care of the self—that led me to see its significance in newly discovered texts.[6] In the ancient world, the longing for well-being was expressed in terms of engaging in "the care of the self," also sometimes called "the therapy of emotions" or "the cure of the passions." Various philosophical schools (for example, Platonic, Stoic, Epicurean, and Cynic) encouraged their members to engage in certain practices of self-formation and self-transformation that would lead to the ability to remain calm and unruffled. The Stoics, in particular, taught that while one might have little or no control over one's circumstances, one did have control over how one responded to them, and the way to achieve that self-control was through these practices or exercises.[7] In the first few centuries C.E. under Roman rule, life could include disease, torture, executions, blood-thirsty spectacles in arenas and colosseums, and other kinds of trauma. The care of the self entailed finding means of living that allowed one to exercise control over one's emotions or passions rather than be controlled by them.

Foucault's recognition of the significance of the care of the self has important implications for reframing the way in which we discuss the diversity among early Christ movements. His emphasis on the importance of practices that would allow for individuals and groups to develop a sense of self and engage in spiritual transformation guided me in looking for the description of any such practices in the writings of early Christ movements. This book is the result. It examines the ways in which various groups identifying themselves with Christ were conceiving of the proper way to

---

Age, 2016; Pearson, "Gnosticism as a Religion," 81–101. For an overview of what can be learned from studying "heresies", see Wilhite, *The Gospel according to Heretics*, 245–256.

[6]Here, I rely primarily on Foucault's lectures near the end of his life published in English as *The Hermeneutics of the Subject* as well as his essay "Technologies of the Self" in *Technologies of the Self*.

[7]The term "exercise" comes from Pierre Hadot, Foucault's colleague, who drew Foucault's attention to the care of the self by describing the practice of philosophy in ancient times as a "way of life" that involved "spiritual exercises." See Hadot, *Philosophy as a Way of Life*, 81–82. Ilsetraut Marten Hadot, Pierre Hadot's wife, a distinguished philosopher in her own right, also did extensive research and produced a monumental work about spiritual direction in antiquity; see Hadot, *Sénèque*.

engage in the care of the self. Moreover, using this lens, this book explores how the categorization of these early groups into the false binary opposites of "proto-orthodox" and "heretical" (or "gnostic") can shift. I argue that these distinctions actually arose out of contending perspectives about the best way to care for one's self in the ever-shifting, hybrid conditions of the ancient Greco-Roman world.

In Chap. 2, I discuss Foucault's argument regarding the importance of the care of the self for understanding ancient history as well as key points in the work of his conversation partner, Pierre Hadot, relating this to the topic of martyrdom. For when we look for differences in attitudes regarding practices among early Christ movements, it is discussion of martyrdom that crops up repeatedly. The work of Judith Perkins has been foundational in describing how the identity of early followers of Christ coalesced around the discourse of a "suffering self." Perkins clearly illustrates the way that many viewed martyrdom as a means of both subverting the moral and political status quo as well as transcending the established social order for union with Christ—that is, "Death as a Happy Ending."[8] Daniel Boyarin also has characterized martyrdom as a discourse, "a practice of dying for God and of talking about it" in ways that created meaning for the groups to which those who died belonged.[9] These compelling, theoretical frameworks provide crucial background for my own analysis of the texts of ancient church "fathers" in the next chapter.

In Chap. 3, I utilize the insights of Elizabeth Castelli in thinking about the process of martyrdom—not just the final act of dying itself but of all that leads up to it—as a way of going about the care of the self. A close reading of the *Letters of Ignatius* cogently demonstrates how Ignatius develops his sense of self and his ongoing process of spiritual transformation through his correspondence about suffering and his impending martyrdom, an example of Foucault's "technology of self-writing."[10] This approach is useful in examining other works as well. I explore the way that not only the *Letters of Ignatius* but also *I Clement*, the *Letter of Polycarp*, and the *Martyrdom of Polycarp* describe the process of suffering in terms of the care of the self. They emphasize patience, endurance, and the belief

---

[8]Perkins, *Suffering Self*, 15–40.
[9]Boyarin, *Dying for God*, 94–95.
[10]Castelli, *Martyrdom and Memory*, 69–103.

that their selves will be fully formed at the end of a process culminating in imitating Christ's death.

In Chap. 4, I juxtapose the discourse of martyrdom in these texts with discussions of the same topic in newly discovered writings from Nag Hammadi and other places in Egypt. Irenaeus, for example, derisively dismissed the "Gnostics" as lacking in the kind of courage that martyrs such as Ignatius exhibited. However, until recently, we have not been able to read the works on which such claims were presumably based. Now that we can, we find that they provide a very different perspective than Irenaeus's and do not reflect his and other opponents' accusations of a lack of courage on the part of the "Gnostics." Rather, in various ways, the authors of these writings disrupt a discourse involving the glorification of martyrdom. At the same time, these authors present alternatives for the care of the self for those in early Christ movements. Texts such as the *Apocalypse of Peter* and the *Testimony of Truth*—both from Nag Hammadi, fragments attributed to Basilides and Valentinus, and the *Gospel of Judas* all provide good examples.

In Chap. 5, I highlight the way that two ancient works of those who identified themselves with Christ represent women in terms of the care of the self. In the *Gospel of Mary*, the writer represents the main character as an unwavering, model figure who functions as a strong, stable leader—a quality resulting from immersion in self-care. In addition, Mary engages in *parrhēsia*, or frank speech, one of the most common practices related to the care of the self and extensively discussed by Foucault in his last lectures.[11] This gospel also includes a description of an "ascent of the soul" that some scholars interpret as happening after death, but I argue that it may well be a description of an ancient contemplative practice related to the care of the self. The second text, *The Martyrdom of Perpetua and Felicity*, an account of the process of facing and undergoing martyrdom, depicts Perpetua, one of its heroines in whose voice the work is partially written, similarly to Mary and in terms consonant with the care of the self. Both of them are courageous women who transgress the norms of social deference expected of them in Greco-Roman society. Perpetua also takes the risk of speaking up directly and boldly, and like Mary, she describes an ascent. In this case, she relates a vision in which she herself has climbed to heaven on a ladder. The only "rub" with respect to *The Passion of Perpetua and Felicity* is that it typifies ancient works that depict women as exemplars

---

[11]See Foucault, *Government of Self and Others* and Foucault, *Courage of Truth*.

of virtue *only* when they subject themselves to suffering or death. It is important to recognize this because all too often women have been immersed in a discourse that encourages them to endure suffering or abuse.

In Chap. 6, I unpack the two hours of lectures that were the last Foucault gave at the Collège de France in 1984. He died just a couple of months later. Here, he traces the way that the meaning of *parrhēsia*, this one specific practice that has been a part of the care of the self, changes over time, splitting into two different directions. Foucault calls them the "poles" of *parrhēsia*. In the Christian tradition, the meaning of *parrhēsia* will shift dramatically and come to be associated with a renunciation of the flesh and the practice of confession—a practice that can only be mediated by ecclesiastical authorities. This provides further support for my argument: that disagreements about the proper way to care for the self are at the heart of differences between early Christ movements rather than doctrinal disputes per se.

In conclusion, then, by relying on key reframings of recent scholarship, this book moves into an active reconstruction of early Christ movements. These are not slight adjustments but substantive changes in thinking about how to understand the second and third centuries C.E. There are several major shifts that open up in this study.

First of all, I provide a reevaluation of what had until recently been assumed to be unanimous agreement among early Christ movements regarding martyrdom as the best and fullest expression of commitment to the way of Christ. Here, my reading of a range of works portrays a much more complex positioning of what Christ people thought about imperial threats of violence. Newly discovered writings show that the so-called Gnostics did not hold the same view about martyrdom as the so called proto-orthodox—the latter seeing it in terms consistent with the care of the self.

Second, there is also a significant reassessment of the status of a number of works relative to the larger emerging mosaic representing the diverse writings of these two centuries. Works from Nag Hammadi and other texts newly discovered in modern times such as the *Gospel of Mary* help us to gain larger understandings of spiritual practices and insights regarding the first three centuries C.E. that have been overshadowed by the partiality shown toward works that were only eventually elevated and canonized. This book elaborates on and nuances the perspectives of extracanonical writings and connects them through comparisons to texts that have enjoyed a privileged status due to their inclusion in the New Testament.

Third, I bring Foucault's notion of the care of the self into conversation with those who stress the importance of practice over belief or even one type of practice over another in the study of early Christ movements and emerging Christianities. This challenges ways of conceptualizing and theologizing that have until recently been granted a certain epistemological immunity. Simultaneously, it opens up an understanding of the variety of ways second and third century Christ movements engaged the process of making meaning in circumstances far less than ideal.

As these three shifts in perspective emerge and interact, the binary opposition of orthodoxy and heresy that has reigned supreme in the telling of Christian history slips quietly into the background. Instead, different models that account for and encompass hybridity, heterogeneity, and practice-based perspectives—those which provide a less misleading perspective regarding the nature of diversity within and among those identifying themselves with Christ—can begin to take root and flourish.

REFERENCES

Ancient Works

Layton, Bentley. Gnostic Scriptures: Ancient Wisdom for the New Age. New York: Doubleday, 1987.
Roberts, Alexander, and James Donaldson, eds. *The Ante-Nicene Fathers: The Writings of the Fathers down to A.D. 325.* American Reprint of the Edinburgh Edition. 10 vols. Edited by A. Cleveland Coxe. New York: Charles Scribner's Sons, 1903.

Modern Works

Boyarin, Daniel. *Dying for God: Martyrdom and the Making of Christianity and Judaism.* Figurae. Stanford: Stanford University Press, 1999.
Brakke, David. *The Gnostics: Myth, Ritual, and Diversity in Early Christianity.* Cambridge: Harvard University Press, 2010.
Burns, Dylan M. "Providence, Creation, and Gnosticism According to the Gnostics." Journal of Early Christian Studies 24.1 (2016): 55–79.
Castelli, Elizabeth A. *Martyrdom and Memory: Early Christian Culture-Making.* New York: Columbia University Press, 2004.

De Conick, April D. *The Gnostic New Age: How a Countercultural Spirituality Revolutionized Religion from Antiquity to Today.* New York: Columbia University Press, 2016.

Dunderberg, Ismo. *Beyond Gnosticism: Myth, Lifestyle, and Society in the School of Valentinus.* New York: Columbia University Press, 2008.

Foucault, Michel. "Technologies of the Self." Pages 16–49 in *Technologies of the Self: A Seminar with Michel Foucault.* Edited by Luther H. Martin, Huck Gutman, and Patrick H. Hutton. Amherst: University of Massachusetts Press, 1988.

Foucault, Michel. *The Hermeneutics of the Subject: Lectures at the Collège de France 1981–82.* Edited by Frédéric Gros. Translated by Graham Burchell. New York: Picador, 2005.

Foucault, Michel. *The Government of Self and Others: Lectures at the Collège de France 1982–83.* Edited by Frédéric Gros. Translated by Graham Burchell. New York: Picador, 2008.

Foucault, Michel. *The Courage of Truth. Lectures at the Collège de France 1983–84.* Edited by Frédéric Gros. Translated by Graham Burchell. New York: Picador, 2011.

Hadot, Ilsetraut Marten. *Sénèque: Direction spirituelle et pratique de la philosophie. Philosophie du present.* Paris: Librairie Philosophique J. Vrin, 2014.

Hadot, Pierre. *Philosophy as a Way of Life: Spiritual Exercises from Socrates to Foucault.* Translated by Arnold I. Davidson. Edited by Michael Chase. Oxford: Blackwell, 1995.

Hall, Stuart, ed. *Representation: Cultural Representations and Signifying Practices.* London: Sage, 1997.

King, Karen L. *What Is Gnosticism?* Cambridge: Belknap Press of Harvard University, 2003.

Marjanen, Antti, ed. *Was There a Gnostic Religion?* Publications of the Finnish Exegetical Society 87. Helsinki: Finnish Exegetical Society, 2005.

Pearson, Birger. "Gnosticism as a Religion." Pages 81–101 in *Was There a Gnostic Religion?* Publications of the Finnish Exegetical Society 87. Edited by Antti Marjanen. Helsinki: Finnish Exegetical Society, 2005.

Perkins, Judith. *The Suffering Self: Pain and Narrative Representation in the Early Christian Era.* New York: Routledge, 1995.

Taussig, Hal. "Preface." Pages xvi-xix in *A New New Testament: A Bible for the Twenty-First Century Combining Traditional and Newly Discovered Texts.* Boston: Houghton Mifflin Harcourt, 2013.

Wilhite, David E. *The Gospel according to Heretics: Discovering Orthodoxy through Early Christological Conflicts.* Grand Rapids, Mich., Baker Academic, 2015.

Williams, Michael A. *"Rethinking Gnosticism": An Argument for Dismantling a Dubious Category.* Princeton, N.J.: Princeton University Press, 1996.

CHAPTER 2

The Importance of the Care of the Self in the History of the Early Christ Movements

THE CARE OF THE SELF AS THE MAIN FOCUS OF GRECO-ROMAN PHILOSOPHIES

For Michel Foucault, being open to new ways of conceptualizing what we think we know is crucial. He puts it this way:

> There are times in life when the question of knowing if one can think differently than one thinks, and perceive differently than one sees, is absolutely necessary if one is to go on looking and reflecting at all . . . . But, then, what is philosophy today—philosophical activity, I mean—if it is not the critical work that thought brings to bear on itself? In what does it consist, if not in the endeavour to know how and to what extent it might be possible to think differently, instead of legitimating what is already known?[1]

Moreover, for Foucault, this "thinking differently" is particularly relevant with respect to the way that modern scholars have conceptualized Greco-Roman philosophies—as the pursuit of abstract knowledge. He argues that philosophers and members of philosophical schools focused on

---

[1]Foucault, *Use of Pleasure*, 9.

© The Author(s) 2017
D. Niederer Saxon, *The Care of the Self in Early Christian Texts*,
The Bible and Cultural Studies, DOI 10.1007/978-3-319-64750-0_2

sets of practices centered on "the care of the self/soul" instead.[2] In *The Hermeneutics of the Self*, he traces the history of this concept and discusses the means through which one goes about it. Such care revolves around what he terms "technologies of the self." He defines these "technologies" as those practices

> which permit individuals to effect by their own means or with the help of others a certain number of operations on their own bodies and souls, thoughts, conduct, and way of being, so as to transform themselves in order to attain a certain state of happiness, purity, wisdom, perfection, or immortality.[3]

These "technologies" are simple practices, or exercises, which effect both identity formation and spiritual transformation.

Foucault's inquiries took place in conversation with his colleague, Pierre Hadot, who had explored the practice of philosophy in the ancient world extensively and also emphasized the idea that the formation of the self was its critical concern.[4] Hadot argued that in order to understand what philosophy was about one had to consider the way in which philosophy was actually a whole way of life. He maintained that there was a difference between talking about philosophical ideas and *doing* philosophy—that philosophy is "an invitation to each human being to transform himself.

---

[2]The Greek term for the care of the self/soul is the *epimeleia heautou*; see Foucault, *Hermeneutics of the Subject*, 2–27; and Foucault, "Technologies of the Self," 16–49. Throughout his work, Foucault uses "self" and "soul" interchangeably; for examples, see Foucault, "Technologies of the Self," 25–57. On page 25, for example, Foucault discusses Socrates's urging Alcibiades to take care of himself and Foucault says, "Alcibiades tries to find the self in a dialectical movement. When you take care of the body, you don't take care of the self. The self is not clothing, tools, or possessions. It is to be found in the principle which uses these tools, a principle not of the body but of the soul. You have to worry about the soul—that is the principal activity of caring for yourself."

[3]Foucault, "Technologies of the Self," 18.

[4]Hadot became the Chair of the Department of Philosophy at the Collège de France in 1983 just after Foucault gave the lectures in 1981–82 that have been transcribed and translated as the *Hermeneutics of the Subject*; see Davidson, *Philosophy as a Way of Life*, 2. Foucault, in fact, cites Hadot's work several times in Foucault, *Hermeneutics of the Subject*, 23, 62, 79, 123, 146, 203, 216, 226, 312, 269, 387, 417, 418, and 434.

Philosophy is a conversion, a transformation of one's way of being and living, and a quest for wisdom."[5] Its goal was "not simply to develop the intelligence of the disciple, but to transform all aspects of his being—intellect, imagination, sensibility, and will" and that it aimed at "an art of living"; Hadot's short passage from Epictetus, a Stoic in the third century C.E., sums up the practice of philosophy nicely: "A carpenter does not come up to you and say 'Listen to me discourse about the art of carpentry,' but he makes a contract for a house and builds it . . . Do the same thing yourself"; Hadot also quotes a passage regarding Epictetus's *Manual* from Simplicius, a sixth-century Greek philosopher, a passage that illustrates the same point:

> If I admire the exegete because he provides good explanations, and if I can understand and myself interpret the text and if, quite frankly, everything falls to my lot except the fact of making use of these writings in life, would I have become anything other than a grammarian instead of a philosopher?[6]

These two passages written centuries apart illustrate why both Hadot and Foucault emphasize self-care as a major thread in philosophy for roughly a thousand years—five hundred years both prior to and after the beginning of the Common Era.[7] Foucault's *The Hermeneutics of the Subject* as a whole lays out the case for this thesis with extensive examples from the time of Socrates to that of the Christian ascetics of late antiquity.[8]

Foucault admits that the care of the self is a concept that has scarcely been thought of as significant in the history of philosophy.[9] Therefore, to illustrate his point, he discusses the famous inscription at the oracle of Delphi, "Know thyself," and shows how the connotation associated with it would have meant something more like "Know your limitations," or

---

[5]Hadot, *Philosophy as a Way of Life*, 275.

[6]Hadot, *Philosophy as a Way of Life*, 27.

[7]Hadot does so in the context of illustrating this principle within the passages just cited. For discussion of this point by Foucault, see Foucault, *Hermeneutics of the Subject*, 11. See also Bernauer and Carrette, *Michel Foucault and Theology*, 8.

[8]Foucault, *Hermeneutics of the Subject*, 2–27 provides a good overview. See also Hadot, *Philosophy as a Way of Life*, 264–267.

[9]Foucault, *Hermeneutics of the Subject*, 2.

"Understand that one should not ask for too much."[10] Then, Foucault provides three examples of Socrates's use of the term in the *Apology*. Socrates's whole discussion revolves around the fact that he has not taken care of himself in terms of trying to acquire fame or fortune. Rather, he sees his role as one who not only does not seek these things for himself but also encourages others to take care of their souls, or selves. He alludes to the fact that if he is forced to leave the Athenians, they will suffer by not having someone to provide such guidance. He feels he deserves to be rewarded by his society rather than punished.[11]

Finally, Foucault points to the dialogue of the *Alcibiades* to further his argument regarding the prominence of the notion of the care of the self for Greek thought, pointing out that the concept is or will come to be important for the Pythagoreans, Stoics, Cynics, Epicureans, and Neo-Platonists—in short, for all of the philosophical schools of ancient Greece and Rome with the exception of the Aristotelians.[12] Initially, Foucault explains, the care of the self is a specific kind of activity that Socrates urges the elite young men who will rule Athens to practice.[13] Socrates's conversation with Alcibiades, an ambitious young man eager to enter public life, is a case in point. Key passages illustrate this. Well into the conversation, Socrates asks if Alcibiades intends to continue in a state of ignorance, even stupidity, or whether he will "take care of" himself (*Alcibiades I* 119A).[14] At first, Alcibiades is not convinced that he needs to

---

[10]Foucault, *Hermeneutics of the Subject*, 3–4.

[11]Foucault, *Hermeneutics of the Subject*, 6–8.

[12]For Foucault, Aristotle is the great exception to the emphasis on the care of the self in Greek thought: "Aristotle is not the pinnacle of Antiquity but its exception"; see Foucault, *Hermeneutics of the Subject*, 17.

[13]Hadot, too, discusses the importance of the care of the self in Socratic dialogue, saying that such a teaching exercise "is not concerned with the exposition of a doctrine, but with guiding an interlocutor to a certain settled mental attitude." See Hadot, *Philosophy as a Way of Life*, 20, plus pages 89–93 where Hadot discusses the role of the representation of Socrates in detail, and page 281 where he refers to Alcibiades's description of Socrates to argue for the definition of a philosopher as "someone who lived in a philosophical way." Also see Harris, *Restraining Rage*, 352–353.

[14]All translations of Socrates are from Johnson, trans., *Socrates and Alcibiades: Four Texts*.

engage in this process, but Socrates points out that though Alcibiades comes from a distinguished, noble family, he must consider that those to whom he will need to measure up, those against whom he may need to protect Athens, are every bit as noble if not more so. He points out that the Persian prince receives an excellent education from the very best tutors: the wisest, the most just, the most moderate, and the most courageous, and he details what is involved:

> The first of these teaches the craft of the Magi, that of Zoroaster, son of Horomazus (this consists of service to the gods), and he also teaches him about being a king. The most just man teaches him to tell the truth throughout his life; the most moderate man teaches him not to be ruled by any pleasure, so that he may be accustomed to be free and truly royal, since he rules first of all over the things within him, and is no slave to them. The most courageous man teaches by preparing him to be fearless and without dread, since to be afraid is to be a slave. (*Alcibiades I* 122A)

The mention of the practices of truth-telling and freedom from being controlled by pleasure or ruled by fear are a part of the ancient idea that one needs to engage in such practices. This is what allows one to be free, or cured, of one's passions. Socrates goes on to discuss how amazed other rulers would be if they knew that Alcibiades did not think it important to take care of himself, and Alcibiades acknowledges the importance of what Socrates is saying and asks how he can do this. Socrates explains that this kind of self-care is not about taking care of things that Alcibiades *owns*, "but that which we use to make ourselves better," (*Alcibiades I* 128E) and that this involves *investigating what we ourselves actually are*; i.e., "knowing our souls" (*Alcibiades I* 130D-E). Near the end of the dialogue, Socrates states: "So you must first get possession of excellence yourself, as must anyone who is going to rule and take care not only of himself and what belongs to him in private but also of the city and what belongs to it" (*Alcibiades I* 134C).

The idea that the one who has engaged in self-care is capable of acting justly will come up repeatedly in Foucault's explication of the care of the self. In particular, Foucault will discuss the practice of *parrhēsia*, or speaking frankly and directly (as Socrates has just done), as both a practice of the care of the self and a consequence of the care of the self.

Much has been written about the value of the Socratic dialogue, but Pierre Hadot's comment is insightful:

For ancient philosophy . . . intended . . . to form people and to transform souls. That is why, in Antiquity, philosophical teaching is given above all in oral form, because only the living word, in dialogues, in conversations pursued for a long time, can accomplish such an action. The written work, considerable as it is, is therefore most of the time only an echo or a complement of this oral teaching.[15]

Most of the texts this book examines in the following chapters include or are in the form of dialogues. The authors who crafted these literary representations were, in a sense, practicing the care of the self by writing narratives (or snippets of them within longer works) that serve two purposes. They are an aid in remembering one's own relationship to the figures depicted and provide models of the process of the care of the self. Presumably, those who heard or read the texts were using them as a means of engaging in self-care in these ways as well. In this sense, the works explored in this book function *in and of themselves* as expressions of the care of the self.

In fact, Foucault argues throughout *The Hermeneutics of the Self* that over time, the care of the self becomes a process practiced by a much wider group of people. It also becomes a lifelong process rather than a shorter preparation for entering public life. As the concept of the care of the self develops over the centuries, it encompasses additional practices. One is corresponding with a spiritual mentor (a written substitute for oral dialogue), Seneca's letters being a prime example.[16] Another is writing down one's thoughts about one's attitudes and actions in a notebook—particularly those related to the examination of conscience—as, for instance, Marcus Aurelius does.[17] This journaling functions as an ongoing dialogue

---

[15]Hadot, *Philosophy as a Way of Life*, 20.

[16]See Ilsetraut Hadot, *Sénèque*, 2014.

[17]See Hadot, *Philosophy as a Way of Life*, 179–180 for pertinent remarks about the *Meditations*. Hadot points out how they function as evidence for the practice of *doing philosophy* but that they are often misjudged for their lack of coherence and for their pessimistic tone. Hadot explains that the *Meditations* are just notes that Marcus Aurelius has jotted down intended for his personal use and that they are not a systematic treatise. Therefore, they should not be analyzed for the kind of coherence that characterizes a formal exposition of philosophical ideas. This point is worth noting with regard to all of the texts we will be examining in this book as well.

with oneself that results in self-exhortations. There are also certain kinds of meditation—particularly reflection on death and consequently, a focus on the value of the present moment, as well as dream interpretation, concentrated mental exercises of a contemplative nature (such as cultivating a bird's eye view of the universe, or "the view from above") and even practices related to medical matters and the care of one's body.

Why Historians Have Not Recognized the Importance of the Care of the Self

Foucault discusses the reasons for a distorted focus on knowledge rather than the care of the self and the obscuring of the latter over time. He argues that historians of philosophy have simply *assumed* that the emphasis was on knowledge. He feels this assumption is a result of what he terms the "Cartesian moment," that is, the moment "when [it came to be thought that] knowledge itself and knowledge alone gives access to the truth."[18] In other words, from Descartes to today, later expositors of ancient times have not properly recognized that the emphasis on "knowing oneself" in ancient Greek and Roman thought is actually subsumed within the broader notion of the care of the self.[19]

Foucault does, however, qualify this by indicating what he feels is an even earlier dissociation between, on the one hand, philosophy conceived of as being about the care of the self and, on the other, philosophy as being about knowledge, the latter occurring as practices of spirituality and the study of theology become separated from each other in Scholasticism. He argues that until the seventeenth century, it is not spirituality and *science* which are at odds but spirituality and *theology*.[20] At that point, the "Cartesian moment" occurs, further obscuring the emphasis on the care of the self in premodern times.

Pierre Hadot's insight into the matter is also very helpful. Hadot basically argues that in the early centuries, particularly in monasticism, Christianity *was* a way of life, but eventually the spiritual exercises that were

---

[18]Foucault, *Hermeneutics of the Subject*, 17.
[19]Foucault, *Hermeneutics of the Subject*, 8.
[20]Foucault, *Hermeneutics of the Subject*, 25–27.

a part of doing philosophy became a part of what was called "spirituality," not "philosophy." Philosophical reasoning isolated from the practice of spiritual exercises was used to engage in theological disputation and buttress theological concepts while philosophy as a way of life disappeared.[21]

Foucault also mentions one other reason for the failure to recognize the importance of the care of the self. Paradoxically, in some respects, an emphasis on one's own self is at odds with the renunciation of self and the focus on non-egoism that has permeated Western, Christian thought.[22] For example, figures such as Gregory of Nyssa as well as Methodius of Olympus and Basil of Caesarea discuss the care of the self, but they associate it with themes of self-renunciation and freedom from marriage. In fact, in the thought of these ascetics, the concept becomes related to austerity and self-restraint rather than being a positive activity that allows for human flourishing.[23]

For all these reasons, then, Foucault argues that later generations have neglected the concept of the care of the self.[24] Hadot argues along similar lines. He, too, feels that the recognition of the importance of "spiritual exercises" has been obscured.[25]

---

[21]Hadot, *Philosophy as a Way of Life*, 32.

[22]Foucault, *Hermeneutics of the Subject*, 13.

[23]Hadot also notes that an earlier writer, Clement of Alexandria, describes *gnosis* as a death which divides the soul and the body." See Hadot, *Philosophy as a Way of Life*, 138. Likewise, Harry Maier has also described the care of the self in Clement of Alexandria in an article that points out the way in which Clement reinterprets the care of the self as renunciation of one's sinful flesh in a process beginning with baptism and mediated from that point on by ecclesiastical authority as one receives the sacraments and participates in the church's life; see Maier, "Clement of Alexandria and the Care of the Self," 719–745. This is a vastly different conception of the care of the self than we see in the Greco-Roman tradition prior to the advent of Christianity and is also distinct from that in the texts examined in Chaps. 4 and 5.

[24]Foucault, *Hermeneutics of the Subject*, 10–13.

[25]Hadot, *Philosophy as a Way of Life*, 33.

Usefulness of the Care of the Self
in Reconceptualizing the History of the Early
Christ Movements

The focus on *knowledge* in modern interpretations of Greco-Roman philosophies parallels the focus on *doctrine* in the way the story of Christianity has been told.[26] In fact, in *Technologies of the Self*, Foucault says that, "Christianity has always been more interested in the history of its *beliefs* than in the history of real *practices*" and that a hermeneutics of technologies of the self "was never organized into a body of doctrine like textual hermeneutics."[27]

Reconceiving the history of early Christ movements to delve more deeply into practices regarding the care of the self rather than merely the history of knowledge, doctrines, or beliefs proves to be just as valuable as reconceiving Greek philosophies in this way.[28] In particular, this yields crucial insights into the fierce conflicts between certain communities in the second and third centuries of the Common Era. We can apply and extend Foucault's insights regarding the care of the self in re-conceptualizing issues of "orthodoxy" and "heresy" particularly with respect to "defining" the problematic category of "Gnosticism," reframing the issue as debates about the care of the self rather than knowledge or doctrine per se (whether or not these disagreements were necessarily explicit or conscious).[29] Therefore, this book will not attempt to catalog and interpret a

---

[26]As discussed in Chap. 1, the terms "Christian" and "Christianity" are problematic with regard to the period preceding Constantine.

[27]Foucault, "Technologies of the Self," 17.

[28]Bernauer and Carrette agree, stating that Foucault's work is not "simply a modernist critique of knowledge: it also continually opens up the space of theology and Christian living to new possibilities. Foucault offers theology the critical apparatus to find new inclusive and non-dualistic forms of living; he offers the possibility of imagining new ways of rethinking theology, as practice rather than belief"; see Bernauer and Carrette, *Michel Foucault and Theology*, 4. See also Carrette, *Foucault and Religion*, 108–128.

[29]Foucault does not seem to be aware of the problems with the categorization of some Christians as "Gnostics." He ironically expresses beliefs stereotypical of discourses of orthodoxy about "Gnosticism" in Foucault, *Hermeneutics of the Subject*, 16–17. He may have known something of the codices discovered near Nag Hammadi in 1945 as his colleague, Henri-Charles Puech, was one of the first

"body of doctrine" but rather to illustrate the ways in which various early Christ movements envisioned the care of the self (and corresponding technologies of the self). It will also articulate the ways in which the discursive strategies they used to do so involved a collision of discourses in the social contexts that these groups inhabited.

Foucault himself provides a clue to the means whereby a reconceptualization of Christian history in terms of its practices (or technologies of the self) might begin. In describing Christianity, Foucault mentions that

> Christianity belongs to the salvation religions. It's one of those religions which is supposed to lead the individual from one reality to another, from death to life, from time to eternity. In order to achieve that, Christianity imposed a set of conditions and rules of behavior for a certain *transformation of the self*.[30]

Foucault then goes on to say that for Christians, this involved *exomologēsis*: "to recognize publicly the truth of their faith or to recognize publicly that they were Christians."[31] For Foucault, this includes "the dramatic recognition of one's status as a penitent."[32]

However, if one who engages in *exomologēsis* can be defined as one who publicly recognizes the truth of one's faith, it sounds strikingly similar to

---

to see them. Puech was a noted history of religions scholar and expert on Gnosticism who taught at the same institution as Foucault. See Foucault, *Hermeneutics of the Subject*, 23–24n49. Puech's student, Doresse, Jean, was the first to examine the codices and Puech was subsequently one of the first, per Dart, *Jesus of Heresy and History*, 5, 11, 13, 24, and 29. The history of religions school, however, would have assumed the texts to be gnostic using the same typological definitions that Karen King, heavily relying on Foucauldian insights, later deconstructs; see especially her "note on methodology" in King, *What is Gnosticism*, 239–247. The works, however, remained untranslated and accessible to only a handful of scholars until the 1970's, shortly before Foucault died. Foucault does mention a "Gnostic self" to be discovered within oneself more positively in one of his lectures: "as a sparkle of the primitive light"; Foucault, "Subjectivity and Truth," 171–172.
[30]Foucault, "Technologies of the Self," 40. Emphasis added.
[31]Foucault, "Technologies of the Self," 41. See also Carrette, *Religion and Culture*, 172–173, 179–181, 203–204.
[32]Foucault, "Technologies of the Self," 41.

the definition of a martyr, or witness. Martyrdom means simply *to bear witness*.[33] Foucault continues:

> [t]he most important model used to explain *exomologēsis* was the model of death, of torture, or of *martyrdom*. The theories and practices of penance were elaborated around the problem of the man who prefers to die rather than to compromise.[34]

Foucault refers to *exomologēsis* within the context of acts of self-punishment that constituted penance.[35] However, such an insight resonates with a certain desire for martyrdom that seems to have been prevalent in some early Christ movements in the first three centuries prior to the Edict of Milan in 313 C.E. when the Roman Empire legally declared the toleration of Christianity. Thus, an examination of discourses related to martyrdom can yield important insights regarding practices in early groups identifying themselves with Christ.

MARTYRDOM AS A DISCURSIVE FORMATION

Judith Perkins has utilized a Foucauldian framework to argue that the very identity of Christianity was being established through the envisioning of the Christian community as the body or bodies of a "suffering self." In particular, Perkins contrasts the comedic ending of Greco-Roman novels in marriage with the comedic ending of martyr accounts, the culmination of suffering in death. Death as a happy ending (the name of her first chapter) turns Greco-Roman morality on its head. In the moral universe of

---

[33]The Latin word *martys* referred to one who gave testimony in a Roman court of law. It acquired the particular connotation of suffering death for one's beliefs in the context of the Roman persecution of Christians. For studies tracing the etymology of this word, see Brox, *Zeuge und Märtyrer*; see also von Campenhausen, *Idee des Martyriums*. Paul Middleton, too, argues that martyrdom functions differently in the Maccabean context and the early Christian context in Middleton, "Sacrifice, Salvation, and Holy War."

[34]Foucault, "Technologies of the Self," 43. Emphasis added.

[35]Foucault jumps abruptly from Greco-Roman philosophy to fourth- and fifth-century Christian monasticism. He recognizes that both martyrdom and asceticism ground themselves in a sense of self-renunciation, but he does not discuss martyrdom as care of the self. See Foucault, "Technologies of the Self," 39–49.

Greco-Roman values, there is no virtue in suffering; therefore, suffering epitomized by an ignominious death, a death that allows the sufferer to transcend the established social order and established hierarchies of this world for union with Christ, actually subverts the moral and political order of the elites who rule this earthly domain.[36] Though Perkins traces the way that the notion of a suffering self is emerging in other Greco-Roman discourse (that of an Asclepius follower, for example), noting that Christian discourse does not emerge out of a complete vacuum, she effectively argues that Christian discourse completely transforms notions of selves and suffering. Moreover, the very emergence of this subject, while not the sole reason for the success of Christianity, is helpful in at least two ways: (a) in constituting an audience of suffering selves to whom Christianity can address itself—the sick, poor, suffering, widowed, and orphaned—all of whom the discourses of Greco-Roman elites largely ignored and (b) the appropriation of the wealth of the rich for the serving of the poor. In this sense, she is articulating the operation of a communal technology of selves in the shaping of Christian identity.[37]

In Perkins's more recent book, *Roman Imperial Identities in the Early Christian Era*, she explores the way that the themes of alienation and estrangement from this world emerge in the construction of collective Christian identity, again by means of discursive analyses of a variety of ancient texts. Perkins points out that the power of the Roman Empire revolved in part around an alliance of elites (the class known as *honestiores*). The law exempted such persons from cruel, physical punishments. The emphasis on the value of martyrdom for Christians whether they were socially and economically of high or low status "opened a crack in the unity of elite self-interest that informed the early empire"[38]—as this strategy stridently opposed the traditional distinction between the elites and the non-elites (*honestiores* and *humiliores*). Thus, the cult of martyrdom served

---

[36]Judith Perkins analyzes this incisively in Chap. 1, "Death as a Happy Ending." See Perkins, *Suffering Self*, 15–40.

[37]Jeremy R. Carrette also discusses Foucault's equating religion with a political force; see Carrette, "Prologue to a Confession of the Flesh," 38. Thierry Voeltzel, too, describes how Foucault refers to the church as an instrument of power in Voeltzel, "On religion (1978)," 106–109.

[38]See Perkins, *Roman Imperial Identities in the Early Christian Era*, 180.

larger social and political purposes as a means of *dis*identification with the status quo—being a member of the Roman Empire—and clear identification with a new institution that eventually served as an alternative space or site of power, the Christian Church. In short, through the praise of martyrdom, Christians were discursively delineating their very self-definition over and against the Roman status quo.[39]

Simultaneously, however, the meaning of martyrdom for the individual was also being shaped discursively with respect to beliefs. Many early Christ followers thought that martyrdom assured one of salvation and was the ultimate means by which the self continued to exist and that it would be resurrected in the same fleshly form—the care of the self par excellence. Such views are prevalent in the works traditionally referred to as the Apostolic Fathers. The next chapter will discuss representative strategies with examples from *1 Clement*, the *Letters of Ignatius*, the *Letter of Polycarp to the Philippians*, and the *Martyrdom of Polycarp* while Chap. 5 utilizes the *Passion of Perpetua and Felicity* as an example. In *Martyrdom and Memory*, Elizabeth Castelli examines early texts such as these and articulates the means by which writing by and about martyrs and elaborations on their lives and deaths constituted a "technology of the self." She specifically invokes Foucault's notion of the technology of self-writing in analyzing the letters attributed to Ignatius, the martyrdom account of Perpetua, and the work of Pionius, thus extending Foucault's ideas to the martyrs themselves.[40]

Perkins's and Castelli's work supplement Daniel Boyarin's development of the idea that discussions of martyrdom functioned as a discourse. As Boyarin explains,

> I propose that we think of martyrdom as a "discourse," as a practice of dying for God and of talking about it, a discourse that changes and develops over time and undergoes particularly interesting transformations among rabbinic Jews and other Jews, including Christians, between the second and the fourth centuries. For the "Romans," it didn't matter much whether the lions were eating a robber or a bishop, and it probably didn't make much of a difference to the lions, either, but the robber's friends and the bishop's

---

[39]See Perkins, *Roman Imperial Identities*, 172–180 for extended discussion.
[40]Castelli, *Martyrdom and Memory*, 69–103; Foucault, "Écriture de soi," 3–23.

friends told different stories about those leonine meals. It is in these stories that martyrdom, as opposed to execution or dinner, can be found, not in "what happened."[41]

Moreover, for Boyarin, accounts of martyrdom are "a particularly fertile site" for the exploration of the permeability of the borders between so-called Judaism and so-called Christianity in late antiquity.[42] In other words, deconstructing this discourse is the basis for showing how various strands of Judaism and Christianity overlapped with each other (rather than there being two separate, monolithic entities) and thus for deconstructing "supercessionist theology" such as that in the work of W. H. C. Frend.[43] Scholars have long considered Frend's work on martyrdom a classic and cite it repeatedly; Frend, however, portrays martyrdom as originating in Judaism and Christians adopting this practice as Christianity "replaces" Judaism. Boyarin argues that such work has obscured, albeit unwittingly, the nature of the relationship between these groups in the early centuries C.E. As evidence, Boyarin points to stories in the Talmud that show that it was possible for the authorities to mistake Jews for Christians even in the second and third centuries. A prime example is the story of the arrest of Rabbi Eliezer for engaging in "sectarianism":

The ruler said to him: A sage such as you having truck with these matters!

He said to him: I have trust in the judge.

The ruler thought that he was speaking of him, but he meant his Father in Heaven. He said to him: Since you trust me, I also have said: Is it possible that these gray hairs would err in such matters? Behold, you are dismissed![44]

---

[41]Boyarin, *Dying for God*, 94–95. Candida R. Moss also defines martyrdom as a discourse in Moss, *Ancient Christian Martyrdom*, 17. Paul Middleton makes a similar point: "Martyrdom is not a category that can be defined. Martyrdom is essentially created when a narrative about a death is told in a particular way. The central character is not the most important element in the creation of a martyrdom; it is the narrator"; Middleton, *Martyrdom*, 29–30.

[42]Boyarin, *Dying for God*, 21.

[43]Boyarin, *Dying for God*, 8, 128.

[44]Boyarin, *Dying for God*, 27.

Boyarin goes on to discuss the fact that "sectarianism" may well have been participation in Christ-related activity and that the boundaries between the two traditions may have been rather unclear to people living at that time.

What is more to the point for the purposes of this book, however, is that the rabbi chooses to avoid martyrdom through the use of clever, ambiguous language ("trust in the judge"). In fact, the Talmud juxtaposes this story against others that embrace martyrdom. Therefore, for Boyarin, given that both kinds of responses are recorded as acceptable, the Talmud demonstrates an openness to questions regarding what the response of a faithful person should be. These positions function as "nodes on a continuum." By contrast, for those Boyarin terms "Christian", the response is almost always a choice to face martyrdom bravely, even with a certain desire for it:

> It is not finally the issues themselves, or even the positions taken on them that divide the traditions, but the forms of textuality and authority that they generate and venerate. Ambrose (and other patristic 'authors') control their texts in ways that the unauthored rabbinic text does not . . . . It should . . . . be emphasized that 'tolerance' for diversity is not what was at issue here. There is no reason to see the Rabbis as any more tolerant than the Fathers. The issue is rather the elasticity or plasticity of the discourse of the different traditions in their ability and desire to allow heterogeneity on certain kinds of questions.[45]

Though we can applaud Boyarin's desire not to label certain groups as more tolerant than others, it is crucial to note the remarkable diversity of opinion —the spectrum of attitudes—regarding martyrdom's value within the early Christ-related groups as well.[46] The statements of some traditionally labeled "Gnostics" serve as a complement that fills out even more completely the continuum about which Boyarin speaks. Boyarin has demonstrated that Judaism and Christianity were not monolithic entities but were each composed of fluid strands that continuously overlapped, and this book illustrates that variety within early Christ movements in Chap. 4.[47]

---

[45]See Boyarin, *Dying for God*, 66.

[46]See King, "Martyrdom and Its Discontents in the Tchacos Codex," 23–42; and Moss, *Ancient Christian Martyrdom*, 155–67.

[47]Boyarin is familiar with King's work, citing her article on "Gnosticism as Heresy" as a "productive influence" on his own. He does mention that some "Gnostics" did

The recognition of a discursive formation of martyrdom so well-elaborated by Boyarin and others accords well with Foucault's notion of the importance of the theme of self-renunciation mentioned above. "Throughout Christianity there is a correlation between disclosure of the self, dramatic or verbalized, and the renunciation of self."[48] Near the end of his essay on "Technologies of the Self," Foucault states that for a Christian, "the acts by which he *punishes* himself are indistinguishable from the acts by which he *reveals* himself."[49] Although Foucault mentions this in the context of exhibiting penitential behavior, it applies to the establishment of both individual and collective identity among the early Christ-related groups as well.

DISRUPTIONS TO THE DISCOURSE OF MARTYRDOM

If, then, the very constitution of identity for early Christ movements revolved around a specific technology of the self, the discourse of martyrdom, that denoted a means of not only caring for one's soul, but indeed, of guaranteeing the eternal salvation of one's soul and one's bodily resurrection, one can well imagine that any disruptions to the discourses of glorifying and exalting the practices of martyrdom may have constituted a challenge, even a threat, to the very means by which the identity of what would become "Christianity" was developing in various circles.[50] As Perkins clearly shows us, this discourse involved not only themes of individual salvation but eventually played a role in the establishment of an alternative power site, the Christian Church of the fourth century, as well. Thus, such disruptions were probably not merely theological but may well have represented challenges to the developing power of the "orthodox" that came to dominate the institutional church eventually centered in Rome. One finds such a challenge in the discourses of certain individuals excoriated as Gnostics (a number of different early Christ-related groups

---

not see martyrdom as valuable, but he repeatedly refers to the "Christian" view as one that did. See Boyarin, *Dying for God*, 137–37n24.

[48]Foucault, "Technologies of the Self," 48.

[49]Foucault, "Technologies of the Self," 42. Emphasis added.

[50]The best exposition of the emergence of a belief in a fleshly resurrection is Caroline Walker Bynum's *Resurrection of the Body in Western Christianity, 200–1336.*

being lumped together under this term).[51] These challenges must be closely examined and understood with this context in mind if we are to better understand the hostility and contentiousness that dominate the tone of certain texts with regard to other groups. Indeed, close reading of the *Apocalypse of Peter*, the *Testimony of Truth*, two fragments preserved in the writings of Clement of Alexandria (one attributed to Basilides and one to Valentinus), and the recently discovered *Gospel of Judas* provides striking insight. We will examine these writings more closely in the fourth chapter.

In summary, rather than conceiving of differences as primarily doctrinal, perhaps it is possible to shed post-Cartesian assumptions. We can begin to understand that orthodoxy and heresy are not binary oppositions. Rather than being centered on doctrinal differences defined in terms of essential characteristics, they are discursive constructions arising out of competing visions regarding the best way to care for one's self (individually or collectively).

REFERENCES

Ancient Works

Plato
Johnson, David M., trans. *Socrates and Alcibiades: Four Texts*. Newburyport, Mass., 2003.

Modern Works

Bernauer, James W. and Jeremy R. Carrette, eds. *Michel Foucault and Theology: The Politics of Religious Experience*. Aldershot, Hampshire: Ashgate, 2004.
Boyarin, Daniel. *Dying for God: Martyrdom and the Making of Christianity and Judaism*. Figurae. Stanford: Stanford University Press, 1999.
Brox, Norbert. *Zeuge und Märtyrer: Untersuchungen zur frühchristlichen Zeugnis-Terminologie*. Studien zum Alten und Neuen Testament 5. Munich: Kösel-Verlag, 1961.
Bynum, Caroline Walker. *The Resurrection of the Body in Western Christianity, 200–1336*. New York: Columbia University Press, 1995.

---

[51]The seminal work for understanding the conflation of several different groups under this one term is Michael Williams's *Rethinking "Gnosticism."*

Carrette, Jeremy R. *Foucault and Religion: Spiritual Corporality and Political Spirituality.* New York: Routledge, 2000.

Carrette, Jeremy R. "Prologue to a Confession of the Flesh." Pages 1–47 in Jeremy Carrette, *Religion and Culture: Michel Foucault.* New York: Routledge, 1999.

Castelli, Elizabeth A. *Martyrdom and Memory: Early Christian Culture-Making.* New York: Columbia University Press, 2004.

Dart, John. *The Jesus of Heresy and History: The Discovery and Meaning of the Nag Hammadi Gnostic Library.* San Francisco: Harper & Row, 1988.

Davidson, Arnold I. "Introduction." Pages 1–45 in *Philosophy as a Way of Life: Spiritual Exercises from Socrates to Foucault.* Edited by Arnold I. Davidson. Translated by Michael Chase. Oxford: Blackwell, 1995.

Foucault, Michel. "L'écriture de soi." *Corps écrit* 5, "L'autoportrait" (February 1983): 3–23. Translated as "Self Writing" by Paul Rabinow in Foucault, *Ethics, Subjectivity and Truth.* Vol. 1 of *Essential Works of Foucault, 1954–1984,* 207–22. New York: New Press, 1994.

Foucault, Michel. *The Hermeneutics of the Subject: Lectures at the Collège de France 1981–82.* Edited by Frédéric Gros. Translated by Graham Burchell. New York: Picador, 2005.

Foucault, Michel. "Subjectivity and Truth" in *The Politics of Truth.* Edited by Sylvère Lotringer. Translated by Lysa Hochroth and Catherine Porter. South Pasadena, CA: Semiotext(e), 2007).

Foucault, Michel. "Technologies of the Self." Pages 16–49 in *Technologies of the Self: A Seminar with Michel Foucault.* Edited by Luther H. Martin, Huck Gutman, and Patrick H. Hutton. Amherst: University of Massachusetts Press, 1988.

Foucault, Michel. *The Use of Pleasure.* Vol. 2 of *The History of Sexuality.* Translated by Robert Hurley. London: Penguin, 1984.

Hadot, Ilsetraut Marten. *Sénèque: Direction spirituelle et pratique de la philosophie. Philosophie du present.* Paris: Librairie Philosophique J. Vrin, 2014.

Hadot, Pierre. *Philosophy as a Way of Life: Spiritual Exercises from Socrates to Foucault.* Edited by Arnold I. Davidson. Translated by Michael Chase. Oxford: Blackwell, 1995.

Harris, William V. *Restraining Rage: The Ideology of Anger Control in Classical Antiquity.* Cambridge: Harvard University Press, 2001.

King, Karen L. "Martyrdom and Its Discontents in the Tchacos Codex." Pages 23–42 in *The Codex Judas Papers: Proceedings of the International Congress on the Tchacos Codex held at Rice University, Houston, Texas, March 13–16, 2008.* Edited by April D. De Conick. Nag Hammadi Manichaean Studies 71. Edited by Johannes van Oort and Einar Thomassen. Leiden: Brill, 2009.

King, Karen L. *What Is Gnosticism?* Cambridge: Belknap Press of Harvard University, 2003.

Maier, Harry O. "Purity and Danger in Polycarp's Epistle to the Philippians: The Sin of Valens in Social Perspective." *Journal of Early Christian Studies* 1 (1993): 229–47.

Middleton, Paul. *Martyrdom: A Guide for the Perplexed.* London: T & T Clark, 2011.

Middleton, Paul. "Sacrifice, Salvation, and Holy War in Maccabean and Early Christian Martyrdom." Paper presented at the annual meeting of the SBL, Chicago, November 18, 2012.

Moss, Candida R. *Ancient Christian Martyrdom: Diverse Practices, Theologies, and Traditions.* New Haven, Conn.: Yale University Press, 2012.

Perkins, Judith. *The Suffering Self: Pain and Narrative Representation in the Early Christian Era.* New York: Routledge, 1995.

Perkins, Judith. *Roman Imperial Identities in the Early Christian Era.* Routledge Monographs in Classical Studies. New York: Routledge, 2008.

Voeltzel, Thierry. "On religion (1978)." Pages 106–09 in *Religion and Culture: Michel Foucault.* Edited by Jeremy R. Carrette. Translated by Richard Townsend. New York: Routledge, 1999.

Von Campenhausen, Hans. *Die Idee des Martyriums in der alten Kirche.* Göttingen: Vandenhoeck und Ruprecht, 1936.

Williams, Michael A. *"Rethinking Gnosticism": An Argument for Dismantling a Dubious Category.* Princeton, N.J.: Princeton University Press, 1996.

CHAPTER 3

Martyrdom Represented as Care of the Self in the Texts of Clement, Ignatius, and Polycarp

MARTYRDOM AS CARE OF THE SELF

In Chap. 2, we have explored Foucault's notion of the care of the self and the way that martyrdom functions as a discourse. According to Judith Perkins, this discourse serves to unify those who view themselves as part of a collective "suffering self."[1] In this chapter, we turn more specifically to the way that texts attributed to Clement of Rome, Ignatius of Antioch, and Polycarp of Smyrna repeatedly represent martyrdom as a form of the care of the self in terms of Stoic ideals. This portrayal circulates in tandem with the signification of martyrdom as an imitation of Christ's sacrifice. Specifically, this depiction of martyrdom as care of the self accords with Foucault's definition of "technologies of the self" as those practices

> which permit individuals to effect by their own means or with the help of others a certain number of operations on their own bodies and souls, thoughts, conduct, and way of being, so as to transform themselves in order to attain a certain state of happiness, purity, wisdom, perfection, or immortality.[2]

As the discourse of early Christ groups begins to emphasize the suffering of the body in enduring torture, imprisonment, and death, it actually becomes the means by which one can become a true disciple who reenacts

---

[1]Perkins, *Suffering Self*, 40.
[2]Foucault, "Technologies of the Self," 18.

© The Author(s) 2017
D. Niederer Saxon, *The Care of the Self in Early Christian Texts*,
The Bible and Cultural Studies, DOI 10.1007/978-3-319-64750-0_3

Christ's own passion and who will become a fully formed self, enjoying a blessed eternal existence, and eventually, the fleshly resurrection of one's body.[3] Contemporary readers may take for granted that these ideas of attaining immortality and resurrection are central concerns of the works discussed in this chapter simply because such doctrines have dominated Christian theology through the centuries. For our purposes, though, the most important aspect is the manner in which these writings refer to the process of martyrdom in terms of how a self becomes fully actualized, the key element in Foucault's delineation of technologies of the self.

This process of transformation, of becoming a certain kind of self, also goes hand in hand with Stoic ideals regarding freedom from passions and an emphasis on the "cure" of the passions, or the "therapy of emotions." Stoics believed that in order to be free, one should extirpate the passions from one's soul. Passions were equated with illnesses. Just as medical cures involved healing and freedom from physical maladies, philosophical "cures" helped one to root out and become free of passions such as fear, anger, jealousy, and greed. "We call on the philosopher as we call on the doctor in cases of illness."[4] The Stoics thought that such passions undermined self-control, and ultimately, it is self-control which allowed one to be truly free.

Foucault illuminates this in *The Hermeneutics of the Subject* in discussing how the term *therapeuein* informs the care of the self.[5] He focuses on three meanings. One is to perform a medical operation in order to effect a treatment or cure. Another is in describing a servant engaged in serving a master. Lastly, *therapeuein* has the connotation of being devoted to oneself in the sense of keeping oneself free and pure of the emotions.[6] One must "protect, defend, respect, worship, and honor oneself."[7] It is in this sense

---

[3]Bynum, *Resurrection of the Body*, 19–58. See also Salisbury, *Blood of Martyrs*, 31–53.
[4]Foucault, *Hermeneutics of the Subject*, 55.
[5]For further in-depth treatment of these issues, see Nussbaum, "The Stoics on the Extirpation of the Passions," 129–177; see also Long and Sedley, *Hellenistic Philosophers*, 410–423.
[6]Foucault, *Hermeneutics of the Subject*, 8–9, 98–99.
[7]For Seneca's elaboration of this, see Foucault, *Hermeneutics of the Subject*, 272.

that Marcus Aurelius says that one must "surround [one's inner self] with sincere service" (*Med.* II.13).[8] He also describes the "intelligence free from passions" as a "citadel," and says that when in this state, a person "has no stronger place into which to withdraw and henceforth be impregnable" and that one's "inner guide" is also unassailable (*Med.*, VIII.48).[9] Seneca likewise discusses the value of curing the passions, saying, "How much wiser to stifle one's own passions than to recount for posterity those of others?" (*Nat.* III, Preface).[10] He then articulates the way in which greatness lies in

> seeing the whole of this world with the eyes of the mind and having carried off the most beautiful triumph, triumph over the vices. Those who have made themselves masters of towns and entire nations are countless; but how few have been masters of themselves . . . . What is great is a steadfast soul, serene in adversity, a soul that accepts every event as if it were desired . . . . What is great is having one's soul at one's lips, ready to depart; then one is free not by the laws of the city but by the law of nature.[11]

Seneca goes on to say,

> I am not surprised that so few people enjoy this happiness: we are our own tyrants and persecutors; sometimes unhappy due to loving ourselves excessively, sometimes from disgust with our existence, in turns the mind is swollen by a deplorable pride or strained by greed; giving ourselves up to pleasure or burning up with anxiety (*Nat.* IV, Preface).[12]

Toward the end of the second century C.E., Galen, the doctor to Commodus, the son of Marcus Aurelius, also discusses these themes in a

---

[8]Translations of Marcus Aurelius and Seneca are Foucault's unless otherwise noted. See Foucault, *Hermeneutics of the Subject*, 105n59.

[9]Foucault, *Hermeneutics of the Subject*, 101n10.

[10]Foucault, *Hermeneutics of the Subject*, 269n36.

[11]Foucault, *Hermeneutics of the Subject*, 269n39.

[12]Foucault, *Hermeneutics of the Subject*, 392n11.

text entitled *On the Treatment of the Passions.*[13] Helmut Koester has commented insightfully that for Stoics,

> the integrity of [the] rational human self is threatened by emotions and affections of the soul. Psychology, therefore, becomes a central and highly refined element of Stoic teaching as a doctrine of the affections . . . which are seen as diseases of the soul. Not only desire, fear, and pleasure, but also regret, sorrow, and compassion, are pathological states, from which the wise man must free himself in order to reach the goal of imperturbability (*apatheia*, later, in Epiktetos, *ataraxia*). In their description of the affections, Stoics borrowed many terms and concepts from the medical sciences. Their view of the affections as diseases of the soul is modeled on pathological insights into the diseases of the body. The philosopher becomes a physician of the soul.[14]

Tuomas Rasimus, Troels Engberg-Pederson, and Ismo Dunderberg have argued that Stoic ideals permeate the first two centuries of the Common Era, that is, in the time in which writers were starting to create accounts of martyrdom.[15] As we closely examine these works we see the process of embracing martyrdom represented in terms of "patient endurance."[16] This term is consonant with the idea of maintaining self-control whatever the circumstances, even in anticipating a painful death which ultimately brings freedom.[17] In fact, the authors of the texts actually represent death as

---

[13]See Foucault, *Hermeneutics of the Subject*, 396–401. The focus on the care of the self also continued to prevail in works Foucault does not discuss explicitly. Gregory the Great, for example, wrote a long treatise entitled "Pastoral Care" in the sixth century C.E. that dealt with the care of souls and was influential throughout the medieval and early modern period; see Oden, *Care of the Souls in the Classic Tradition.* Boethius' *Consolation of Philosophy,* also written in the sixth century C.E., delineates the role of virtue in attaining happiness as well; see Boethius, *Consolation of Philosophy.*

[14]Koester, *History, Culture, and Religion of the Hellenistic Age,* 145. See also Hadot, *Philosophy as a Way of Life,* 82–89 for discussion of the Stoic notion of the care of the self and its therapeutic connotations.

[15]Rasimus, Engberg-Pedersen, and Dunderberg, eds., *Stoicism in Early Christianity,* vii.

[16]In most of the passages discussed below, the Greek term for "patient endurance" is *hypomoné.*

[17]Brent D. Shaw has also noticed the prominence of this theme and refers to it as "an ideology of patience" in Shaw, "Body/Power/Identity," 296.

desirable and the process of facing it successfully as the means of gaining an eternal reward.[18]

Close readings of the works of the so-called apostolic fathers and acts of Christian martyrs (accounts of martyrdom) reveal ample evidence of early Christ people conceiving of martyrdom itself, including the whole process leading up to the final event, as a kind of care of the self. The idea that martyrdom assures one of salvation is prevalent. The suffering of the body could serve to ensure one's eternal health and happiness and the body's fleshly resurrection. Thus, suffering had a purpose—the care of the self in ultimate and eternal terms. This seems to be in line with a shift Judith Perkins discusses: from the Greco-Roman philosophical belief that the rational mind could control the body to a focus on the body itself as in pain and need of care.[19] In turn, we shall examine *1 Clement*, the *Letters of Ignatius*, and both the *Letter of Polycarp to the Philippians* and the *Martyrdom of Polycarp* for the ways in which notions about freedom and self-control appear in characterizations of selves as cured of enslaving passions. As we shall see, these notions merge with the representation of martyrdom as a sacrifice which imitates Christ's own.

1 Clement

The book opens with those in Rome addressing the problem of "schism" among the followers of Christ at Corinth (*1 Clem.* 1.1).[20] Primarily at stake are matters of authority. The author emphasizes the importance of humility

---

[18]A key debate concerns to what extent those in early groups identifying themselves with Christ even actually sought martyrdom. Lack of hard, factual evidence regarding the extent of and degree of persecution in the first centuries of the Common Era makes studying martyrdom in the first centuries of the Common Era problematic; see Moss, *Ancient Christian Martyrdom*, 8–16, 171–73. Some scholars have argued that a desire for it existed at times; see de Ste. Croix, *Papers by De Ste. Croix Christian Persecution, Martyrdom, and Orthodoxy*.

[19]Perkins, *Suffering Self*, 173.

[20]All citations and translations of *1 Clement* are from Holmes, *Apostolic Fathers*. Most scholars date this text to 65–110 C.E. Probably a leader or leaders of an early Christ movement in Rome wrote it during the reign of Domitian (81–96 C.E.) or perhaps earlier at the end of the reign of Nero (54–68 C.E.); for a good introduction and overview, see Jefford, *Reading the Apostolic Fathers*, 103–121. See also Holmes, *Apostolic Fathers*, 33–43; and Andrew Gregory, "*1 Clement*," 21–31.

and submissiveness, and the way in which one demonstrates having them is by respect for hierarchy—that of the bishop and leaders in the line of the Roman apostolic succession. In accord with the Stoic notion of the need for the therapy of emotions, the writer frames the schism as the result of improper control of unruly emotions, particularly an excess of jealousy (*1 Clem.* 3.2), and jealousy is characterized as leading to death (*1 Clem.* 9.1).

In descriptions of the martyrdoms of Peter and Paul, the author depicts these two apostles as the particular targets of jealousy and as exemplifying the very antithesis of those who are subject to it. Consider the following passage:

> Let us consider the noble examples that belong to our own generation. Because of jealousy and envy the greatest and most righteous pillars were persecuted and fought to the death. Let us set before our eyes the good apostles. There was Peter, who because of unrighteous jealousy endured not one or two but many trials, and thus having given his testimony went to his appointed place of glory. Because of jealousy and strife Paul showed the way to the prize for patient endurance. After he had been seven times in chains, had been driven into exile, had been stoned, and had preached in the east and the west, he won the genuine glory for his faith . . . . Finally, when he had given his testimony before the rulers, he thus departed from the world and went to the holy place, having become an outstanding example of patient endurance. (*1 Clem.* 5.1–7)

Here, the writer does not directly discuss details of the martyrdoms of Peter and Paul themselves but rather simply refers to them as events with which the readers would be familiar, merely stating that they have "given witness/testimony" and then gone on to their rewards (*1 Clem.* 5.7).[21] What the author notes is not their imitation of Christ or an association with atonement but rather the fact that they patiently endured trials and suffering. Thus, the author describes them in terms of facing persecution with the proper attitudes or emotions. It is as though the suffering they face enables them to practice the therapy of the emotions and actually *become* the kinds of selves who demonstrate properly "cured" passions. The writer does not describe their witness in dramatic terms; there is no sense of

---

[21]The phrase used for "witness" contains the same root as that in the noun, "martyr." Thus we see an early usage of the linking of "witnessing" and "martyrdom." As explained in Chap. 2, the very definition of a "martyr" is a "witness."

spectacle involved. Rather, the manner in which they face suffering exemplifies the attitude of one who is taking care of the self properly while maintaining self-control and exercising restraint through patient endurance. Simultaneously, the author reminds those who are not able to subdue their passions of the witness of Peter and Paul as persons who *were* in control, which, in turn, prompts the reader to remember their authority as apostles. Over and over, the readers of the text (or those listening to it being read) receive exhortations to proper behavior: kindness, gentleness, and peacefulness like that exhibited by the apostles (*1 Clem.* 13, 14). In fact, the ultimate desired goal for the group is "peace" (*1 Clem.* 19.2).

Christ is also lifted up as an example of a "pattern" to "imitate" (*1 Clem.* 16.7, 33.8), and this involves modeling oneself on his example in terms of one's emotions and attitudes (*1 Clem.* 17.1). The author emphasizes that the proper sacrifice is that of a "broken spirit" (*1 Clem.* 52.4) rather than a "burnt offering" (*1 Clem.* 18.16–17). Conceivably, this writer is advocating following Christ in terms of imitating him with respect to notions of the therapy of the emotions.[22] Likewise, the author describes God in terms consonant with the therapy of emotions as one who is "patient" and "free of anger": "Let us observe [God] with our mind, and let us look with the eyes of the soul on his patient will. Let us note how free from anger he is toward all his creation" (*1 Clem.* 19.3).

At the same time, as quoted above, there is language of sacrifice. *1 Clement* does represent Christ's death as an atoning sacrifice which can mediate in the lives of those who practice repentance:

Wash and be clean; remove the wickedness from your souls out of my sight. Put an end to your wickedness; learn to do good; seek out justice; deliver the one who is wronged; give judgment on behalf of the orphan, and grant justice to the widow. And come, let us reason together, he says: even if your sins are as crimson, I will make them white as snow, and if they are as scarlet, I will make them white as wool. (*1 Clem.* 8.4)

---

[22]For discussion of the way that *imitatio Christi* functions in works related to martyrdom, see Moss, *Other Christs*, with pages 105–109, 253–255 relevant in discussing martyrdoms as models or "embodiments of Christian virtues" (105).

Letters of Ignatius

In the *Letter of the Ephesians*, Ignatius states that it is his hoped-for success as a martyr that will allow him to become a disciple (*Eph.* 1.2).[23] In other words, this is what will allow the complete formation of his identity as a self totally committed to Christ. He clearly feels that he has not yet attained this status. Paradoxically casting his impending death as "success," he states,

> For when you heard that I was on my way from Syria in chains for the sake of our shared name and hope, and was hoping through your prayers to succeed in fighting with wild beasts in Rome—in order that by so succeeding I might be able to be a disciple—you hurried to visit me (*Eph.* 1.2).

A little later on, he says,

> For even though I am in chains for the sake of the Name, I have not yet been perfected in Jesus Christ. For now I am only beginning to be a disciple, and I speak to you as my fellow students. For I need to be trained by you in faith, instruction, endurance, and patience. (*Eph.* 3.1)[24]

The theme continues as Ignatius repeatedly implies that successfully facing and enduring martyrdom, rather than apostatizing, will lead to true discipleship. In other words, performing an operation on the body that requires grueling endurance allows one to become a perfected self. Ignatius refers to his chains as "spiritual pearls" (*Eph.* 11.2); just as there are irritants that produce something as worthy and beautiful as pearls, his chains will be

---

[23]All citations and translations of the *Letters of Ignatius* are from Holmes, *Apostolic Fathers*. Ignatius was a bishop who wrote letters as he was being transported to the city of Rome for punishment. Some scholars argue that his desire for death is pathological; see de Ste. Croix, *Christian Persecution*, 133; Perkins, *Suffering Self*, 33; Bowersock, *Martyrdom and Rome*, 6–7; Frend, *Martyrdom and Persecution*, 197; and Riddle, *The Martyrs*. See also the discussion in Moss, *Ancient Christian Martyrdom*, 6–8, 49–52, 165–166, 170–171, 178–179, 202–203 warning readers against too easily conceiving of martyrdom in this way.

[24]Often, "brother" or "sister" was used in the texts of early Christ people. "Fellow students" is a term used for other members of a philosophical school where the care of the self would have been practiced. This phrasing in terms of "endurance" and "patience" also echoes that of *1 Clement*.

the means of his spiritual perfection. This is true only, of course, if he is successful in persevering to the end (*Eph.* 14.2). Moreover, just as the author of *1 Clement* refers to Christ as a "pattern" (*1 Clem.* 16.7, 33.8), so Ignatius talks about suffering as an imitation of Christ's forbearance toward his persecutors and of his patience and gentleness with them, portraying the Savior as one who exercised proper self-control with regard to his emotions when he was persecuted.

In the *Letter to the Trallians* and the *Letter to the Magnesians*, Ignatius briefly reiterates these themes. In the former, he talks about his desire to suffer and then speaks of his need for "gentleness" in order to be able to do so (*Trall.* 4.1). Likewise, in the latter, Ignatius states that reaching God is possible for those who "patiently endure all the abuse of the ruler of this age and escape" (*Magn.* 1.2). Toward the end of the letter, Ignatius even maintains that a desire for death or at least a willingness to die is not just admirable but *necessary* when he says that Christ's "life is not in us unless we voluntarily choose to die into his suffering" (*Magn.* 5.2). Over and over again, Ignatius frames suffering as a means of discipline that allows one to develop proper attitudes and emotions. It is an opportunity to engage in such therapy. This practicing of self-control in a manner consonant with those who engage in the therapy of emotions is the means of ultimate care for one's eternal self. Those who "patiently endure" are the ones who "may be found to be disciples of Jesus Christ" (*Magn.* 9.1).

In his *Letter to the Romans*, Ignatius mentions these ideas yet again, speaking of his impending martyrdom as "an opportunity . . . to reach God" (*Rom.* 2.1). He implores his community to allow him to "be food for the wild beasts . . . ground by the teeth of the wild beasts, so that I may prove to be pure bread" (*Rom.* 4.1). Simultaneously, however, issues of the formation of self-identity are at stake. Ignatius asks the Romans to whom he is writing to

> pray that I will have strength both outwardly and inwardly so that I may not just talk about it but want to do it, so that I may not merely be called a Christian *but actually prove to be one*. For if I prove to be one, I can also be called one, and then I will be faithful when I am no longer visible to the world. (*Rom.* 3.2)[25]

---

[25]Emphasis added.

He says that it is only *after* he has been martyred that "I will truly be a disciple of Jesus Christ, when the world will no longer see my body" (*Rom.* 4.2). Finally, he says, "I am even now still a slave. But if I suffer, I will be a freedman of Jesus Christ and will rise up free in him" (*Rom.* 4.3). Perkins also sees this passage as meaning that Ignatius actually

> understood his real existence as beginning with his suffering and martyrdom . . . . the 'self' did not really come into being until it suffered; suffering was not simply something that happened to a person. Rather, it was the means of achieving real selfhood.[26]

Likewise, a little later, Ignatius says

> Bear with me—I know what is best for me. Now at last I am beginning to be a disciple. May nothing visible or invisible envy me, so that I may reach Jesus Christ. Fire and cross and battles with wild beasts, mutilation, mangling, wrenching of bones, the hacking of limbs, the crushing of my whole body, cruel tortures of the devil—let these come upon me, only let me reach Jesus Christ! (*Rom.* 5.3)[27]

Again, in Chap. 6, he begs and pleads to be allowed to suffer as he refers to death as "life" and life in this world as "death":

> Bear with me, brothers and sisters: do not keep me from living; do not desire my death. Do not give to the world one who wants to belong to God or tempt him with material things. Let me receive the pure light, for when I arrive there I will be a human being. Allow me to be an imitator of the suffering of my God. If anyone has him within, let that person understand what I long for and sympathize with me, knowing what constrains me. (*Rom.* 6.2–3)

In fact, Ignatius even says that he is "in love with death" (*Rom.* 7.2). In the *Letter to the Philadelphians*, Ignatius also talks about not yet being perfected:

---

[26]Perkins, *Suffering Self*, 190–191. See also Moss, *Ancient Christian Martyrdom*, 56, 179–180.

[27]Ignatius alludes in this passage to a gladiator's oath; see Straw, "'A Very Special Death,'" 45–46.

My brothers and sisters, I am overflowing with love for you, and greatly rejoice as I watch out for your safety—yet not I, but Jesus Christ. Though I am in chains for his sake, I am all the more afraid, because I am still imperfect. (*Phld.* 5.1)

And, in the *Letter to the Trallians*, Ignatius alludes to the idea that a certain *practice*—that of suffering—is the way in which he can fully achieve a sense of self-identity as a disciple of Christ. He actually contrasts the kind of self-care that suffering enables as opposed to that which mere comprehension "of heavenly things" allows. He claims that the latter does not make him a disciple; it is suffering that does (*Trall.* 5.2).

Finally, in the *Letter to Polycarp*, Ignatius repeats this theme once again. Ignatius mentions that he has learned that there is peace among the early Christian group at Antioch. He says that he has "become more encouraged in a God-given freedom from anxiety—provided, of course, that through suffering I reach God, *so that I may prove to be a disciple* by means of your prayer" (*Pol.* 7.1).[28]

Elizabeth Castelli examines the *Letters of Ignatius* and analyzes the way in which Ignatius crafts his very self-identity through the process of writing, linking the achieving of selfhood specifically to the technology of the self that Foucault terms "the technology of self-writing."[29] She discusses the way in which Ignatius emphasizes the ongoing process of his spiritual transformation as a process of "attaining God or Christ": "Ignatius's preparation for martyrdom is a spiritual exercise in focusing his wants and gaining control over his desires. It is, in essence, a form of askesis *avant le letter*."[30] In short, the self that he is crafting through language is located "at the place where language and the body intersect."[31]

---

[28]Emphasis added.

[29]Castelli, *Martyrdom and Memory*, 85; Foucault, "L'écriture de soi," 207–222.

[30]Castelli, *Martyrdom and Memory*, 82.

[31]Castelli, *Martyrdom and Memory*, 85. Emphasis added. Castelli discusses the fact that Foucault did not refer to martyrdom in terms of the care of the self, focusing on Christian asceticism in the fourth and fifth centuries instead. However, Castelli argues that "techniques of self-formation" are "also very much on display" in "second- or third-century texts related to Christ's martyrdom" (71). It is actually hard to know the full extent of Foucault's thought on these matters as he was planning to publish a fourth volume in his History of Sexuality series, *Confessions of the Flesh*, exploring the history of early Christ movements in greater detail.

Robin Darling Young also discusses the function of letter-writing in the formation of collective identity among Christ-related groups. She says,

> Those in training to become martyrs are shaped by the letters of people who have previously trained for and thought about this contest . . . . Certainly those Christians who joined this apostolic tradition of witness knew that their testimonies and deaths would be written about and that these accounts would be circulated. But the training went further than that. Because martyrs bore the name of Christ, *they were themselves like letters* meant to be read by the community and the world, letters from Christ that were recognizably like Christ.[32]

In this way, the technology of self-writing takes on a much broader meaning.

At the same time, the *Letters of Ignatius* emphasize martyrdom as an imitation of Christ's sacrifice.[33] Moss points out that this is only one of the ways martyrdom is represented in the Apostolic Fathers and martyr acts themselves; yet, the idea that Christ died as a sacrifice is most definitely present. In the *Letter to the Ephesians*, for example, Ignatius addresses his audience by saying: "Being imitators of God, once you took on new life through the blood of God you completed perfectly the task so natural to you" (*Eph.* 1.1). A little later, Ignatius tells the Ephesians: "I am a humble sacrifice for you and I dedicate myself to you" (*Eph.* 8.1). Near the end of the letter, he says,

> My spirit is a humble sacrifice for the cross, which is a stumbling block to unbelievers but salvation and eternal life to us . . . . For our God, Jesus the Christ, was . . . . born and baptized in order that by his suffering he might cleanse the water (*Eph.* 18.1–2).

Unfortunately, he died before it could be published, asking that it never appear in print. See Carrette, "Prologue to a Confession of the Flesh," 2n6; and Bernauer, *Michel Foucault's Force of Flight,* 160.

[32]Young, *In Procession Before the World,* 9–10.

[33]For a summary of the function of sacrifice in martyr acts specifically, see Moss, *Other Christs,* 77–87, and Castelli, *Martyrdom and Memory,* 51. Some scholars explore this idea in-depth: Young, *Sacrifice and the Death of Christ;* Young, *Use of Sacrificial Ideas in Greek Christian Writers;* Daly, *Christian Sacrifice;* and Daly, *Origins of the Christian Doctrine of Sacrifice.*

In the *Letter to the Romans*, he begs the readers: "Grant me nothing more than to be poured out as an offering to God while there is still an altar ready" (*Rom.* 2.2).

POLYCARP

The themes common in *1 Clement* and the *Letters of Ignatius* also appear in the two works related to Polycarp, the *Letter of Polycarp to the Philippians* and the *Martyrdom of Polycarp*. Polycarp is traditionally thought to have been the bishop of Smyrna in the mid-second century C.E. and to have been martyred circa 155–160. Polycarp is mentioned in Ignatius's *Letter to the Ephesians* 21.1 and his *Letter to the Magnesians* 15.1, and presumably, Ignatius writes an entire letter to Polycarp as mentioned above. Polycarp also refers to Ignatius and his letters, mentioning that he is passing the letters of Ignatius that he has received on to the Philippians for their own encouragement (Pol. *Phil.* 13.1–2).[34]

Letter of Polycarp to the Philippians

The *Letter of Polycarp to the Philippians* clearly depicts martyrs in a favorable way as Polycarp immediately commends the Philippians for "help[ing] on their way those confined by chains suitable for saints" (Pol. *Phil.* 1.1). He exhorts the Philippians to follow God faithfully, reminding them that "the Lord said . . . 'blessed are the poor and those who are persecuted for righteousness' sake, for theirs is the kingdom of God" (Pol. *Phil.* 2.3). Later, the narrator depicts martyrs in a manner similar to that in *1 Clement*, as those who "exercise[d] unlimited endurance" (Pol. *Phil.* 9.1–2). This and the frequent calls for "self-control" are quite reminiscent of *1 Clement*.[35] Moreover, such "endurance" is attributed to Paul and the apostles as well as the martyrs Ignatius, Zosimus, and Rufus. In particular, Polycarp mentions that the *Letters of Ignatius*, which he is attaching to his own letter, will be of "great benefit . . . for they deal with faith and patient

---

[34]All citations and translations of the *Letter of Polycarp to the Philippians* are from Holmes, *Apostolic Fathers*.

[35]Michael W. Holmes notes that "Polycarp seems to be particularly familiar with 1 Peter and *1 Clement*," in Holmes, *"Martyrdom of Polycarp,"* 273. Jefford notes familiarity or access to *1 Clement* in Jefford, *Reading the Apostolic Fathers*, 82.

endurance and every kind of spiritual growth that has to do with our Lord" (Pol. *Phil.* 14.2). Such phrasing resonates with the overtones of the kind of technologies of the self that are associated with the care of the self.[36] Michael Holmes has analyzed this emphasis on behavior and practicing virtue rather than doctrine per se:

> This understanding of the letter makes sense of the way Polycarp stresses so strongly the behavioural aspects of what is usually viewed as a purely "theological" concept, i.e. "righteousness". For him, orthopraxy is the other side of the coin of orthodoxy; if the community is behaving properly, it is also likely believing properly. This position may explain the vigour with which he reinforces (what he thinks should be) the community's sense of behavioural norms and standards throughout the letter.[37]

Stanley K. Stowers has written extensively on the role that letter-writing played in advocating ethical ideals in antiquity. He notes that a letter like that of Polycarp's provides a "model of what it means to be a good person in a certain role." It also "attempts to persuade and move the audience to conform to that model and to elicit corresponding habits of behaviour."[38]

Martyrdom of Polycarp

The *Martyrdom of Polycarp* is the only martyr account per se included in the works of the *Apostolic Fathers*.[39] Moreover, scholars have long considered it the oldest martyrdom account outside the New Testament

---

[36]Jefford also notes the ethical emphasis in Jefford, *Reading the Apostolic Fathers*, 80.

[37]Holmes, "Polycarp of Smyrna," 57. Regarding the function of the epistle as *paraenesis*, or moral exhortation, see also Maier, "Purity and Danger in Polycarp's Epistle to the Philippians," 229–247. Holmes analyzes the strengths and weaknesses of Maier's argument in Holmes, "Polycarp of Smyrna," 56–57.

[38]Stowers, *Letter-Writing in Greco-Roman Antiquity*, 94. See also Holmes' discussion in Holmes, "Polycarp of Smyrna," 54.

[39]The *Martyrdom of Polycarp* is often considered the first of the acts of the martyrs, but its provenance and dating have proven hard to establish. The many textual variants have provoked considerable scholarly debate. For discussion of these, see Dehandschutter and Leemans, *Polycarpiana*, 3–42.

although Moss compellingly argues for a date as late as the mid-third century.[40] Scholars repeatedly note its high quality as literature and defend its authenticity. The writer has discursively shaped it to parallel that of Jesus's own death in order for it to be "in accord with the gospel" (*Mart. Pol.* 1.1). For example, the name of the captain of the police who arrests Polycarp is Herod (*Mart. Pol.* 6.2); Polycarp sits on a donkey (*Mart. Pol.* 8.1) to be taken before the official who will condemn him just as Christ entered Jerusalem on a donkey, and Polycarp also hears a "voice from heaven" (*Mart. Pol.* 9.1) just as Christ did at his baptism. In addition, Polycarp is very kind toward his persecutors, inviting them to eat a meal and praying for them when they come to arrest him (*Mart. Pol.* 7.2–3).[41] Clearly, these elements are in keeping with a martyrdom account that the author is shaping to

---

[40]Moss summarizes the reasons for questioning the integrity, dating, and authenticity of the account, pointing instead to its elegance as a literary text. Certain elements are not historically plausible. As just one example, Polycarp's trial occurs in an amphitheater rather than a judicial basilica. Such was not normal legal precedent. The work also explicitly condemns voluntary martyrdom, carefully contrasting Polycarp's flight from persecution with that of Quintus, a man who presents himself to the Roman authorities but demonstrates cowardice when he actually faces the beasts. Such direct criticism of the practice leads some to date the text as late as the mid-third century C.E., for example, Moss, *Ancient Christian Martyrdom*, 62, 181. Scholars also use the fact that the writing shows evidence of well-developed ideas about a martyr's function and status, ideas consonant with those at a time when the cult of the saints was more solidly in place, to support this later dating. For general discussion of these issues, also see Jefford, *Reading the Apostolic Fathers*, 87–101; Moss, *Ancient Christian Martyrdom*, 57–76, 180–185; Moss, *Other Christs*, 57, 231n60, 196–198.

[41]Jefford provides a table listing all of the similarities between the representation of Christ in the New Testament gospels and the representation of Polycarp in the martyrdom account; see Jefford, *Reading the Apostolic Fathers*, 97. For in-depth, scholarly analysis of parallels between Christ's passion and Polycarp's martyrdom, see Dehandschutter, *Martyrium Polycarpi*, 241–254; and Moss, *Other Christs*, 56–69, 231–238. For discussion of the difficulty in making intertextual parallels, however, see Lieu, *Image and Reality*, 59–63; and Holmes, "*Martyrdom of Polycarp*," 407–432.

represent Polycarp as a Christ-like figure rather than a literal recounting of the story.[42]

The theme of martyrdom as an imitation of Christ's sacrifice definitely appears as well. At the end of the account, Polycarp looks up toward heaven and prays, "May I be received . . . in your presence today, as a rich and acceptable sacrifice" (*Mart. Pol.* 14.2). Moreover, the narrator then goes on to represent Polycarp's body in terms that bring the Eucharist to mind—as fragrant, baking bread:

> For the fire, taking the shape of an arch, like the sail of a ship filled by the wind, completely surrounded the body of the martyr, and it was there in the middle, not like flesh burning but like bread baking or like gold and silver being refined in a furnace. For we also perceived a very fragrant aroma, as if it were the scent of incense or some other precious spice (*Mart. Pol.* 15.1–2).

In this passage, the idea of being refined like pure metal resonates with the idea of martyrdom as a process that develops one's virtuous qualities, and indeed, as in other texts of the apostolic fathers, the narrator represents martyrdom as a means of developing and exhibiting "patient endurance" consonant with self-care (*Mart. Pol.* 2.2) throughout the work.[43] In fact, the writer explicitly mentions the fact that Polycarp does "not collapse in fright" (*Mart. Pol.* 12.1) and that he does not need to be nailed to a post to prevent him from escaping the fire because he is so in control of his

---

[42]With respect to martyrdom accounts in particular, Candida Moss advocates for looking at what martyrdom texts can teach us about the practices of early Christ movements and deconstructing the labeling of such works as *Kleinliteratur* written only for the masses, a designation used by Franz Overbeck and Adolf Deissmann. She also helpfully points to Gamble, *Books and Readers in the Early Church.* Her work dispels the notion that martyr acts "represent the tawdry underbelly of Christian literature" in Moss, *Other Christs*, 45, 225n1. Moreover, Moss also urges us to consider the variety of contexts in which such accounts may have functioned: "liturgical, catechetical, intra-ecclesial, pedagogical, apologetic, and heresiological" and to remember that even within any one of these contexts, a text can function in multiple ways, in Moss, *Other Christs*, 17, 210n61. The idea that a martyrdom account could serve a heresiological function is an important one to keep in mind.

[43]Michael Holmes also notes that Polycarp is portrayed in ways that embody Greco-Roman virtues as well as Christian ones. See Holmes, *Apostolic Fathers*, 300.

emotions (*Mart. Pol.* 13.3).[44] Many scholars note parallels to the noble death of Socrates.[45] Others note similarities to the literary representation of the binding of Isaac, a scene in which Issac was almost a martyr and in which both Abraham and Isaac exhibit a virtuous sense of self-control and patience.[46]

DEVELOPMENT OF A COLLECTIVE IDENTITY THROUGH THE DISCOURSE OF MARTYRDOM

The cultivations of individual selves through the process of facing and enduring martyrdom accompanied the formation of a corporate self among those in early Christ movements. In fact, as discussed briefly above, Judith Perkins utilizes a discursive, Foucauldian framework to show us how the identity of Christ followers was being established through the envisioning of themselves as a collective "suffering self." She argues that in the moral universe of Greco-Roman values, there was no virtue in suffering; therefore, suffering epitomized by an ignominious death, a death that allowed the sufferer to transcend the established social order and hierarchies of this world for union with Christ, actually subverted the moral and political order of the elites ruling this earthly domain.[47] Moreover, through the praise of martyrdom, those associating themselves with Christ were discursively delineating their very self-definition over and against the Roman status quo, opening "a crack in the unity of elite self-interest that informed the early empire."[48]

---

[44]Jefford also discusses the way that Polycarp's martyrdom is represented as a "noble death" as well as an example par excellence of an imitation of Christ's suffering that is "painted against the canvas of similar events in the life of Jesus of Nazareth," in Jefford, *Reading the Apostolic Fathers*, 97; see also his discussion of the representation of these deaths as atoning sacrifices associated with the Eucharist on pages 95–96, and his description of the ways that the account supports the developing doctrine of the resurrection of the flesh on page 99.

[45]See Geffcken, "Die christlichen Martyrien," 8–22; also Sterling, "*Mors philosophi*," 383–402; and Moss, *Ancient Christian Martyrdom*, 182n47.

[46]Moss, *Ancient Christian Martyrdom*, 65, 182.

[47]Perkins, *Suffering Self*, 15–40.

[48]Perkins, *Roman Imperial Identities*, 180.

Nicola Denzey argues for understanding the discourse of martyrdom differently. She asserts that martyrdom reflects a conservative social perspective highlighting the virtue of those identifying with Christ in terms that resonate with Stoic sensibilities regarding freedom from emotions and noble death.[49] Seemingly, this argument is at odds with the one Perkins makes in *The Suffering Self*. Perkins argues that Christian martyrdom is a radical social move that aligns the members of the Christian community with each other and, in fact, creates an institution at odds with the values of Roman society as a whole. In actuality, both Denzey and Perkins illuminate important parts of the way martyrdom is being represented. Perkins's argument about the ways in which the representation of martyrdom helps to create a new institution is persuasive. Nonetheless, the Roman elites are challenged by means of a kind of discourse they can understand—a discourse of virtue attained through proper care of the self. Several scholars have argued that Stoic philosophical ideas permeated the Roman world at the time the early Christian martyr acts were being written although there were "borderlines" between the various philosophical traditions and those associated with Jewish communities and early groups of Christ followers (these latter two also being characterized by diverse points of view). Platonists might borrow from Stoics, Stoics from Platonists, Christians from Stoics, and so on.[50] If so, it would have been hard for those belonging to Christ-related communities to think of presenting themselves in any other way.

Such notions were part of the philosophical "deep structure" in which they lived. Chomsky argues that there is a universal grammar wired into the brains of all infants that allows them to quickly acquire language. What particular language is acquired depends on the social context the infant inhabits. One acquires the language one hears, but the underlying basis of all cognitive linguistic development is the universal grammar that is intrinsically part of the human brain. Another name for this universal

---

[49]Denzey, "Facing the Beast," 176–198, esp. 193–194; see also David Aune, "Mastery of the Passions," 125–158; and Straw, "A Very Special Death," 39–57.
[50]See Rasimus, Engberg-Pedersen, and Dunderberg, ed., *Stoicism in Early Christianity* especially Rasimus, "Introduction," 8–10. The term "borderlines" has been, of course, popularized by Boyarin, *Border Lines*.

grammar is "deep structure."[51] The grammar of the specific language an infant learns is a "surface structure."[52] George Tinker and Loring Abeyta have pointed out that this concept can be applied to the world of culture, arguing that while it is possible to think differently in terms of "surface structure," it is impossible to change one's cultural view in terms of "deep structure." Such an argument resonates with what seems to be happening with regard to martyrdom. Early Christ movements are representing martyrdom in ways consonant with the philosophical tenets that pervaded the Roman cultural view. However, as Judith Perkins has argued cogently, they are investing the meaning of martyrdom with allegiance to a new community, one that will eventually become an alternative site of political power, the Christian Church. In this sense, Denzey's insights ring true. In other words, those inhabiting the social contexts of the Roman Empire in the first two centuries of the Common Era utilized strategies that were understandable to those living in that time. Those of lower socioeconomic status are engaged in this process, and these arguments appear in martyr acts whose narrative form was popular with all classes rather than merely in philosophical or theological treatises accessible only to the elites. However, they are in service of an alternative group, one with a different hierarchy, that of the "proto-orthodox" group that will rise to power in the fourth century.

I fully concur with Perkins's arguments about this group's constructing an alternative site of power although the degree to which such a community granted equality to its members is not clear-cut. Certainly, the discourse speaks of equality, but the very texts that the members of the community value the most speak unceasingly of obedience to and respect for the bishop, deacons, and presbyters. The *Letters of Ignatius* are a prime example. Repeatedly, Ignatius tells each of the groups to whom he writes that they must do nothing without the bishop:

> For Jesus Christ, our inseparable life, is the mind of the Father, just as the bishops appointed throughout the world are in the mind of Christ. Thus, it is proper for you to run together in harmony with the mind of the bishop, as you are in fact doing. For your council of presbyters, which is worthy of its name and worthy of God, is attuned to the bishop as strings to a lyre.

---

[51] I am grateful to George Tinker and Loring Abeyta for making this analogy and emphasizing its significance with me and others in discussions at the Iliff School of Theology.

[52] Chomsky's seminal work in laying out his theory is *Syntactic Structures*, 1972.

Therefore in your unanimity and harmonious love Jesus Christ is sung. You must join this chorus, every one of you, so that by being harmonious in unanimity and taking your pitch from God you may sing in unison with one voice through Jesus Christ to the Father, in order that he may both hear you and, on the basis of what you do well, acknowledge that you are members of his Son. It is, therefore, advantageous for you to be in perfect unity, in order that you may always have a share in God (*Eph.* 3.2–4.2).[53]

1 Clement reiterates this theme, simultaneously defining and reinforcing a hierarchy:

Let us fear the Lord Jesus Christ, whose blood was given for us. Let us respect our leaders; let us honor the older men; let us instruct the young with instruction that leads to the fear of God. Let us guide our women toward that which is good: let them display a disposition to purity worthy of admiration; let them exhibit a sincere desire to be gentle; let them demonstrate by their silence the moderation of their tongue; let them show their love, without partiality and in holiness, equally toward all those who fear God (*1 Clem.* 21.6–7).

Shelly Matthews, however, points out the way that the discourse of martyrdom can work both to subvert the existing sites of power and authority and yet also generate new ones in a manner that illuminates the insights of both Perkins and Denzey:

As a discourse that attempts to wrest meaning out of violence through inverting categories of strength and weakness, victory and loss, and life and death, martyrdom narratives can subvert hegemonic powers, providing a language of, and hence a means for, resistance to those facing similar violent circumstances . . . . Paradoxically, the anti-judgment, anti-authority alignment of Christian martyrdom discourse can work in the service of generating new sites of authority."[54]

Beth Berkowitz also describes the way that Ignatius links the themes of martyrdom with those of obedience and submission to the bishop:

---

[53]As discussed previously, all citations come from Holmes, *Apostolic Fathers*, unless noted otherwise.

[54]Matthews, *Perfect Martyr*, 4–5.

> We have [in Ignatius] martyrdom on top of martyrdom on top of martyr-
> dom: Ignatius martyrs himself for those church members who in turn
> "martyr" themselves for the bishop, all of whom imitate the originary mar-
> tyrdom of Christ for God. Yet Ignatius also demands obedience as a bishop:
> He is both the subject of suffering and the object for whom one suffers.[55]

In the end, it seems that social norms regarding hierarchy and gender
remain largely intact.

INTERMINGLING OF MARTYRDOM AS THE CARE OF THE SELF WITH THE RESURRECTION OF THE FLESH AND APOSTOLIC AUTHORITY

In works such as the *Letters of Ignatius* and *1 Clement*, the discourse of
martyrdom as care of the self and other topics intermingle. One is the love not
only of Christ himself but love of his "suffering and resurrection." A second is
linking participation in the Eucharist with certain notions of Christ's suffering, death, and resurrection and promising immortality to the faithful, and a
third is respect for apostolic authority. The text links medical imagery and the
notion of an "undisturbed mind" with these ideas. Such language resonates
with the idea of a properly cared for soul and the notion of "immovability"
and emotional stability discussed later in Chap. 5. Ignatius says, for example:

> If Jesus Christ, in response to your prayer, should reckon me worthy, and if it
> is his will, in a second letter . . . I will explain to you the subject about which
> I have begun to speak, namely, the divine plan with respect to the new man
> Jesus Christ, involving faith in him and *love for him, his suffering and res-
> urrection* . . . . All of you, individually and collectively, gather together in
> grace, my name, in one faith and one Jesus Christ . . . in order that you may
> obey the bishop and the council of presbyters with an *undisturbed mind,
> breaking one bread*, which is the *medicine of immortality*, the antidote we
> take in order not to die but to *live forever* in Jesus Christ (*Eph.* 20.2).[56]

In this passage, participating in the Eucharist, a symbol of Christ's sacrifice,
goes hand in hand with obedience to the ecclesial authorities. Ignatius

---

[55]See Berkowitz, *Execution and Invention*, 200. See also Matthews, *Perfect Martyr*,
139n6.
[56]Emphasis added.

makes this clearer in his *Letter to the Smyrneans* when he accuses heretics of "abstain[ing] from Eucharist . . . because they refuse to acknowledge that the Eucharist is the flesh of our savior Jesus Christ, which suffered for our sins and which the Father by his goodness raised up" (*Smyr.* 6.2). He then goes on to tell the readers to avoid these kinds of people (*Smyr.* 7.2) as he emphatically thunders,

> You must all follow the bishop as Jesus Christ followed the Father, and follow the council of presbyters as you would the apostles; respect the deacons as the commandment of God. Let no one do anything that has to do with the church without the bishop. Only that Eucharist which is under the authority of the bishop (or whomever he himself designates) is to be considered valid. Wherever the bishop appears, there let the congregation be; just as wherever Jesus Christ is, there is the catholic church. It is not permissible either to baptize or to hold a love feast without the bishop. But whatever he approves is also pleasing to God, in order that everything you do may be trustworthy and valid. Finally, it is reasonable for us to come to our senses while we still have time to repent and turn to God. It is good to acknowledge God and the bishop. The one who honors the bishop has been honored by God; the one who does anything without the bishop's knowledge serves the devil (*Smyr.* 8.1–9.1).

Indeed, in such passages, it is hard to delineate the point where one theme ends and another begins. Ignatius compares his chains to "spiritual pearls," describes those very chains as the means of resurrection, and then intermingles notions of agreement with or submission to apostolic authority as well:

> Let nothing appeal to you apart from him, in whom I carry around these chains (my spiritual pearls!), by which I hope, through your prayers, to rise again. May I always share in them, in order that I may be found in the company of the Christians of Ephesus, who have always been in agreement with the apostles by the power of Jesus Christ (*Eph.* 11.2).

Though Ignatius does not use the term "flesh" in speaking of the resurrection, he carefully notes that Jesus Christ "*really* was raised from the dead when his Father raised him up" (*Trall.* 9.2).[57]

In *1 Clement*, the author speaks of resurrection, invoking the image of the phoenix and a passage from Job, and the notion of a *fleshly* resurrection

---

[57]Emphasis added.

is clear: "[Y]ou will raise this flesh of mine, which has endured all these things" (*1 Clem.* 26.3). Likewise, Polycarp's words are represented as follows:

> I bless you because you have considered me worthy of this day and hour, so that I might receive a place among the number of the martyrs in the cup of your Christ, to the resurrection to eternal life, *both of soul and of body*, in the incorruptibility of the Holy Spirit (*Mart. Pol.* 14.2).[58]

Theologians such as Tertullian make the insistence on this idea of a fleshly resurrection extremely plain:

> If God raises not men entire, He raises not the dead. For what dead man is entire, although he dies entire? Who is without hurt, that is without life? What body is uninjured, when it is dead, when it is cold, when it is ghastly, when it is stiff, when it is a corpse? When is a man more infirm, than when he is entirely infirm? When more palsied, than when quite motionless? Thus, for a dead man to be raised again, amounts to nothing short of his being restored to his entire condition,—lest he, forsooth, be still dead in that part in which he has not risen again. God is quite able to remake what He once made. This power and this unstinted grace of His He has already sufficiently guaranteed in Christ; and has displayed Himself to us (in Him) not only as the restorer of the flesh, but as the repairer of its breaches . . . . Thus our flesh shall remain after the resurrection—so far indeed susceptible of suffering, as it is the flesh, and the same flesh, too; but at the same time impassible, inasmuch as it has been liberated by the Lord for the very end and purpose of being no longer capable of enduring suffering (*De res.* 57).[59]

It is important to note the interweaving of these themes as all of them will play a part in discussing the ways that other works disrupt the meaning of martyrdom as a kind of care of the self linked with notions of martyrdom as a sacrifice, notions of apostolic authority, and the doctrine of a fleshly resurrection. Caroline Walker Bynum shows the means by which this

---

[58]Emphasis added.

[59]All translations of Tertullian come from Roberts, *Ante-Nicene Fathers* unless otherwise noted.

doctrine actually arises in the context of persecution. I will discuss it more fully in Chap. 4 as I put both those who promoted it and those who disagreed with it in conversation.[60]

In summary, the main argument of this chapter is that writers identifying with Christ in the second and third centuries C.E. represent martyrdom in terms consonant with the care of the soul, particularly in its Stoic conception. In signifying the meaning of martyrdom in this way, suffering becomes a good and martyrdom something to be desired. In some cases, the texts also link martyrdom with the imitation of Christ's sacrifice as a blood atonement for sin, a sacrifice pleasing to God. In addition, it is linked with the development of belief in a bodily resurrection of the very flesh of one's existing, earthly body. Moreover, the discourse of martyrdom appears to be used to uphold the legitimacy of the insistence on the authority of the bishops in the line of the apostolic succession from Peter and Paul. Finally, all of these together make the discourse of martyrdom one of the significant ways by which the Roman Empire's claim to authority is challenged as a whole other sense of corporate selfhood develops and an alternative site of power starts to coalesce in what will become the Christian Church of the fourth century. Chap. 4 delineates the ways that so-called gnostic writings disrupt this discourse in two ways: by articulating views about how to care for the self using practices that reflect more traditional Greco-Roman notions regarding the therapy of emotions while simultaneously critiquing the glorification of martyrdom, disrupting the increasingly dominant discourse.

References

Ancient Works

Ante-Nicene Fathers

Roberts, Alexander, and James Donaldson, eds. *The Ante-Nicene Fathers: The Writings of the Fathers down to A.D. 325*. American Reprint of the Edinburgh Edition. 10 vols. Edited by A. Cleveland Coxe. New York: Charles Scribner's Sons, 1903.

---

[60]Bynum, *Resurrection of the Body*, 21–58.

Apostolic Fathers

Holmes, Michael W., ed. and trans. *The Apostolic Fathers: Greek Text and English Translations*. 3d ed.; Grand Rapids: Baker Academic, 2007.

Boethius, Ancius

Watts, Victor, ed. *The Consolation of Philosophy*. Rev. Ed. London: Penguin, 1999.

Modern Works

Aune, David E. "Mastery of the Passions: Philo, 4 Maccabees, and Early Christianity." Pages 125–158 in *Hellenization Revisited: Shaping a Christian Response within the Greco-Roman World*. Edited by W. E. Hellerman. Lanham, Md.: University Press of America, 1994.

Berkowitz, Beth. *Execution and Invention: Death Penalty Discourse in Early Rabbinic and Christian Cultures*. New York: Oxford University Press, 2006.

Bernauer, James W. *Michel Foucault's Force of Flight: Toward an Ethics of Thought*. London: Humanities Press International, 1990.

Bowersock, G. W. *Martyrdom and Rome*. Cambridge: Cambridge University Press, 1995.

Boyarin, Daniel. *Border Lines: The Partitioning of Judaeo-Christianity*. Divinations: Rereading Late Ancient Religion. Edited by Daniel Boyarin, Virginia Burrus, Charlotte Fonrobert, and Robert Gregg. Philadelphia: University of Pennsylvania Press, 2004.

Bynum, Caroline Walker. *The Resurrection of the Body in Western Christianity, 200–1336*. New York: Columbia University Press, 1995.

Carrette, Jeremy R. "Prologue to a Confession of the Flesh." Pages 1–47 in Jeremy Carrette, *Religion and Culture: Michel Foucault*. New York: Routledge, 1999.

Castelli, Elizabeth A. *Martyrdom and Memory: Early Christian Culture-Making*. New York: Columbia University Press, 2004.

Chomsky, Noam. *Syntactic Structures*. 2d ed. Berlin: de Gruyter, 1972.

Daly, Robert J. *Christian Sacrifice: The Judaeo-Christian Background before Origen*. Washington, D. C.: Catholic University of America Press, 1978.

Daly, Robert J. *The Origins of the Christian Doctrine of Sacrifice*. Philadelphia: Fortress, 1978.

De Ste. Croix, G. E. M. *Papers by De Ste. Croix: Christian Persecution, Martyrdom, and Orthodoxy*. Edited by Michael Whitby and Joseph Streeter. Oxford: Oxford University Press, 2006.

Dehandschutter, Boudewijn. *Martyrium Polycarpi: Ein literair-krittisch studie.* Biblioteca Ephemeridum Theologicarum Lovaniensium 52. Leuven: Peeters, 2005.

Dehandschutter, Boudewijn and Johan Leemans, *Polycarpiana: Studies on Martyrdom and Persecution in Early Christianity.* Leuven: Leuven University Press, 2007.

Denzey, Nicola. "Facing the Beast: Justin, Christian Martyrdom, and Freedom of the Will." Pages 176–198 in *Stoicism in Early Christianity.* Edited by Tuomas Rasimus, Troels Engberg-Pedersen, and Ismo Dunderberg. Grand Rapids: Baker Academic, 2010.

Foucault, Michel. *The Hermeneutics of the Subject: Lectures at the Collège de France 1981–82.* Edited by Frédéric Gros. Translated by Graham Burchell. New York: Picador, 2005.

Foucault, Michel. "Technologies of the Self." Pages 16–49 in *Technologies of the Self: A Seminar with Michel Foucault.* Edited by Luther H. Martin, Huck Gutman, and Patrick H. Hutton. Amherst: University of Massachusetts Press, 1988.

Frend, W. H. C. *Martyrdom and Persecution in the Early Church: A Study of a Conflict from the Maccabees to Donatus.* 1965. Repr., Cambridge: James Clarke, 2008.

Gamble, Harry Y. *Books and Readers in the Early Church: A History of Early Christian Texts.* New Haven, Conn.: Yale University Press, 1995.

Geffcken, Johnannes. "Die christlichen Martyrien." *Hermes* 45 (1910): 481–505.

Gregory, Andrew. "*1 Clement*: An Introduction." Pages 21–31 in *Writings of the Apostolic Fathers.* Edited by Paul Foster. London: T&T Clark, 2007.

Hadot, Pierre. *Philosophy as a Way of Life: Spiritual Exercises from Socrates to Foucault.* Edited by Arnold I. Davidson. Translated by Michael Chase. Oxford: Blackwell, 1995.

Holmes, Michael W. "The *Martyrdom of Polycarp* and the New Testament Passion Narratives." Pages 407–432 in *Trajectories Through the New Testament and the Apostolic Fathers.* Edited by Andrew F. Gregory and Christopher Tuckett. Oxford: Oxford University Press, 2005.

Holmes, Michael W. "Polycarp of Smyrna, Letter to the Philippians." *Expository Times* 118.2 (2006): 53–63.

Jefford, Clayton N. *Reading the Apostolic Fathers: A Student's Introduction.* 2d ed. Grand Rapids: Baker Academic, 2012.

Koester, Helmut. *History and Literature of Early Christianity.* 2 vols. New York: de Gruyter, 2000.

Koester, Helmut. *History, Culture, and Religion of the Hellenistic Age.* 2 vols. 2d ed. New York: de Gruyter, 1995.

Lieu, Judith M. *Image and Reality: The Jews in the World of the Christians in the Second Century.* Edinburgh: T&T Clark, 1996.

Long, A. A., and D. N. Sedley. *The Hellenistic Philosophers.* Vol. 1. Cambridge: Cambridge University Press, 1987.

Maier, Harry O. "Purity and Danger in Polycarp's Epistle to the Philippians: The Sin of Valens in Social Perspective." *Journal of Early Christian Studies* 1 (1993): 229–47.

Matthews, Shelly. *Perfect Martyr: The Stoning of Stephen and the Construction of Christian Identity.* Oxford: Oxford University Press, 2010.

Moss, Candida R. *Ancient Christian Martyrdom: Diverse Practices, Theologies, and Traditions.* New Haven, Conn.: Yale University Press, 2012.

Moss, Candida R. *The Other Christs: Imitating Jesus in Ancient Christian Ideologies of Martyrdom.* New York: Oxford University Press, 2010.

Nussbaum, Martha. "The Stoics on the Extirpation of the Passions." *Apeiron* 20 (1987): 129–77.

Oden, Thomas C. *Care of the Souls in the Classic Tradition* in Theology and Pastoral Care Series. Edited by Don S. Browning. Philadelphia: Fortress, 1984.

Perkins, Judith. *Roman Imperial Identities in the Early Christian Era.* Routledge Monographs in Classical Studies. New York: Routledge, 2008.

Perkins, Judith. *The Suffering Self: Pain and Narrative Representation in the Early Christian Era.* New York: Routledge, 1995.

Rasimus, Tuomas. "Introduction" Pages 8–10 in *Stoicism in Early Christianity.* Edited by Tuomas Rasimus, Troels Engberg-Pedersen, and Ismo Dunderberg. Grand Rapids: Baker Academic, 2010.

Rasimus, Tuomas, Troels Engberg-Pedersen and Ismo Dunderberg, eds. *Stoicism in Early Christianity.* Grand Rapids: Baker Academic, 2010.

Salisbury, Joyce E. *The Blood of Martyrs: Unintended Consequences of Ancient Violence.* New York: Routledge, 2004.

Shaw, Brent D. "Body/Power/Identity: Passions of the Martyrs." *Journal of Early Christian Studies* 4.3 (1996): 269–312.

Sterling, Gregory E. "*Mors philosophi*: The Death of Jesus in Luke." *Harvard Theological Review* 94.4 (2001): 383–402.

Stowers, Stanley K. *Letter-Writing in Greco-Roman Antiquity.* Philadelphia: Westminster, 1986.

Straw, Carole. "'A Very Special Death': Christian Martyrdom in its Classical Context." Pages 39–57 in *Sacrificing the Self: Perspectives on Martyrdom and Religion.* Edited by Margaret Cormack. Oxford: Oxford University Press, 2002.

Young, Frances M. *Sacrifice and the Death of Christ.* Philadelphia: Westminster, 1975.

Young, Frances M. *The Use of Sacrificial Ideas in Greek Christian Writers from the New Testament to John Chrysostom.* Patristic Monograph Series 5. Philadelphia: Philadelphia Patristic Foundation, 1979.

Young, Robin Darling. *In Procession Before the World: Martyrdom as Public Liturgy in Early Christianity.* Milwaukee: Marquette University Press, 2001.

CHAPTER 4

Competing Visions of the Care of the Self in the *Apocalypse of Peter*, the *Testimony of Truth*, *Fragments of Basilides and Valentinus*, and the *Gospel of Judas*

Given what we see in reading *1 Clement*, the *Letters of Ignatius*, and texts associated with Polycarp, I have argued that the constitution of some Christ-related identities was revolving around a conception of the care of the self as the process of facing and enduring martyrdom.[1] If this is the case, one can well imagine that works of other early Christ groups criticizing this idea of the care of the self may well have constituted a challenge, even a threat, to the imagination of the early Christian self in relation to martyrdom. One indeed finds such a challenge in the discourses of certain other individuals and groups who also identified with the Christ. In contrast to the way that the meaning and significance of martyrdom are represented in the texts of *1 Clement*, the *Letters of Ignatius*, the *Martyrdom of Polycarp*, and the *Letter of Polycarp to the Philippians*, these other writers, including the authors of some of the books discovered near Nag Hammadi, Egypt, offer a broad range of interpretations. Just as the authors of the works discussed in Chap. 3, these writers also describe the care of the self in terms consonant with Stoic philosophy, particularly regarding the therapy of emotions and healing, which results in freedom from enslavement to desires or passions.[2]

---

[1] Of course, this by no means implies that the discourse in these texts is itself monolithic. See Moss, *Other Christs*, 87 for further discussion of this point.

[2] For an excellent discussion of this idea, see Nussbaum, *Therapy of Desire*, 1994. Chapters 9 and 10 consider Stoic conceptions of self-government and the extirpation of the passions. In contrast to Foucault, Nussbaum emphasizes the focus on reason in Greek texts.

© The Author(s) 2017
D. Niederer Saxon, *The Care of the Self in Early Christian Texts*,
The Bible and Cultural Studies, DOI 10.1007/978-3-319-64750-0_4

However, for them, Christ is the teacher and healer who can effect a "cure" from passions such as fear and anger through his teaching, his revelation, and his wise interpretations of the visions his followers have. It is through being acquainted with Christ, knowing him, and interacting with him that freedom comes.[3] Moreover, these thinkers see entrapment in desire of any kind as weakness; therefore, while advocating for a therapy of the emotions based on one's relationship to Christ, they simultaneously adopt a discursive strategy of criticizing those who glorify or even desire martyrdom as "filled with passion," representing them as lacking in self-control.[4] This criticism disrupts a discourse increasingly dominated by such praise.

Moreover, those responsible for the texts discussed in this chapter do not necessarily agree with the particular significance some ascribe to the death of Christ—an atonement needed to appease a God who requires

---

[3]Bentley Layton's analysis of the Greek *gnōsis* is helpful here. Layton explains that in Greek, "knowledge" is represented by several different words. Some knowledge is propositional while other knowledge is relational, involving personal acquaintance with something or someone. There are different words for each. The verb for propositional knowledge is *eidenai*, and the verb for relational knowledge is *gignoskein*. A sentence stating that one "knows" that Athens is the capitol of Greece would contain a form of *eidenai* whereas a statement about knowing Athens well or having known a person for many years would contain a form of the verb *gignoskein*. The noun that is related to *gignoskein* is *gnōsis*. When people are introduced to each other, they have *gnōsis* of each other. Layton goes on to say, "If one is introduced to god, one has *gnōsis* of God. The ancient Gnostics described salvation as a kind of *gnōsis* or acquaintance, and the ultimate object of that acquaintance was nothing less than god." He then explains that he therefore translates *gnosis* as "acquaintance with." See Layton, *Gnostic Scriptures*, 9. I think, this distinction helps us to understand the connotations of *gnōsis* as having to do with one's relationship to knowledge provided by Christ and even to Christ himself rather than the acquiring of esoteric knowledge.

[4]Even Romans who are not part of Christ-related groups employ this critique. For example, the Stoic emperor Marcus Aurelius remarks in *Meditations* 11.3, "What a soul that is which is ready, if at any moment it must be separated from the body, and ready either to be extinguished or dispersed or continue to exist; but so that this readiness comes from a man's own judgment, not from mere obstinacy, as with the Christians, but considerately and with dignity and in a way to persuade another, without tragic show." Translation from Eliot, *Meditations of Marcus Aurelius*, 285.

sacrifice.[5] In addition, while they agree that there is a life (or lives) beyond this one, they do not necessarily agree with the developing theology of the resurrection of the *flesh*. They do believe in immortality but not necessarily that of the very same material body one inhabited prior to death.

HERESIOLOGICAL FRAMING

Unfortunately, these differences have long been refracted through the lens of heresiologists who accused their opponents of disloyalty or a lack of courage in not embracing martyrdom. Criticism begins with Justin, who observes that "they [Gnostics] are neither persecuted nor put to death" (*I Apol.* 26).[6] Irenaeus, too, accuses the Gnostics:

> [s]ome of these men have proceeded to such a degree of temerity, that they even pour contempt upon the martyrs, and vituperate those who are slain on account of the confession of the Lord, and who suffer all things predicted by the Lord, and who in this respect strive to follow the footsteps of the Lord's passion, having become martyrs of the suffering One; these we do also enrol with the martyrs themselves. For, when inquisition shall be made for their blood, and they shall attain to glory, then all shall be confounded by Christ, who have cast a slur upon their martyrdom (*Haer.* 3.18.5).

Later, Irenaeus returns to this theme:

> Wherefore the Church does in every place, because of that love which she cherishes towards God, send forward, throughout all time, a multitude of martyrs to the Father; while all others not only have nothing of this kind to point to among themselves, but even maintain that such witness-bearing is

---

[5]Moss discusses the way in which sacrifice is represented in various martyr acts. In some, as well as in other genres, such as the *Letters of Ignatius*, language and imagery associated with sacrifice is present, but in others, such language is rare or altogether lacking, and martyrs are represented as conquering Satan in accord with a *Christus Victor* theory of atonement or as moral exemplars. See Moss, *Other Christs*, 75–111, 240–255. Thus, it is crucial to understand that early followers of Christ in a wide variety of groups and social and geographical contexts are responding and reacting to a wide range of representations.

[6]As noted above, all citations and translations of Justin and other so-called "orthodox" pre-Constantinian writers come from Roberts and Donaldson, *Ante-Nicene Fathers*, unless otherwise specified.

not at all necessary, for that their system of doctrines is the true witness [for Christ], with the exception, perhaps, that one or two among them, during the whole time which has elapsed since the Lord appeared on earth, have occasionally, along with our martyrs, borne the reproach of the name (as if he too [the heretic] had obtained mercy), and have been led forth with them [to death], being, as it were, a sort of retinue granted unto them. For the Church alone sustains with purity the reproach of those who suffer persecution for righteousness' sake, and endure all sorts of punishments, and are put to death because of the love which they bear to God, and their confession of His Son; often weakened indeed, yet immediately increasing her members, and becoming whole again (*Haer.* 4.33.9).

Irenaeus actually uses an analogy in which he places himself in the role of a martyr in the arena and depicts those he deems heretics as the animals and beasts who are attacking him. In other words, he uses the discourse of martyrdom itself as a discursive strategy of "othering."[7] In the first chapter of the *Scorpiace*, Tertullian, too, refers to some who scorn martyrdom:

This among Christians is a season of persecution. When, therefore, faith is greatly agitated and the church burning, as represented by the bush, then the Gnostics break out; then the Valentinians creep forth; then all the opponents of martyrdom bubble up, being themselves also hot to strike, penetrate, kill. For, because they know that many are artless and also inexperienced, and weak moreover, that a very great number in truth are Christians who veer about with the wind and conform to its moods, they perceive that they are never to be approached more than when fear has opened the entrances to the soul, especially when some display of ferocity has already arrayed with a crown the faith of martyrs . . . . we are in the midst of an intense heat, the very dog-star of persecution . . . . Of some Christians the fire, of others the sword, of others the beasts, have made trial; others are hungering in prison for the martyrdoms of which they have had a taste in the meantime by being subjected to clubs and claws besides. We ourselves, having been appointed for pursuit, are like hares being hemmed in from a distance; and heretics go about according to their wont.

---

[7]See Moss, *Other Christs*, 175.

At the end of the chapter, he says,

> But woe to them who turn sweet into bitter, and light into darkness. For, in
> like manner, they also who oppose martyrdoms, representing salvation to be
> destruction, transmute sweet into bitter, as well as light into darkness; and
> thus, by preferring this very wretched life to that most blessed one, they put
> bitter for sweet, as well as darkness for light.

In fact, the entire *Scorpiace* is an antidote to what Tertullian considers the
poison of heretics who are akin to small but very dangerous scorpions.
Finally, in the fourth chapter of Book IV of the *Stromata*, sometimes
referred to as "miscellanies" or even a "carpet bag" due to its loosely
organized and eclectic nature, Clement of Alexandria says,

> Now some of the heretics who have misunderstood the Lord, have at once an
> impious and cowardly love of life, saying that the true martyrdom is the
> knowledge of the only true God (which we also admit), and that the man is a
> self-murderer and a suicide who makes confession by death; and adducing
> other similar sophisms of cowardice.[8]

The style and tone of such writers varies somewhat, but in the end, some
would argue that all these critiques are "hostile sources" whose framing of
the issues as doctrinal disputes has long perpetuated the discourse of
"orthodoxy" and "heresy."[9]

Ismo Dunderberg notes that so-called Gnostic texts have not often been
examined for what they have to say about "moral exhortation, views about
emotions, and critical analysis of power and society" simply because such
topics have not been considered main themes of "the core of Gnostic
thought," and as he succinctly points out, "None of these features has been
regarded as constituting the distinct essence, or the 'spirit,' of
Gnosticism."[10] In effect, the focus of scholarship has been influenced by
presuppositions about what the main themes of gnostic writing are. Philip
Tite reinforces this point in his comprehensive discussion of the ways that

---

[8]There are other examples as well, particularly in Origen's *Exhortation to
Martyrdom*; see O'Meara, trans., *Prayer: Exhortation to Martyrdom*.

[9]Dunderberg, *Beyond Gnosticism*, 8.

[10]Dunderberg, *Beyond Gnosticism*, 1.

scholars usually explicate works deemed gnostic in terms of their esoteric myths, arguing that these writings are worth reexamining with respect to their ethical teachings.[11] Likewise, Lance Jenott also discusses the impossibility of presupposing a gnostic point of view and the distorted perspective that evolves from doing so.[12]

In addition, most of the texts we will examine in this chapter and the next are in the form of a dialogue or have a dialogical component with speech-like qualities. A general point that Hadot makes with respect to the genre of dialogue is relevant here. He explains that dialogue is not "a theoretical and dogmatic account . . . it is not concerned with the exposition of a doctrine, but with guiding an interlocutor to a certain settled mental attitude." He goes on to say, "Rather than aiming at the acquisition of a purely abstract knowledge, these exercises aimed at realizing a transformation of one's vision of the world and a metamorphosis of one's personality."[13] It is worth keeping in mind that often newly discovered writings have been analyzed for what they have to say about doctrine when their main thrust may be something quite different than an exposition of doctrine or a set of propositions for their readers to "believe" in and, in fact, when analyzing them this way is anachronistic, imposing formulations of doctrine on them that had not been articulated at the time they were written.

Existential issues are involved, and Hadot also talks about the difficulty of discussing topics that involve "our feeling of existence, our impressions when faced by death, our perception of nature, our sensations, and a fortiori the mystical experience." He says that it is almost impossible to communicate about these things in language that is other than "conventional and banal"—that "we realize this when we try to console someone over the loss of a loved one." He then goes on to say that often "a poem or a biography are more philosophical than a philosophical treatise, simply because they allow us to glimpse this unsayable in an indirect way."[14] Most of the texts that this book explores have a biographical component though they are literary representations. They are useful not in proving the truth of a set of logical assertions about exactly who Jesus was or is. Rather, they

---

[11]Tite, "*Valentinian Ethics*" 1–2, 6–102 and 192–195.

[12]Jenott, *Gospel of Judas*, 2, 10.

[13]Hadot, *Philosophy as a Way of Life*, 20.

[14]Hadot, *Philosophy as a Way of Life*, 285.

provide a glimpse of the way in which people in the early Christ movements conceived of their relationship to him and the way in which that
relationship, particularly the way that they interpreted Jesus's teachings,
informed their own understanding of the existential. The literary representations of Jesus's death and resurrection also served to help them
overcome any passions—including fear or anger—that would keep them
from preaching the gospel with boldness and courage; that is, from sharing
the teachings and the way of living embodied in Jesus with others, a form
of *parrhēsia*.

ALTERNATIVE PERSPECTIVES

Therefore, in this chapter, we take a fresh look at some of these newly discovered works with respect both to what they have to say about the care of the
self as the therapy of emotions and their simultaneous critique of martyrdom
discourse prevalent in their time. In particular, the texts of the *Apocalypse of
Peter*,[15] the *Testimony of Truth*,[16] two fragments preserved in the writings of
Clement of Alexandria (one attributed to Basilides[17] and the other to

---

[15]Citations and translation for the *Apocalypse of Peter* are from Brashler, trans.,
Apocalypse of Peter, 201–247. There are actually two texts by this name, the con-
tents of which are completely different. The one discussed in this chapter is the
Coptic *Apocalypse of Peter* (codex VII) found at Nag Hammadi. It is in Coptic but
was probably originally in Greek. Andreas Werner dates it to the late second or early
third century; see Werner, "Coptic gnostic Apocalypse of Peter," 702. The other
work of the same name, surviving in Ethiopic, was probably also originally written
in Greek. An English translation is available in Schneemelcher, *New Testament
Apocrypha*, 2:620–638. This name was also given to some other apocalypses written
considerably later, which now exist in Arabic and Ethiopic; Desjardins,
"Introduction to the *Apocalypse of Peter*," 201–216.

[16]Citations and translation from the *Testimony of Truth* are from Pearson, trans.,
Testimony of Truth. Birger A. Pearson discusses the difficulty in dating the text. He
argues that the "most plausible hypothesis" is the late second or early third century
of the Common Era; Pearson, *Testimony of Truth*, 118–120.

[17]All citations and translation of Fragment G come from Layton, *Gnostic Scriptures*,
440–443, which also includes Layton's commentary on the fragment.

Valentinus),[18] and the *Gospel of Judas*[19] offer insight into these interpretations. In these five works, a discourse that articulates the positive value of the therapy of emotions intersects with a discourse challenging the meaning of martyrdom as described in the previous chapter. These writings challenge the conception of the ultimate care of the self as an imitation of Christ's atoning sacrifice, the doctrine of the fleshly resurrection, and notions of apostolic succession.

Close examination of these texts reveals not the existence of two opposed religions—"Christianity" and "Gnosticism"—but rather a shifting, fluid web of interactions among those who will come to be thought of as the orthodox and a variety of other Christ movements such as those that scholars increasingly refer to as Sethians, Basilideans, and Valentinians. Of course, the boundaries among groups such as these were not necessarily clearly defined or fixed. Such groups may have been marked by internal diversity as well.[20]

These differences are in many ways analogous to those between the strands of the various groups Daniel Boyarin has explained so well as "Judaisms" and "Christianities." Boyarin also discusses the ways in which attitudes toward martyrdom reflect a spectrum of religious identities. He describes Christians as those who embrace martyrdom, and he maintains that Jews hold a variety of positions regarding its value, but a closer examination of Christ-related texts previously deemed gnostic actually serves to extend Boyarin's thesis regarding the variety of attitudes toward martyrdom. His ideas about the ways that attitudes toward martyrdom

---

[18]All citations and translation of Fragment F come from Layton, *Gnostic Scriptures*, 240–241, which also includes Layton's commentary on it.

[19]All citations and translation of the *Gospel of Judas* come from Kasser et al., *Gospel of Judas*. Irenaeus of Lyon may have known about this work, which would place its dating prior to ca. 180 of the Common Era. See discussion below.

[20]Lance Jenott describes why labeling such groups can be problematic: "If we choose to use such labels as Sethian (or Valentinian, or any other) to typologically sort texts according to the unique features they share, we must also remember that our typologies do not represent monolithic 'systems' with no internal diversity. When one looks closely at the specific details of each work, it is clear that they also tell drastically different narratives and advocate different theological perspectives. This raises a larger question that historians of early Christianity are only beginning to explore, namely, what sorts of controversies there were *within* the various 'schools' of thought that we typologically construct by blurring differences among their members." Jenott, *Gospel of Judas*, 132.

serve as markers of identity can be applied to debates among various Christ movements regarding its value as well.[21]

Apocalypse of Peter

The single extant manuscript of the *Apocalypse of Peter* in Nag Hammadi Codex VII, 3 (70,13–84,14) articulates a vision of the care of the self as healing from the destructive effects of one's emotions.[22] This text revolves around Peter's need for a therapy of emotions and the portrayal of Jesus as being able to provide such a cure. At the same time, it serves as a critique of those whom the author sees as blindly attributing the source of liberation from one's passions to an exaltation of suffering centered in theologies of a substitutionary atonement and a fleshly resurrection.[23]

The main thrust of the text is that Peter lacks courage. In short, he is consumed by his passions and in need of the kind of healing that a therapy of the emotions can provide. The work progresses with Jesus repeatedly telling Peter not to be afraid. Indeed, as the editor of the Brill edition points out, exhortations to Peter to be strong, perfect, or unafraid frame the entire narrative, appearing at both the introduction and the end as well as throughout the text (71,16; 71,22; 80,32–33; 82,18; 84,7–12). Specifically, Peter expresses his fear three times, and Jesus reassures him in each case, instances that are discussed below. First, Peter fears that both he and Jesus will be killed when a mob runs toward them with stones. Later, he expresses fear regarding who will win the battle for control of the "little ones." Finally, Peter expresses fear in his vision of the crucifixion, begging Jesus to flee. In each case, Jesus carefully explains why Peter does not need to be afraid and exhorts him to be "perfect" (71,16) or "strong" (71,22).[24]

---

[21] Boyarin, *Border Lines;* Boyarin, *Dying for God.*

[22] For discussion of the text, see Desjardins, *Apocalypse of Peter,* 201–216; Koschorke, "Die Polemik der Petrusapokalypse," 11–90.

[23] The editors of the Brill edition note that this work could be as early as 150 C.E.; Desjardins, *Apocalypse of Peter,* 214. Scholars have often assumed a third century composition because the text clearly reflects the existence of discord among Christ movements rather than the supposed unity that characterized the earliest groups. Such reasoning, however, is circular. The notion of an original unity within which heresy arose has been deconstructed; see Bauer, *Orthodoxy and Heresy.*

[24] See Brashler, *Apocalypse of Peter (NHC VII, 3),* 230.

The term "perfect" also appears in Seneca, Philo, the *Book of Thomas the Contender*, and the *Secret Revelation of John*.[25] The Stoic notion of perfection entailed the absence of the passions, or *apatheia*. It is used in the *Gospel of Judas* as well. Judas is the one who more closely approaches the status of "the perfect human" (35,4) than do any of the other disciples (although scholars debate whether, in the end, he is portrayed positively or negatively).

Repeatedly in the *Apocalypse of Peter*, Peter fails to demonstrate such *apatheia*. Near the beginning, he says, "I saw the priests and the people running toward us with stones, as if they were about to kill us. And I was afraid that we were going to die" (72,5–9). Some scholars feel this scene takes place on the night of Jesus's arrest. Others argue it occurs in a heavenly temple.[26] In any case, it is Peter's sense of fear that is highlighted, the same fear recorded in all four gospels of the New Testament, which results in Peter's threefold betrayal of Jesus. The *Apocalypse of Peter* does not explicitly mention this betrayal, but it comes to mind when the text says that Jesus "will correct you three times in this night" (72,2–4). Through these corrections, which actually function as special insights, Jesus provides the words of revelation Peter needs to help him overcome his fears.

Parallels also exist with the transfiguration that Peter, James, and John witness in the Gospel of Mark (Chap. 9), the Gospel of Matthew (Chap. 17), and the Gospel of Luke (Chap. 9). In the *Apocalypse of Peter*, Peter sees Jesus bathed in light: "For I saw a new light greater than the light of day. Then it came down upon the Savior" (72,22–26). This allusion serves to remind the reader of Peter's lack of full understanding and his fear. In that transfiguration scene, Peter wants to honor Jesus, Moses, and Elijah equally (Mark 9:5; Matt 17:4). A voice from heaven has to tell him to listen only to Jesus (Mark 9:7; Matt 17:5). Moreover, Peter and the others (James and John) are afraid (Mark 9:6; Matt 17:6). Jesus has to tell them explicitly

---

[25]Dunderberg, "Judas' Anger and the Perfect Human," 201–221.

[26]Michael Desjardins' comment is pertinent here: "Brashler (125–135) and Dubois ("Le preambule," 387–390) argue that the author sets his work in a heavenly temple, with the revelation given by the risen Savior. Koschorke (13), Perkins (*Gnostic Dialogue*, 116), and Brown and Griggs (133) posit an earthly, pre-crucifixion setting and do more justice to the passage. In fact, however, the Savior's spiritual nature moves the revelation to a non-earthly sphere regardless of the option one chooses," in Desjardins, *Apocalypse of Peter*, 203n15.

not to fear (Matt 17:7). When they come down from the mountain, a man with a son in need of healing immediately confronts them, but in spite of the experience they have just had, they are unable to cure him (Mark 9:18; Matt 17:16). The father has to bring him to Jesus (Mark 9:17; Matt 17:17). Jesus tells them that they are still lacking in belief (Matt 17:20) and that a cure is possible only with prayer and fasting (Mark 9:29; Matt 17:21). The limited understanding Peter and the others exhibit in these passages seems similar to Peter's lack of awareness in the *Apocalypse*.

As the narrative progresses, Jesus understands and responds to Peter even though Peter has never voiced his fear out loud. Peter does tell Jesus what he has seen, and Jesus gives a lengthy response (72,29–79,31) in which he tells Peter that those whom he fears are "blind and deaf" (73,13–14) and that they are "dry canals" (79,31). In other words, they are not drinking of and filled with Jesus, the living water (John 4:10), the "spring of water gushing up to eternal life" (John 4:14), or the bubbling spring (*Gospel of Thomas*, Logion 13). It is in this context that a long conversation ensues in which a clear critique of those who embrace martyrdom appears (as discussed below). In fact, it is those "who name themselves bishops"—that is, those who falsely claim authority—that Jesus is describing as "dry canals."[27]

Jesus also alludes in this passage to his "forgiveness of their transgressions into which they fell through their adversaries, whose ransom I got from the slavery in which they were, to give them freedom" (78,9–16). Here are allusions to a *Christus Victor* theory of atonement (an atonement in the sense of a ransom paid to Satan).[28] Those who are blind and ignorant do not properly understand the significance of Jesus's death. The

---

[27]This closely parallels the critique of the apostles in the *Gospel of Judas* that will be further discussed below.

[28]Gustaf Aulén discusses this theme in detail in a book not published until 1966, *Christus Victor: An Historical Study of the Three Main Types of the Idea of Atonement*. His work is based on lectures he gave in 1930. In the texts discussed in this book, we have seen an example of a *Christus Victory* theory of atonement in the *Martyrdom of Polycarp*, but it is also conceivably present in the *Apocalypse of Peter* and the *Gospel of Judas*, and it is quite prominent in the *Passion of Perpetua and Felicity*.

implication may well be that they instead insist on a substitutionary atonement theory in which Jesus's blood serves to appease a wrathful God.

However, once again, Peter is afraid. He is worried that the wrong leaders will prevail. He says,

> I am afraid because of what you have told me—that indeed little ones are in our view counterfeit. Indeed, there are multitudes that will mislead other multitudes of living ones, and they will be destroyed among them. And when they speak your name, they will be believed (79,32–80,6).

Again, the text shows Jesus reassuring Peter, saying, "You, oh Peter, will stand in their midst. Do not be afraid because of your cowardice" (80,31–33). In fact, Jesus has already affirmed Peter's leadership over these "blind and deaf" ones. He has told Peter, "But you yourself, Peter, become perfect in accordance with your name, along with me, the very one who chose you. For from you I have made a beginning for the remnant whom I have summoned to knowledge" (71,15–71,21).

However, even toward the end of the narrative, after Jesus has revealed many things to him, Peter is still afraid. His visions continue, and he starts to see the crucifixion of Jesus. The divine part of Jesus, which cannot die, actually comes and stands beside him, and he and Jesus watch the crucifixion together. He pleads with Jesus saying, "Lord, no one is looking at you. Let us flee this place" (81,26–28).

Again, Jesus responds with words of reassurance, telling Peter that those who think they are killing him are blind and ignorant (81,30–32), and he once again exhorts Peter: "Be strong!" (82,18). Again, he names Peter as "the one to whom these mysteries have been given" (82,18–19). He tells Peter that the "living Savior, the primal part in him whom they seized" (82,28–29) cannot be destroyed. In fact, "he has been released" (82,30).

A scene such as this may reflect a two-natures Christology rather than Docetism per se. Docetism is the belief that Jesus only *appeared* to be human; thus, he could not actually suffer and die. A two-natures, or *pneumatic*, Christology affirms that the preexistent Son of God either transformed into or inhabited a human body. In this latter case, it is still possible that the human body could suffer and die efficaciously for humankind.[29] Ultimately, Christ triumphs. Jesus is making all of this clear to Peter, and, therefore, Peter does not need to feel any fear.

At the very end, Jesus says, "You, therefore, be courageous and do not fear anything. For I will be with you so that none of your enemies will prevail over you. Peace be to you! Be strong!" (84,6–11). The text ends by saying that Peter "came to his senses" (84,12–13). Perhaps this implies that Peter comes to his senses on a couple of levels—he comes back to regular consciousness after being in a visionary state, and, seemingly, he is now equipped with the knowledge he needs to serve and lead courageously. The text does not state this explicitly, but the story ends as the task of healing Peter of his fear has apparently been accomplished.

In summary, the fact that Peter feels or expresses fear three times seems to be in keeping with the fact that he betrayed Jesus three times in the canonical gospels. Here, though, it is Peter's emotions that are emphasized along with a representation of Jesus as the one who can heal Peter of these disturbing passions. The pro-Petrine emphasis seems to be stronger in this work than in the Gospel of John where Peter (and the reader) are reminded of the fact that Peter betrayed Jesus three times by Jesus's asking Peter three times if he will "feed his sheep" (John 21:15–17). In both work, Jesus affirms that Peter will ultimately have the courage to be loyal to Jesus, but in the Gospel of John, this courage is linked to martyrdom, whereas in the *Apocalypse of Peter*, it is not. In the Gospel of John, Jesus says to Peter,

> Very truly, I tell you, when you were younger, you used to fasten your own belt and to go wherever you wished. But when you grow old, you will stretch out your hands, and someone else will fasten a belt around you and take you where you do not wish to go . . . . Follow me (John 21:18–19).

In the context of the *Apocalypse of Peter*, Peter is not asked explicitly to follow Jesus to a martyr's death but to be strong and unafraid. Indeed, Jesus continues believing in Peter as one who will ultimately be healed of his fear and become a suitable leader. Although these two perspectives are not necessarily at odds, the emphasis is different regarding what Peter needs in order to be a strong leader. The source of his apostolic authority in

---

[29]See Kelly, *Early Christian Doctrines*, 141–158. Lance Jenott's discussion of this issue with regard to the *Gospel of Judas* is pertinent here as well; see especially Jenott, *Gospel of Judas*, 23–30. Jenott builds on the classic work of Elaine Pagels: Pagels, "Gnostic and Orthodox Views of Christ's Passion," 262–288.

the *Apocalypse of Peter* stems from his ability to perceive things in such a way that he is cured of the passion of fear. As Desjardins notes:

> In the *Apoc. Pet.*, Peter needs the strength not only to realize that those putting Jesus to death can do him no harm but especially to await the Savior's Parousia (78,4–6; perhaps also 71,22–23) which ends the rule of the present generation of Christians, thereby allowing Peter to resume his rightful leadership over the 'remnant' (71,18–19).[30]

Indeed, Jesus's teaching provides this strength.

Moreover, the source of Peter's authority does not derive from his understanding Jesus as an atoning blood sacrifice who was then resurrected into a fleshly body. The knowledge that Peter needs in order to develop the courage that will enable him to lead others comes *before Jesus actually dies*. While still alive, Jesus interprets Peter's visions and clothes them with significance, revealing why Peter need not fear. As Pheme Perkins comments, "*Apocalypse of Peter* has turned Peter, the witness of the sufferings of Jesus, *into the witness of the true meaning of those sufferings*; they did not touch the heavenly redeemer."[31]

However, this means of effecting Peter's transformation from fear into boldness does not involve Peter's buying into a discourse in which sacrifice and suffering are exalted in and of themselves. In fact, the writer sharply critiques those who extol martyrdom, those immersed in the discourse of what Perkins has termed the "suffering self." While this discourse of the suffering self, elaborated in Chap. 2, also seeks to eradicate fear and incite its subjects to boldness in the face of death, in the *Apocalypse of Peter*, Jesus explains that this is an improper understanding and a false means of overcoming fear. He clearly disrupts the discourse of this type of glorification, saying that such people

> are without perception. And the guileless, good, pure one is pushed to the executioner, even into the kingdom of those who praise a restored Christ. And they praise the men of the propagation of falsehood, who will succeed you. And they will hold fast to the name of a dead man, while thinking that they will become pure. But they will become greatly defiled. And they will fall into an explicit error and into the hand of an evil, cunning man with a

---

[30]Desjardins, *Apocalypse of Peter*, 203–204.
[31]Perkins, *Gnostic Dialogue*, 121. Emphasis added.

multifarious doctrine. And they will be ruled heretically. For some of them will blaspheme the truth and proclaim evil teaching. And they will say evil things to each other (74,3–27).

The allusion to a "restored Christ" and a "multifarious doctrine" may be that of the resurrection of the flesh. To "hold fast to the name of a dead man" may also imply disputes over whether the human part of Jesus was resurrected in the flesh. The writer may feel not that Christ only *appeared* to be human but that he did indeed have a human nature that died. However, he also had an immortal nature that triumphed over Satan, demons, and death. Such would be consistent with a two-natures Christology. This triumph, though, would not necessarily have resulted in the restoration of the fleshly body.

Jesus goes on to say that the "deaf and blind ones" (76,21–22) "will create an imitation remnant in the name of a dead man" (78,15–17). The referent may well be those who exalted martyrdom. He then states,

> These are the ones who oppress their brothers, saying to them, "Through this our God has pity, since salvation (allegedly) comes to us through this." They do not know the punishment of those who are delighted by what has been done to the little ones whom they sought out and imprisoned. And there will be others of those who are outside our number who name themselves "bishop" and also "deacons," as if they have received their authority from God. They submit to the judgment of the leaders. Those people are dry canals (79,11–20).

Michel Desjardins notes that

> the context suggests that the term "allegedly" in line fifteen begins a parenthetical and ironic comment expressing the author's rejection of the oppressors' motivation that they are promoting the salvation of the Gnostics by forcing orthodox doctrine upon them.[32]

Unfortunately, such a statement perpetuates the notion of a unified, orthodox group versus a unified Gnostic group. It also perpetuates the idea that differences originate in doctrine rather than practice. However, it does

---

[32]Desjardins, *Apocalypse of Peter*, 237n37.

clearly show us that the editor recognizes the tensions between different groups.

Pheme Perkins has also commented insightfully on the contrast between the way that some see martyrdom as a source of victory and the way that other early Christ movements (which she describes as Gnostic) locate it elsewhere:

> The Christian may also be said to triumph over the powers through the victory that Christ works in him or her. Orthodox Christians saw this victory represented in the martyrs (Origen, *Comm Matt* XII 25; *Exhort ad Martyr.* XL 1). We have seen that Gnostics locate the Christian's share in the victory in the preaching of Gnosis as the Savior had done (e.g., *SJC CG* III 119,1–9, *PetPhil* VIII 137,20–25). *ApocPet* also associates the victory with the Docetic account of the crucifixion. The powers are crucifying what they think is the Savior, while the living Jesus is standing aside and laughing at them (*CG* VII 81,15–24). Patristic authors could never go this far and deny that Christ died, but they do agree that those who crucified him were deceived in thinking that they had gained power over him. Origen even speaks of Christ laughing with scorn at the ignorance of those who accepted the Son handed over to them (*Comm Matt* xiii, 9). Thus, Gnostic preaching shares broad lines of thought with other Christian preaching. These similarities show how a Gnostic soteriology might find a sympathetic audience in larger Christian circles.[33]

Finding a "sympathetic audience" would be particularly likely if the account of the crucifixion is not that of a Docetic one but that of a two-natures Christology in which Jesus did indeed triumph over the power of death, such that the proponents of the view at issue were not actually denying that Christ died, at least in his human nature.

Even Jesus's laughing (81,11; 81,16–17; 82,6) may serve to disrupt a discourse in which martyrdom is being idealized as an imitation of Christ's own death with that death being given a very specific interpretive twist— that of a substitutionary blood sacrifice. Jesus's laughter may function as a kind of signal to the reader pointing out his recognition of a lack of understanding on the part of a group regarding the meaning of his death. Indeed, in this case, the writer of the *Apocalypse of Peter* explains, "he laughs at their lack of perception" (83,1–2). Jesus is not condemning or

---

[33]Perkins, *Gnostic Dialogue*, 179–180.

cursing those who persecute them but simply laughing at the lack of awareness. This response shows Jesus himself to be in control of his emotions. He is neither afraid nor angry.[34]

By reading the text in terms of what it says about the care of the self, it is possible to see the relationship between what has often been characterized as two separate themes: Peter's strengthening and the debates among those identifying themselves with Christ. For example, Michel Desjardins mentions in his introduction to the work that there seem to be two issues: "Koschorke, noticing that the *Apoc. Pet.* deals with two issues, and considering the inner-Christian polemic to be more important than the discussion about Jesus's passion, has postulated a tripartite structure."[35] He goes on to give his own analysis:

> The inner-Christian polemic which dominates the central discourse is all but excluded from the rest of the work, where the focus is on Jesus's coming death, Peter's need to be strong, and the necessity of distinguishing the physical Jesus who dies on the cross from the spiritual one who remains unaffected by the passion.[36]

Thus, he sees these issues as separate and not necessarily bearing a relationship to each other.

In effect, however, these issues are intimately related if one reads the text in terms of competing perspectives regarding the care of the self. The *Apocalypse of Peter* articulates a vision elaborating a particular kind of self-care while simultaneously challenging a competing point of view regarding martyrdom as the ultimate care of the self. Tradition has long held that Peter ultimately gave his own life as a martyr. In the *Apocalypse of*

---

[34]Often scholars have simply assumed laughter to be mockery, but one must be very careful about attributing a certain significance to laughing, crying, or other expressions of emotion given the fact that these can have quite different meanings in varying social and narrative contexts. Jesus's laughter is not consistently interpreted as mockery. For example, Rodolphe Kasser describes Jesus's laughter as "an affectionate smile, tinged with pity and gentle irony"; Kasser, *Gospel of Judas*, 24.

[35]Desjardins, *Apocalypse of Peter*, 202.

[36]Desjardins, *Apocalypse of Peter*, 203.

Peter, however, an alternative explanation for Peter's boldness is given. Peter does not achieve the status of a holy martyr but that of one healed of his fear by Christ's intervention in a whole other way, his explanations of Peter's visions.

Of course, there is yet another twist. We cannot discount the possibility that the readers of the work would actually have thought that Peter had suffered and died for the faith whether or not such is mentioned specifically here. Although we have no hard proof that this is the case, Peter's martyrdom is a part of long-standing tradition.[37] Moreover, there is a crucifixion scene in this text. The body of Jesus does indeed endure pain. What differs from works like those discussed in the chapter above, however, is the meaning and significance the text ascribes to Christ's suffering and that of his followers. Such pain should not necessarily be desired or sought, but if it comes as a result of proclaiming the gospel, Jesus's teaching clearly allows Peter to see that it is *not to be feared* either.

In this respect, the *Apocalypse of Peter* can be compared with the *Letter of Peter to Philip*, the *Apocalypse of James*, and the *Gospel of Mary* (discussed further in Chap. 5).[38] In each of these writings, fear of persecution is real, and the likelihood of such is not denied. In short, in the *Apocalypse of Peter*, suffering is not to be sought. It is not represented as the imitation of an atoning blood sacrifice that aids in the forgiveness of sin nor does it result in a fleshly resurrection. However, it certainly can come as the result of proclaiming the gospel boldly, as doing so often brings one into conflict with the evil powers that dominate this world. These texts do not represent those depicted in them as having a lack of courage or refusing to embrace martyrdom. In fact, the opposite may be true as they empower the reader in understanding Jesus's teaching and thus can serve to encourage the reader to proclaim the gospel boldly and face suffering bravely as she/he realizes that Christ has triumphed over these powers.

---

[37] *Clement*, for example, as discussed in the previous chapter, mentions it.

[38] Karen King discusses the fact that the *Letter of Peter to Philip* and the *Apocalypse of James* were found in the same codex containing the *Gospel of Judas*. In each of these texts, the possibility of persecution and death is real. She suggests that it may be helpful to see them as representing a range of viewpoints for readers to consider with respect to the meaning and significance of martyrdom: King, "Martyrdom and Its Discontents," 23–42.

Testimony of Truth

Another work found near Nag Hammadi, the *Testimony of Truth*, is also relevant to our discussion for describing the way a text discusses the care of the self while simultaneously disrupting a discourse that glorifies martyrdom.[39] One copy has surfaced and appears in Nag Hammadi Codex IX,3, but unfortunately, in a heavily fragmentary condition. Only about 45% of the work is decipherable. However, in what remains, this work also presents the care of the self in a manner consonant with the therapy of emotions. Simultaneously, it voices concerns about the practice of martyrdom.

The first major section of the text resembles a homily. Here, the language concerns the Son of Man revealing the "word of truth" (*TTruth* 31,8) and the importance of our receiving it. The section concludes, "This therefore is the true testimony. When man knows himself and God who is over the truth, he will be saved and he will be crowned with the crown unfading" (*TTruth* 44,30–45,6). The text bears no name, but based on this passage, modern scholars have assigned it the title *the Testimony of Truth*.[40]

In the context of the ways in which Foucault has highlighted the significance of "knowing" within the broader context of "caring for the self," this choice of vocabulary strikes a chord. So does the fact that the author associates this kind of knowing with receiving an athlete's crown as this crown is typically a symbol of martyrdom. However, as we will see, in this work, such knowing goes along with being able to struggle against the passions successfully while the exaltation of martyrdom is actually critiqued.[41] Several references to overcoming passion resonate with the

---

[39]All citations and translation come from Pearson, *Testimony of Truth*, 122–203; see also his introduction to the work on pages 101–120. Another useful translation is that of Pearson in Meyer, *Nag Hammadi Scriptures*, 613–628. For more discussion of this text, see also Koschorke, "Polemik von Testimonium Veritatis," 92–174; Pearson, "Anti-Heretical Warnings in Codex IX from Nag Hammadi," 183–193; Pearson, "Gnostic Interpretation of the Old Testament in *The Testimony of Truth*," 311–19; Pearson, "Jewish Haggadic Traditions in *The Testimony of Truth*," 39–51.

[40]For discussion regarding choosing the title, see Pearson, *Introduction*, 101.

[41]Bas van Os has argued that this text may not necessarily be referring to martyrdom per se but rather to ascetic practices; van Os, "The *Testimony of Truth* Reconsidered." Van Os has argued similarly regarding the *Gospel of Judas* as will be discussed below. It is difficult to interpret a work such as this because baptism and

terminology of the therapy of emotions. A close examination of the passage containing the phrase "word of truth" brings out more detail:

> And this is what the Son of Man reveals to us: It is fitting for you (pl.) to receive the word of truth. If one will receive it perfectly,—. But as for one who is [in] ignorance, it is difficult for him to diminish his works of [darkness] which he has done. Those who have [known] Imperishability, [however,] have been able to struggle against [passions] (*TTruth* 31,5–31,15).

Thus, the text actually seems to focus on an ability to rid one's self of harmful desires. Esoteric knowledge is not a goal in and of itself but rather a means of engaging in the therapy of emotions.[42]

The work also discusses the idea that the subjugation of desire is important for salvation. The author praises the one who has "subdued desire" (*TTruth* 41,12) and is in the state of "having examined himself" (*TTruth* 41,14). Likewise, it talks about the need for "endurance" (*TTruth* 44,9) and "patience" (*TTruth* 44,13–19), terms frequently associated with those who are sufficiently healed of their emotions to be able to practice self-control: "He rejects for himself loquacity and disputations, and he

---

martyrdom were both associated with a purifying death. Jesus himself is represented as associating his death with a kind of baptism in Luke 12:50. Tertullian writes: "Uncleanness is washed away in baptism, of course, but the stains of it are made immaculately white through martyrdom" (*Scorp.* 12.10). All citations of Tertullian come from Roberts, *Ante-Nicene Fathers*. In the *Martyrdom of Perpetua and Felicity*, too, the editor represents Saturus's martyrdom as a drenching with blood, at which the crowd yells, "Well washed!" The editor describes it as their witness to Saturus's second baptism (*Mart. Perpet.* 21.7). See Church, "Sex and Salvation in Tertullian," 97. See also Moss, *Other Christs*, 14; Jeanes provides a detailed overview of associations between baptism and martyrdom, but the thrust of Jeanes' argument is that language associated with martyrdom enters into baptismal rites *after actual martyrdoms are no longer occurring*; Jeanes, "Baptism Portrayed as Martyrdom," 174. Quite likely, however, martyrdom is the referent in the *Testimony of Truth*, as Pearson argues in Pearson, *Testimony of Truth*, 614.

[42]Pearson attributes an Alexandrian origin to the text and argues that it can be dated to the late second or early third century, possibly as early as 189 C.E. See discussion in Pearson, *Testimony of Truth*, 117–118. If the *Apocalypse of Peter* can be dated as early as 150 C.E. and the *Gospel of Judas* can be dated prior to 180 C.E., these three works may belong to a similar time period.

endures the whole place; and he bears up under them, and he endures all of the evil things. And he is patient with every one" (*TTruth* 44,4–14).

Moreover, this kind of knowing contrasts with the ignorance of those who desire martyrdom. In fact, the work severely critiques the glorification of martyrdom:

> The foolish, thinking [in] their heart [that] if they confess, "We are Christians," in word only (but) not with power, while giving themselves over to ignorance, to a human death, not knowing where they are going nor who Christ is, thinking that they will live, when they are (really) in error, hasten towards the principalities and the authorities. They fall into their clutches because of the ignorance that is in them. For (if) only words which bear testimony were effecting salvation, the whole world would endure this thing [and] would be saved. [But] in this way, they [drew] error unto themselves (*TTruth* 31,22–32,14).

The author goes on to argue that it would be "vainglorious" for the Father to desire a human sacrifice (*TTruth* 31,22–32,21). Such an attitude would implicate the Father himself in passionate emotions. This implies a clear critique of Christ's death as a substitutionary blood atonement necessary for the appeasement of God (though not necessarily a critique of an atonement as a ransom paid to Satan, the *Christus Victor* perspective).

Rather, just following the passage above, the writer not only represents Christ as bringing freedom to those in Hades but also freedom to those on earth in that Christ "granted healing" (*TTruth* 33,7–8) to "the lame, the blind, the paralytic, the dumb, (and) the demon-possessed" (*TTruth* 33, 5–7). This connotes healing from both physical and emotional infirmities.

This is followed by another passage that disrupts the glorification of martyrdom. The author calls those who seek martyrdom "empty martyrs" (*TTruth* 33,25) who "bear witness only to themselves" (*TTruth* 33,26–27). They are described as "sick" and unable "to raise themselves" (*TTruth* 33,28–34,1). Then follows a section with multiple flavors of meaning. The author says that when those he or she has been describing above "are filled with passion, this is the thought that they have within them: 'If we deliver ourselves over to death for the sake of the Name, we will be saved'" (*TTruth* 34,1–6). But, the author disagrees, saying, "These matters are not settled in this way" (*TTruth* 34,6–7). The Coptic reads as follows (Fig. 4.1):

$\overline{\lambda \lambda}$

ΟΥΑΑΥ· ϩΟΤΑΝ ΔΕ ΕΥϢΑΝ

2   ΧⲰⲔ ΕΒΟΛ ⲚΟΥⲠΑΘΟⲤ· ⲠΑⲒ
ⲠΕ ⲠⲘΕΕΥΕ ΕΤΟΥΚⲰ ⲘⲘΟϥ

4   ⲚϨⲢΑⲒ ⲚϨⲎΤΟΥ· ΧΕ ΕⲚϢΑⲚ
ⲠΑⲢΑΔΙΔΟΥ ⲘⲘΟⲚ ΕⲠⲘΟΥ

6   ϨΑ ⲠⲢΑⲚ ⲦⲚⲚΑΟΥΧΑΕⲒ· ⲚΑⲒ
ΔΕ ⲤⲘΟⲚⲦ ΑⲚ Ⲛ⳨ϨΕ· ΑΛΛΑ

Fig. 4.1   *TTruth* 34, 1–6

The initial translation of this passage in the first edition of the *Nag Hammadi Library* reads,

> Themselves. But when they are
> "perfected" with a (martyr's) death, this
> is the thought that they have
> within them: "If we
> deliver ourselves over to death
> for the sake of the Name we will be saved." These
> matters are not settled in this way. But . . . .

The context of the passage clearly refers to those who desire martyrdom, but the author is literally accusing them of being filled with "passion," that is, a state which is the opposite of being healed of emotions; in this sense, when one seeks death, one is simultaneously "passionate," or "ignorant." For this author, salvation lies in being healed of passion, not filled with it.

Birger Pearson has translated the Coptic phrase "filled with passion" into English as "perfected with a martyr's death." The term πάθος, or *passion*, is translated as "death." The term *martyr* is not actually in the Coptic. This is signified by placing the word *martyr* in parentheses. Pearson mentions that the phrase has been translated as "filled with passion."[43] However, here he states that "it probably means the suffering of

---

[43]Pearson, *Testimony of Truth* 132–133 ('Wenn sie aber ihr [Leben voller] Leidenschaft vollenden').

martyrdom." The Coptic word for "passion" can, of course, refer to death as when we talk about "the passion of Christ." However, Pearson himself notes that at three other places in the *Testimony of Truth* (30,5; 42,28; 58,7) the best translation of the Greek πάθος is just "passion."

I would argue that the precise translation of this term is crucial as the author of the *Testimony of Truth* cleverly associates those who seek passion (or death) with those who are "filled with passion" and in need of the kind of healing that Christ can bring. In fact, Pearson recognizes this as the better translation and has recently changed it to "filled with passion" in *The Nag Hammadi Scriptures: The International Edition* where the passage reads: "But when they are full of passion, this is their motivating idea: 'If we give ourselves up to death for the sake of the name, we will be saved.' That is not the way things are. Rather . . . ."[44]

In addition, if we examine the other three places where πάθος is used, the term clearly connotes the kinds of desire or emotion that need to be dealt with through the therapy of emotions. πάθος is the "desire which constrains the souls of those who are begotten here" (*TTruth* 30,5–7). It is associated with ignorance (*TTruth* 31,11; 31,28) and a lack of knowledge of the truth. People afflicted thus are said to be filled with the "old leaven" of the Pharisees (*TTruth* 29,13), which is equated with "errant desire" (*TTruth* 29,16). In the second passage where πάθος is used, the phrase "he struggled against their passions" (*TTruth* 42,28) occurs within a long passage endeavoring to discern why some are lame, rich, poor, and so on (*TTruth* 42,8–21). Unfortunately, these three adjectives are the only ones that can be deciphered, as the text is partly missing, but clearly, the author seems to be asking why sickness, both physical and emotional, exists. Struggling against the passions seems to be a way of discussing the effort to heal people enslaved to illness in a certain sense. In the final passage containing πάθος (*TTruth* 58,7), the context is not at all clear. πάθος seems to refer to the attitude of a group that the author does not necessarily approve of; but other than this, it is hard to understand what the passage is about as the manuscript is again very fragmented.

The author also critiques the notion that those who seek martyrdom will be resurrected in the flesh. The author discusses the misperceptions of those who expect a "carnal resurrection" (*TTruth* 36,31):

---

[44]Pearson, *Nag Hammadi Scriptures*, 618.

[Do not] expect, therefore, [the] carnal resurrection, which [is] destruction, [and they are not] [stripped] of [it (the flesh) who] err in [expecting] a [resurrection] that is empty. [They do] not [know] the power [of God,] nor do they [understand the interpretation] of the Scriptures [on account of their] double-mindedness (36,30–37,10).

In fact, Pearson cleverly notes in his introduction that in this context, the author equates such persons with the Sadducees whom Jesus criticizes (Matt 22:29).[45] In this passage, the author of the *Testimony of Truth* seems to be talking about the fact that knowledge of Christ has already allowed for a different kind of resurrection, which involves some people having come to know themselves. The translators' footnote says that lines 35,22–36,3 refer to "the process of gnostic awakening," but such phrasing may simply be the author's conception of the way Christ helps his followers to care for their selves/souls. These people are described as being in "the place [in] [which] they will rest from their senselessness, [arriving] at knowledge" (*TTruth* 35,28–36,3).

Finally, in lines 38,6–8, the author seems to be reiterating that when people try to sacrifice themselves "they die [in a] human [way]." However, it is difficult to be certain given that the text is rather corrupt at this point.

The end of the first major portion of the writing invokes "the crown unfading" (*TTruth* 45,5–6). The athlete's crown was, of course, as just mentioned above, a primary symbol for the martyr who faced death bravely and successfully. This allusion nicely contrasts the "achievement" of martyrdom with a different kind of triumph—engaging successfully in the therapy of emotions and becoming healed and whole.[46]

There is also a reference to a salamander: "[like a] salamander. [It] goes into the fiery oven which burns exceedingly; it slithers into the [furnace]" (*TTruth* 71,26–29). In antiquity, the salamander was thought unsusceptible to harm by fire. Although much of the context of this passage has been lost due to the fragmentary form of the manuscript, Pearson explains that "the author of *Testim. Truth* may have utilized the salamander for allegorical purposes . . . in praise of the Gnostic who can live untouched by

---

[45]Pearson, *Testimony of Truth*, 104.

[46]See Dylan M. Burns, "Sethian Crowns, Sethian Martyrs?" for insights regarding the way crown imagery functions in early texts of Christ movements although the *Testimony of Truth* is not discussed specifically since it is not Sethian.

the fires of passion (for this metaphor see Sir 9:8; 23:16; Philo, *Rev. Div. Her.* 64; I Cor 7:9)."[47]

In summary, this text repeatedly discusses the need for one who follows Christ to overcome "passion." In this sense, it is not esoteric knowledge that one needs but rather the ability to live in a manner free of entanglement in harmful desires. Those who seek martyrdom are not living in this way as they associate salvation with a carnal resurrection of a material body that is enslaved to the emotions.

FRAGMENTS OF BASILIDES

Yet another representation of the proper way for one who identifies with Christ to live comes from Basilides, a second-century Alexandrian teacher widely credited with being one of the first to write commentaries on the gospels. Bentley Layton astutely describes Basilides as "a skilled, independent, and outrageously original philosopher *within* Christianity."[48] Unfortunately, the vast majority of his writings have been lost, making it difficult for modern readers to access his thought although a few fragments remain in the quotations of Clement of Alexandria and Origen.[49]

Basilides also portrays the care of the self in terms consonant with Stoic philosophy. For example, according to Clement of Alexandria, Basilides says, "that one part of the so-called 'will' of god is to love all . . . . A second, is to desire nothing; and a third, is to hate nothing."[50] This admonition accords well with the Stoic virtue of freedom from passion.[51]

---

[47]Pearson, *Testimony of Truth*, 114.

[48]Layton, *Gnostic Scriptures*, 413. Emphasis added.

[49]All citations and translation of the fragments of Basilides come from Layton, *Gnostic Scriptures*, 417–444. Bentley Layton has translated eight of the fragments into English with a brief commentary. For another translation and commentary, see Löhr, *Basilides und seine Schule*, 42–254; Foerster, *Gnosis*, 74–83.

[50]Fragment D in Layton, *Gnostic Scriptures*, 435.

[51]Bentley Layton notes that this loving all is "in accordance with the strong Stoic element in Basilides' ethical theory" and that it "must mean to live in complete harmony with the rational order of the universe, accepting all of one's fate without regret or protest; accordingly, there is no place for desire or revulsion, since all is dictated by providence." See Layton, *Gnostic Scriptures*, 435 and also 418 for Stoic influence. More recent interest in linking Stoic thought with a) the New Testament and b) developments in the first three centuries of the Common Era by Troels

Moreover, it provides a marked contrast to the kind of desire or craving for martyrdom present in works such as those discussed in the chapter above. For Basilides, it is liberation from desire of any kind that marks the spiritually mature soul, for it is only when one realizes and accepts the order in all things preordained by Providence that one can be liberated.

However, Basilides does see martyrdom as providing possible benefit in terms of spiritual development. His ideas are found in Fragment G, which is by far the longest fragment preserved for us by Clement, mirroring, perhaps, the degree to which debates surrounding the interpretation of martyrdom dominated conversations among Christ people in the second century. In this fragment, Basilides holds that the soul "receives benefit, profiting by many unpleasant experiences" when it "experiences suffering" (*Basilides* 4.82.1).[52] This statement is strikingly *similar* to the kind of benefit described in the Apostolic Fathers when various writers discuss "patient endurance," which is elaborated in the previous chapter.[53]

Basilides also describes a martyr's death as an honorable one, a "good end" (*Basilides* 4.81.2), saying that such a death is preferable to death for murder or adultery or other crimes as one is likely to believe that in this case one's death has purpose and meaning and thus one may not necessarily feel oneself to be suffering:

> Through the kindness of that which leads each one of them about, they are actually accused of an extraneous set of charges so they might not have to suffer as confessed criminals convicted of crimes, nor be reviled as adulterers or murderers, but rather might suffer because they are disposed by nature to be Christian. And this encourages them to think that they are not suffering (*Basilides* 4.81.2).[54]

Basilides, however, provides clear disruptions to the discourse of martyrdom as a sacrifice willed by and pleasing to a God who must be appeased

---

Engberg-Pedersen and other scholars (as discussed in the previous chapter) accord with Layton's assertion.

[52]Layton, *Gnostic Scriptures*, 442.

[53]Le Boulluec comments that chastisement and punishment were commonly viewed as beneficial purifications, remarking that both Clement and Basilides accepted this idea: Boulluec, *Notion d'hérésie dans la littérature grecque*, 1:306.

[54]Fragment G, in Layton, *Gnostic Scriptures*, 442.

through a substitutionary blood sacrifice along with the accompanying theology of the resurrection of the flesh. He clearly states that "suffering is not caused by the plotting of some power" (*Basilides* 4.81.3); in fact, Basilides actually represents the agonizing death of a martyr as possible punishment for previous sin: "I believe that all who experience the so-called 'tribulations' must have committed sins other than what they realize" (*Basilides* 4.81.2).[55] While there are many theological alternatives to this point of view, it is the way in which Basilides reconciles his belief in the goodness of Providence with the fact of brutal physical suffering endured by those who follow Christ in times of persecution. He asserts, "For I will say anything rather than call Providence evil" (*Basilides* 4.82.2).[56] In other words, if God is good, it cannot be *necessary* for Christ or those who identify with Christ to suffer to appease God, but their doing so may indeed be the means of their spiritual development or "benefit." Basilides carefully notes that since seeming suffering may be of value, it is even possible that an innocent person may suffer. He thinks that such cases are rare, but he does not rule out the possibility (*Basilides* 4.81.3).[57] Although it is hard to be sure given the scanty evidence remaining to us, it seems that Basilides may be referring to Jesus himself as one such person when he writes,

> Nevertheless, let us suppose that you (sing.) leave aside all these matters and set out to embarrass me by referring to certain (famous) figures, saying perhaps, "And consequently so-and-so must have sinned, since he suffered!" If you permit, I shall say that he did not sin, but was like the newborn baby that suffers. But if you press the argument, I shall say that any human being that you can name is human; god is righteous. For no one is "pure of uncleanness," as someone once said (*Basilides* 4.81.1).[58]

---

[55]Fragment G, in Layton, *Gnostic Scriptures*, 442.

[56]Fragment G, in Layton, *Gnostic Scriptures*, 442. One can only wonder what a thorough comparison of writings by writers who are criticized as "deterministic," such as Basilides, with those of Calvin, who is praised as one of the greatest orthodox theologians of all time yet who similarly espouses deterministic beliefs in "predestination" and "election," would yield.

[57]Fragment G, in Layton, *Gnostic Scriptures*, 442.

[58]Fragment G, in Layton, *Gnostic Scriptures*, 442.

Such an idea is hardly representative of the supposed Docetism attributed to some Gnostics.[59]

Secondly, Basilides does not promote a doctrine of the resurrection of the flesh. He appears to believe in the transmigration of souls. For example, in Fragment F, Origen refers to Basilides's belief in this concept and quotes him as saying, "Indeed, the apostle has said, 'I was once alive apart from the law,' at some time or other. That is (Paul means), before I came into this body, I lived in the kind of body that is not subject to the law; the body of a domestic animal or a bird."[60] Likewise, Irenaeus accuses Basilides of believing that "salvation belongs only to the soul; the body is by nature corruptible" (*Haer.* 1.24.5).[61]

Such views might constitute merely a theological difference but for the fact that the discourse of suffering and martyrdom is becoming increasingly key to the way that some early Christ movements are consolidating the "Christian" story in a triumphal way. Martyrs and the resurrection of the flesh are being linked with the order of apostolic succession. It appears that Basilides opposes such conceptions and thus, not surprisingly, writers such as Irenaeus angrily denounce him.

As mentioned above, Fragment F is preserved only in Clement of Alexandria's writings. Clement includes it in Book IV of his *Stromata* (which can be translated as *Miscellanies* or even literally as *Carpet Bags*). Clement explains that Book IV is devoted entirely to a discussion of martyrdom, and indeed he lays out the relevant issues in a careful manner,

---

[59]There is also the matter of Irenaeus's accusation regarding Basilides's supposed assertion that Simon of Cyrene actually died rather than Jesus himself. This example is often used to support Basilides's supposed Docetism. However, we have only Irenaeus's word regarding this. Given Irenaeus's propensity for distortion of the ideas of his opponents, it is hard to be sure what Basilides actually said or meant. Irenaeus represents Basilides as saying that Jesus was laughing while Simon was crucified. It is important to note that such laughing is not necessarily mere mockery. In many texts of those identifying with Christ, Jesus's laughing serves as a signal to the reader that Jesus is aware of spiritual ignorance on the part of those with whom he is interacting. They misunderstand him. Jesus does not curse or condemn them, but his laughter serves to show that he is not subject to passions of anger or fear with regard to them. Christ also laughs in the *Apocalypse of Peter* and the *Gospel of Judas.*
[60]Fragment F, in Layton, *Gnostic Scriptures,* 439.
[61]Fragment F, in Layton, *Gnostic Scriptures,* 423.

discussing the nuances of the kinds of significance attributed to martyrdom by various groups and figures. He includes this particular fragment in order to refute Basilides's teaching. Alain Le Boulluec points out Clement's methodology, noting that Clement uses an ancient rhetorical technique of question and response that involves imagining what an opponent would say if present, presenting this in the form of a question, and then refuting this question in a response, as one would in an oral debate. Unfortunately, helpful as such a technique might be as an exercise, it can result in attributing an argument to an adversary that the opponent never actually made. This could be the case regarding Basilides's teaching on martyrdom.[62]

Irenaeus of Lyons also discusses Basilides's remarks. Irenaeus does not quote the fragment verbatim as Clement does, but he does comment on it. However, Irenaeus's description of Basilides's thought differs dramatically from what is preserved in Clement. Irenaeus writes that the Basilideans say, "Recognize them all, But let none recognize you!" and then he goes on to say, "For this reason, such people are prepared to deny; or, rather, they are not even susceptible to suffering on behalf of the name" *(Haer.* 1.24.6).[63] However, in Fragment G, Basilides does *not* denounce the martyrs or even fail to recognize that their suffering has meaning and purpose; he simply attributes a different kind of significance to such suffering. In short, then, even though only miniscule portions of Basilides's writings remain for us to examine, what seems clear is Basilides's disruption of a discourse that glorifies martyrdom and presents its importance in simple, black-and-white terms linked strongly with notions of apostolic authority.

Christoph Markschies and Bentley Layton have both noted the discrepancies between the actual text of Basilides and the accusations of Irenaeus. Layton is careful to point out that Basilides was accused by later theologians of "disparaging" or "opposing" martyrdom although nothing in this fragment actually bears that out.[64] Markschies goes so far as to maintain that Irenaeus has probably not read Basilides directly, mentioning that Irenaeus's accusation—that Basilides encourages the avoidance of

---

[62]Le Boulluec, *Notion d'hérésie dans la littérature grecque*, 306.

[63]Layton, *Gnostic Scriptures*, 425.

[64]Layton, *Gnostic Scriptures*, 441.

martyrdom and denial of the faith—simply does not correspond to the pastoral manner in which Basilides addresses the issue of persecution.[65]

Basilides also subverts the typical accusation against Gnostics regarding dualism. His insistence on the ultimate goodness of Providence extends all the way to the circumstances of individuals' material, earthly existence. In this sense, it is markedly less dualistic than the views of those who represent this life as one filled with darkness and suffering and the afterlife alone as happy and peaceful.

FOURTH FRAGMENT OF VALENTINUS

Clement of Alexandria has preserved the fourth fragment of Valentinus in Book IV of his *Stromata*. This short passage, like the one just discussed, fails to exhibit what might be considered "gnostic" elements, presenting instead a perspective regarding the care of the self that intersects the dominant discourse of the glorification of martyrdom. Clement quotes Valentinus as saying,

> From the beginning, you (plur.) have been immortal, and you are children of eternal life. And you wanted death to be allocated to yourselves so that you might spend it and use it up, and that death might die in you and through you. For when you nullify the world and are not yourselves annihilated, you are lord over creation and all corruption (*Strom.* 4.89.1–3).[66]

This passage provides an excellent example of the way Valentinus discusses the care of the self in terms of a therapy of the emotions while simultaneously critiquing the way in which the care of the self is represented in the increasingly dominant discourse of martyrdom. Scholars usually argue that Valentinus is doing one or the other. However, in actuality, the language contains a marvelous ambiguity lending itself to both interpretations—as an affirmation of the therapy of emotions and a critique of the glorification of martyrdom.

---

[65]Markschies, *Gnosis*, 79, 81.

[66]All citations and translation of Valentinus are from Layton, *Gnostic Scriptures*, this quote is from Layton, *Gnostic Scriptures*, 241. For another translation and commentary, see Foerster, *Gnosis*, 239–243. See also Markschies, *Valentinus Gnosticus?*, 118–152.

As mentioned above, in the introduction to Book IV, Clement specifically remarks that he will be dealing with the topic of martyrdom, and he goes on to address a great many issues in a complex way, presenting the points of many different thinkers. He does not espouse a simple "pro" or "con" approach but tries to consider the issues thoughtfully from many different angles. It is within this context that he critiques Valentinus (and Basilides). Thus, he clearly represents the passage as having something to do with the issue of martyrdom.

Most modern scholars have assumed Clement's interpretation of this passage to be a Valentinian critique of martyrdom.[67] Hans Holzhausen focuses on the fiscal imagery contained in the text. The phrase, *use it up,* could indicate the idea that the "immortal ones" wish to pay for eternal life with their own martyrdom.

However, Ismo Dunderberg explicates the fourth fragment in a completely different way. He argues that it may well demonstrate Valentinus's characterization of the way those who follow Christ should take on a proper attitude of detachment from the world, an explanation similar to teaching regarding the therapy of the emotions in Stoic philosophy.[68] Dunderberg makes several convincing arguments. First of all, he points out that the present tense is used in the first line, "You *are* immortal from the beginning, and you are children of eternal life." Such phrasing would indicate that the readers or listeners already understand themselves to have eternal life; they do not need to become martyrs in order to gain it. Second, Dunderberg notices that previous interpretations of this fragment have translated the passage as though the second sentence begins with the word *but.* However, in Dunderberg's reading, the second sentence simply affirms the character and wishes of the hearers. In other words, "you are immortal" *and* you wished to have "death bestowed upon you." If this is the case, "death" may well be referring to the death of passions, desires, and emotions, not the physical death of martyrs. This kind of death is a way of "nullify[ing] the world." "Death" becomes paired with "self-control." When one has self-control, one is able to rule over oneself and all of the creation. Such a reading evokes Socrates's sense of the care of the self as necessary for being a good ruler of others. Later, in the context of

---

[67]Holzhausen, "Gnosis und Martyrium," 116–131; Holzhausen, "Valentinus and Valentinians," 1144–1157.

[68]Dunderberg, *Beyond Gnosticism*, 45.

discussing the Valentinian myth of wisdom, Dunderberg suggests that the Valentinians described this therapy, the curing of excessive emotion, as a kind of gift that Christ could give to those who followed him.[69] This focus on the issues of spiritual transformation accords with the kind of care of the self that Foucault discusses as prevalent.

I would argue that this passage might represent a kind of "both/and" argument on the part of Valentinus. Its language works both to provide a positive vision of what is possible for those who come to realize that they can indeed overcome their passions and attain self-control through following Christ, those who see Christ as the one who helps them to achieve self-control and maintain freedom from their emotions here and now. At the same time, the passage also simultaneously provides a critique of those who try to "nullify the world" by literally seeking death. It is cleverly written ambiguously such that both readings are possible with careful sensitivity to the position of those who feel a glorification of martyrdom to be a distortion of the care of the soul/self.

Dunderberg's reading is astute, but one wonders if Clement would have included this passage in Book IV—all of which is devoted to a discussion of martyrdom—had the fragment been totally irrelevant to that issue. On the other hand, while Clement's tone toward figures such as Valentinus and Basilides is considerably less hostile than that of an Irenaeus or a Tertullian, Clement still utilizes a certain adroitness with respect to discursive strategies. He cleverly categorizes this passage as a refusal to embrace martyrdom rather than merely in terms of Stoic detachment from the world.

Le Boulluec argues that Clement attributes ideas to Basilides that he does not actually express. It may well be that Clement indulges in a similar tactic with respect to Valentinus. However, it seems more plausible that the strategy here is one of omission. Clement is thoroughly versed in the idea that the perfection of those who are part of Christ movements involves the therapy of emotions. This theme occurs repeatedly in the *Stromata*. For example, in the *Paedagogus* (or "instructor"), Clement describes Christ as follows:

> The Instructor being practical, not theoretical, His aim is thus to improve the soul, not to teach, and to train it up to a virtuous, not to an intellectual life . . . . Hence accordingly ensues the healing of our passions . . . the Paedagogue strengthening our souls, and by His benign commands, as by

---

[69]Dunderberg, *Beyond Gnosticism*, 117.

gentle medicines, guiding the sick to the perfect knowledge of the truth (*Paed.* I.I).

In fact, at times Clement seems to echo Valentinus. Consider the following passages where Clement discusses martyrdom as "confession to God" and death to passion, which may or may not entail a martyr's physical death:

> If the confession to God is martyrdom, each soul which has lived purely in the knowledge of God, which has obeyed the commandments, is a witness both by life and word, in whatever way it may be released from the body,— shedding faith as blood along its whole life till its departure. For instance, the Lord says in the Gospel, "Whosoever shall leave father, or mother, or brethren," and so forth, "for the sake of the Gospel and my name," he is blessed; not indicating simple martyrdom, but the gnostic martyrdom, as of the man who has conducted himself according to the rule of the Gospel, in love to the Lord (for the knowledge of the Name and the understanding of the Gospel point out the gnosis, but not the bare appellation), so as to leave his worldly kindred, and wealth, and every possession, in order to lead a life free from passion (*Strom.* IV.4).

Clement even describes the sacrifice that is truly acceptable to God in terms of liberation from passion:

> Now the sacrifice which is acceptable to God is unswerving abstraction from the body and its passions. This is the really true piety. And is not, on this account, philosophy rightly called by Socrates the practice of Death? For he who neither employs his eyes in the exercise of thought, nor draws aught from his other senses, but with pure mind itself applies to objects, practises the true philosophy . . . . For the gnostic soul must be consecrated to the light, stript of the integuments of matter, devoid of the frivolousness of the body and of all the passions, which are acquired through vain and lying opinions, and divested of the lusts of the flesh. But the most of men, clothed with what is perishable, like cockles, and rolled all round in a ball in their excesses, like hedgehogs, entertain the same ideas of the blessed and incorruptible God as of themselves (*Strom.* V.XI).

It is well known that Clement himself left Alexandria at one point when persecution broke out. Given his love of philosophy and his possible affinity for fellow Alexandrians such as Basilides and Valentinus, he may simply have felt a need to set himself apart from thinkers such as these and establish his own orthodoxy. Characterizing the passage he attributes to

Valentinus as a critique of martyrdom would have been a clever discursive means of doing so.

Candida Moss also picks up on the ways in which Clement discursively shapes martyrdom as a "middle position" in accord with his own purposes:

> The distinctions between Clement's position and those of his interlocutors are hardly the radical breaks in thought that his rhetoric leads us to believe. In pushing the heretics to the margins, Clement acquires power. In creating and claiming the middle position, he also assumes the rhetorical high ground that the Aristotelian mean affords him. His own perspective, grounded as it is in a philosophy of love, emerges as a middle course and thus as the default position on martyrdom. Much has been made of the ways in which Clement is influenced by the positions of his opponents and takes a reasonable middle position . . . . Much more should be made, however, of the ways in which he creates this middle position and sets himself firmly on it. Scholars have tended to treat Clement's categories of true martyrdom, enthusiasm, and anti-martyrdom as an adequate description of the various positions on martyrdom in his day, yet perhaps he is more constructive than descriptive.[70]

In short, we must remember that we are reading Valentinus as Clement represents him and keep in mind that Clement may be using particular discursive strategies in his reading of a passage that seems to offer insights regarding the care of the self but that can be interpreted in more than one way. Valentinus may well be offering a critique of seeking martyrdom as well, but this position in no way implies a lack of devotion to the way of Christ. It simply reflects a different perspective than that of those discussed in the previous chapter.

Gospel of Judas

Finally, we turn to the *Gospel of Judas*. In this section, we examine first the representation of Judas and its relation to the care of the self in terms of the therapy of emotions. In order to do so, we will examine most closely the interpretations of Judas as an ambiguous moral figure. We then turn to the critique of apostolic succession and of the practices of sacrifice and martyrdom. Finally, we explore the way in which this work may have served as a reflection for those facing persecution.

---

[70]Moss, *Ancient Christian Martyrdom*, 149, and also 145–158.

Background

Irenaeus sarcastically refers to a text called the *Gospel of Judas* as a "fictitious history:"

> Others again declare that Cain derived his being from the Power above, and acknowledge that Esau, Korah, the Sodomites, and all such persons, are related to themselves. On this account, they add, they have been assailed by the Creator, yet no one of them has suffered injury. For Sophia was in the habit of carrying off that which belonged to her from them to herself. They declare that Judas the traitor was thoroughly acquainted with these things, and that he alone, knowing the truth as no others did, accomplished the mystery of the betrayal; by him all things, both earthy and heavenly, were thus thrown into confusion. They produce a fictitious history of this kind, which they style the *Gospel of Judas* (*Haer.* 1.31.1).

However, until the late 1970s, not a single copy was known to exist; therefore, it was impossible to discern the merit of Irenaeus's critique.[71] Most scholars think the work released to the world by National Geographic in 2006 is the one to which Irenaeus is referring. The actual manuscript that was found around 1970 dates to the fourth century C.E., but it is most probably a copy of a text composed by the time at which Irenaeus is writing, the latter half of the second century.[72]

---

[71] Pseudo-Tertullian, Epiphanius, and Theodoret also refer to either this work or ideas contained in it; see Turner, "Place of the *Gospel of Judas* in Sethian Tradition," 190–195.

[72] By means of comparison, our oldest copy of the Bible, the Codex Sinaiticus, also dates to the fourth century, but the New Testament gospels contained therein were composed mostly in the first century. Although the *Gospel of Judas* is of a later date than most of the books of the New Testament, recent scholarship has also pointed to a later date than previously thought for Luke-Acts. This, too, may be a second-century composition rather than a first-century one. It is difficult to establish exact dates for the composition of many writings of those identifying with Christ. Acts in particular contains the sole account of what was later widely perceived as a martyrdom (though this term is not actually used in Acts itself)—the stoning of Stephen. Shelly Matthews' overview discusses the ways in which the representation of Stephen's death functions to strengthen the proto-orthodox discourse of martyrdom. See Matthews, *Perfect Martyr*, 2010.

Johannes van Oort argues that Irenaeus had actually read and had firsthand knowledge of the *Gospel of Judas*.[73] Likewise, Lance Jenott, the author of a newer critical edition of the manuscript, an edition that incorporates fragments to which the National Geographic team did not have access, also argues for a second-century composition.[74]

Scholars unanimously agree that the text is not a literal recounting of actual conversations between Jesus and Judas. It tells us nothing about their historical relationship in the first century of the Common Era. However, the work provides invaluable insight into debates among those identifying themselves with Christ in the second or third century, particularly concerning attitudes regarding the care of the self.[75]

Parts of the *Gospel of Judas* are quite harsh. Hadot discusses the fact that "to rectify distorted opinions, tenacious prejudices, [and] irrational terrors," a writer might have "to twist them in the other direction, to

---

[73]See van Oort, "Irenaeus on the *Gospel of Judas*," 43–56.

[74]Jenott, *Gospel of Judas*, 5–6. For dissenting opinions, see Logan, "Tchacos Codex," 3; Robinson, "*Gospel of Judas*, 90–94; Turner, "Sethian Myth in the *Gospel of Judas*, 131–133.

[75]The discovery of the text and its modern history is in and of itself a fascinating story that has been shrouded in a great deal of mystery. Rodolphe Kasser, one of the scholars chiefly responsible for the manuscript's restoration, describes what is summarized below in detail. It appears that Egyptian farmers found the codex containing this text in a tomb on the Nile River north of the town of Al Minya. The manuscript came into the hands of local antiquities dealers and was divided up into several parts, as the owners thought doing so would be a more profitable way to sell it. The portion containing the *Gospel of Judas* was shown to scholars in the early 1980s, but although its value was recognized, none of the institutions with which they were associated were willing to part with the three million dollar asking price. Unfortunately, the manuscript simply sat in a vault in New York for several years, deteriorating in a humid climate. It was finally sold and resold, but this, too, resulted in further deterioration. In fact, one of the new owners decided to freeze the manuscript, thinking that this would be the best way to preserve it. However, when the papyrus was removed from the freezer, it started to crumble. Finally, the text was purchased by Frieda Tchacos, and several years of painstaking restoration ensued in which crumbled fragments had to be pieced together with tweezers under high definition microscopes. An estimated 10–20% of the manuscript could not be recovered. See Kasser, "Introduction: Lost and Found: The History of Codex Tchacos," 1–25.

exaggerate in order to compensate."[76] Certainly, that dynamic seems to be at work in this gospel as well as in the heresiologists' writings and some other extracanonical works. All took pains to make their arguments as persuasive as possible using strategies popular in ancient times.

Judas's Moral Character

National Geographic acquired the right to publish what has become known as the Codex Tchacos and put together a team of scholars to prepare a critical edition in Coptic, English, and French; however, each person involved was forced to sign a nondisclosure agreement, and the text could not be widely and freely discussed.[77] This work was not published in any form until 2006. Then, it appeared only online at www.nationalgeographic.com/lostgospel/document.html.

In this version, the editors represented Judas as a hero, one actually doing Jesus a favor by releasing his immortal spirit from entrapment in a human body. Bart Ehrman promoted this view widely in a popular book released immediately for publication as well:

> In late Christian anti-Semitic rhetoric he (Judas) becomes the prototypical Jew: a greedy, money-grubbing, God-denying Christ-killer. The Christian tradition has consistently and increasingly portrayed Judas in a bad light. The *Gospel of Judas* provides an alternative vision . . . . The *Gospel of Judas* stands alone in insisting that Judas was not only close to Jesus but also was the only one among the disciples who understood who Jesus was and did what he wanted.[78]

The critical edition (containing photographic plates of the actual manuscript) was then published in a hardback copy in 2007.[79] Shortly thereafter, Karen King and Elaine Pagels published an additional translation and interpretation called *Reading Judas* that largely followed that of the

---

[76]Hadot, *Philosophy as a Way of Life*, 21.

[77]See De Conick, *Thirteenth Apostle*, 181 for a concise summary of the ways that the profit-making motives of corporations impede the cause of scholarship. See also John D. Turner's article in which he sharply critiques the lack of access to the text on the part of National Geographic as well as the interpretation of the team; Turner, "The Sethian Myth in the *Gospel of Judas*," 187–188.

[78]Ehrman, *Lost Gospel of Judas Iscariot*, 138.

[79]Kasser, et al., *Gospel of Judas*.

National Geographic team. Einar Thomassen provides a nice summary of the positive portrayal of Judas:

> According to one interpretation, Judas Iscariot is the hero of the gospel. He alone of all the disciples understands who Jesus really is and where he has come from. He is favoured by Jesus with a special revelation about the divine realm and about the origins and structure of the cosmos. Finally, he is entrusted with the painful but necessary task of handing Jesus over to the authorities, in order that the Saviour may be liberated from the prison of his earthly body. This is the interpretation of the *Gospel of Judas* that was promulgated together with the publication of the text on April 6, 2006, and which no doubt contributed to the sensationalism surrounding the event of the publication: here is an ancient gospel that turns on its head what the Church has always taught by making the greatest villain of the canonical gospels into the hero of the passion story.[80]

He then notes, "Already, however, dissenting voices are beginning . . . ."[81]

Indeed, when the photos became available, a wider circle of scholars was able to look at the actual manuscript, and fierce debates over translation choices ensued particularly regarding the nature of Judas's moral character. April De Conick soon provided a translation that differed substantially, discussing the disputes in detail.[82] As one example, she talks about the fact that Judas is referred to as a *daimon*. The National Geographic team chose to translate this as "spirit," avoiding the negative connotation of the English "demon" and in fact, using this translation as support in interpreting Judas as a positive figure. Such a translation is possible, but De Conick argues that it is not likely in the time period the text was written. She maintains that *pneuma* would be the more probable term if "spirit" had been intended.[83] She sees Judas represented not as a hero but as the one who is condemned to the fate of betraying Jesus. Such a betrayal is motivated by the demons that control him.

---

[80]Thomassen, "Is Judas Really the Hero," 157.

[81]Thomassen, "Is Judas Really the Hero," 157.

[82]In fact, several scholars mention critiques of the National Geographic team's translation, surfacing first at the Université de Laval in Québec, Canada under scholars, such as Wolf-Peter Funk and Louis Painchaud; for a good overview of the critiques, see Painchaud, "Polemical Aspects of the *Gospel of Judas*," 171–186.

[83]De Conick, *Thirteenth Apostle*, 48–51.

Judas's Ambiguous Representation

Some scholars, however, interpret the portrayal of Judas as ambiguous rather than either wholly good or bad. In such case, Judas then serves as a moral exemplar for the care of the self but not a perfect one. Ismo Dunderberg argues persuasively for this interpretation of Judas's character. Dunderberg focuses on the way that the work elaborates Stoic ideals of ethics and morality regarding the value of total extirpation of the passions.[84] He thinks it is important to "move beyond the polarized hero-or-villain debate,"[85] which he feels is often too simplistic and "far too dualistic."[86] He finds the alternative interpretation offered by the revisionists plausible, but he does not feel they necessarily offer convincing proof of the original editors of the text necessarily being wrong or of their interpretation being impossible.[87] Thus, he carefully points out the ways that the work seems to be focused on the theme of overcoming the passion of anger with Judas serving as a model of one who is partially (but *only* partially) able to do so. Dunderberg explains that while at first, he read the text as more aligned with the Platonic and Aristotelian ideals that allow for the expression of anger when injustice needs to be addressed and combated, he came to find the work more in agreement with Stoic ideals that uplift a total rooting out of and abandonment of anger.[88]

The theme of anger emerges in the following passage:

> And one day he was with his disciples in Judea, and he found them seated and gathered together practicing their piety. When he [approached] his disciples, gathered together and seated and offering a prayer of thanksgiving over the bread, [he] laughed. [And] the disciples said to him, "Master, why are you

---

[84]The discussion below is based on Dunderberg, "Judas' Anger and the Perfect Human," 201–221. For discussions of anger in antiquity, see also Harris, *Restraining Rage*, 2001. Finally, Tage Petersen also discusses the *Gospel of Judas* as engaged in philosophical dialogue in Petersen, "From Perplexity to Salvation, 413–434.

[85]Dunderberg, "Judas' Anger and the Perfect Human," 203.

[86]Dunderberg, "Judas' Anger and the Perfect Human," 219.

[87]Dunderberg, "Judas' Anger and the Perfect Human," 202n5.

[88]Dunderberg notes that for the Stoics, even anger for a just cause, or *metropatheia*, (as advocated by Aristotle) was inappropriate for those who were truly advanced in caring for their selves; Dunderberg, "Judas' Anger and the Perfect Human," 203–205.

laughing at [our] prayer of thanksgiving? Or what did we do? [This] is what is right (to do)." He answered and said to them, "I am not laughing at you. You are not doing this because of your own will but because it is through this that your god [will receive] thanksgiving." They said, "Master, you [—] are the son of our god. Jesus said to them, "In what way do [you] know me? Truly [I] say to you, no generation of the people that are among you will know me." And when his disciples heard this, [they] started getting angry and infuriated, and began blaspheming against him in their hearts. And when Jesus observed their lack of understanding, [he said] to them, "Why has this agitation led (you) to anger? Your god who is within you and [his —] have become angry together with your souls. [Let] any one of you who is [strong enough] among human beings bring out the perfect human and stand before my face." And they all said, "We have the strength." But their spirits could not find the courage to stand before [him], except for Judas Iscariot (*GJudas* 33,22–35,9).[89]

Using the analogy of a "morality ladder" to discuss the idea that in antiquity, figures could be thought of as more or less advanced in terms of moral perfection, Dunderberg argues that Judas himself is positioned ambiguously. On the one hand, he is not classed with the disciples referred to in this passage, who exhibit a great deal of anger and are later roundly criticized, and he is the one who will have special visions in the passages that follow and the one to whom Jesus will impart certain secrets regarding the Kingdom. He is the only one who even begins to approach the status of the "perfect human" as he alone dares to stand before Jesus in this passage. Referring to Seneca's *Epistle 75*, Dunderberg explains:

> The concept of "the perfect human" looms large in the works of ancient philosophers as indicating the ultimate goal of moral progress. The most prominent characteristic of the perfect human is freedom: this figure is free of emotions, of all worldly concerns, and, as Seneca summarizes, of the fear of humans and gods.[90]

The fact that Judas "stands" is indeed important. "Standing" often connotes a sense of being firmly positioned in an unwavering state of rest, free

---

[89]All citations and translations of the *Gospel of Judas* are from Kasser, et al., *Gospel of Judas*. Jesus laughs here just as he laughs in the *Apocalypse of Peter*. He carefully clarifies, however, that he is *not* laughing *at* the disciples.

[90]Dunderberg, "Judas' Anger and the Perfect Human," 205.

of passion and entanglement in the world of sense perceptions. To be "immovable" is to be stable and at rest–cured of volatile, shifting emotions. Such is impossible for a person who has not been cured of passions.[91]

However, Judas seems to represent someone who will never be among the few who become completely perfect. He is characterized as a *daimon*, and like many other scholars, Dunderberg feels this term has a negative connotation. Moreover, Dunderberg acknowledges that Judas is not allowed to enter the divine realm that he sees in his vision, but is subject instead to a certain fate related to his star (*GJudas* 45,12–14; 56,23). What the text embodies is his struggle, his wrestling with the whole issue of caring for his self/soul with Jesus's help. Such a representation provides an honest portrayal of the struggle involved in being a follower of Christ, one that brings to mind Paul's confession of doing that which he does not wish to do (Romans 7:15).

This ambiguity in the text is quite enlightening, especially as Judas's struggles are fully represented. He receives both special revelation and Jesus's teaching, but wrestles with understanding and acting as one who is "perfect." If perfection could be equated with reaching the top rung on a ladder of moral progress, Judas has climbed only partway up. In this sense, his portrayal parallels Peter's in the *Apocalypse of Peter* (as discussed above). Both figures seem to function usefully as tools in a pedagogical discussion of what it would mean to be fully healed of the crippling and destructive effects of anger or fear. Such portraits are compelling and perhaps easier to relate to than those of the glorified heroes in the line of apostolic succession. Stephen Emmel suggests that the *Gospel of Judas* may have been intended for those who "stand apart from the ordinary group of Christians . . . but do not (or may not, or do not clearly, or do not yet) belong among the most spiritual."[92] Such a suggestion fits well with the kind of pedagogical purpose Dunderberg ascribes to the work and seems applicable to the *Apocalypse of Peter* as well.

---

[91]See Williams, "Stability as a Soteriological Theme in Gnosticism," 819–829, as well as his discussions on this topic in *Immovable Race*. Lance Jenott picks up on Williams' important discussion in his translation in Jenott, *Gospel of Judas*, 35, 475. Pagels and King also discuss Williams' explication of this theme; Pagels and King, *Reading Judas*, 131–132.

[92]Emmel, "Presuppositions and the Purpose of the *Gospel of Judas*," 38.

It is worth noting that the parallels between the *Apocalypse of Peter* and the *Gospel of Judas* are particularly striking. Both are revelation dialogues that take place with disciples of Jesus prior to his crucifixion. These are the very two men whom the canonical gospels portray as having betrayed Jesus. In each of the texts respectively, Peter and Judas are represented as struggling with destructive passions—Peter with fear and Judas with anger. The *Apocalypse of Peter* shows Jesus patiently revealing the way of liberation and transformation to Peter in spite of his repeated failures to comprehend Jesus's teaching while the author of the *Gospel of Judas* portrays Judas as the one who comes closer than any other disciple to being "the perfect human" (*GJudas* 35.4). Some scholars feel that, ultimately, Judas fails miserably in this role, but others feel just as strongly that he models it (as discussed below). Still, others feel that he is portrayed ambiguously. Likewise, Peter's portrayal—in the *Apocalypse of Peter* and elsewhere—is also riddled with ambivalence.[93] Thus, similarities regarding a need for healing and Jesus's insight regarding a cure, the care of the self in terms of the therapy of emotions, emerge. Other remarkable affinities arise as well: a critique of apostolic succession, a critique of practices of sacrifice (including martyrdom conceived of as a particular kind of sacrifice), and two-natures Christology (with the divine nature engaging in laughter). In addition, neither work interprets Jesus's death as a substitutionary blood atonement or advocates a belief in a fleshly resurrection.[94]

Several other scholars see Judas as represented ambiguously as well. By comparing several texts in which Judas features prominently, Pierluigi Piovanelli insightfully demonstrates that it is not information about a historical Judas that can be gleaned from them but rather insights about how he is represented. Overall, Piovanelli argues that the *Gospel of Judas*

---

[93]For similarities between the portrayals of Judas and Peter, see Dubois, "Évangile de Judas et la Tradition Basilidienne," 145–154.

[94]One other parallel concerns the date of the works. Although the dating of neither work is clear, and both have often been characterized as "late" simply because of their anti-orthodox remarks, a gospel featuring Judas is mentioned by Irenaeus in *Adversus Haereses (Against Heresies)*, circa 180 C.E. As noted above, Michael Desjardins states that the *Apocalypse of Peter* could possibly be dated as early as 150 C.E. Therefore, the *Apocalypse of Peter* and the *Gospel of Judas* may come from a similar time period.

provides us "a more sophisticated and humanized picture of the disciple"—not a simplistic hero or villain.[95]

The idea that Judas may change within the pages of the text is also mentioned by Marvin Meyer who is not sure whether *daimon* is the final characterization of Judas in this work.[96] He goes on to suggest certain parallels between Judas and the figure of Sophia. These parallels bring to mind the striking analysis of Ismo Dunderberg regarding the way in which the Sophia myth may be a Valentinian reflection on the therapy of emotions as Christ actually heals Sophia of her passions.[97] Specifically, in tracing the struggle to translate the term "set apart" and whether Judas is "set apart *for*" or "set apart *from*" others (45,13–46,18), Meyer says that he is increasingly convinced that the translation should be the latter and that "Judas is one who is enlightened but estranged in this world—rather like Allogenes the Stranger in the next tractate, also Sethian, in Codex Tchacos, and perhaps like Sophia in *Pistis Sophia*."[98]

In particular, with regard to Judas ruling over the thirteenth aeon, Meyer discusses the fact that on the one hand, the realm of the evil demiurge is that of thirteen aeons. Here the implication may be "that the fate of Judas is that he is destined to become no more than a lackey of the demiurge by joining him in the thirteenth aeon." He then goes on to note that the text ultimately says that Judas will rule over the thirteenth aeon:

> In that case, perhaps the text means to proclaim that, in the end, Judas—like Sophia elsewhere—will overcome the demiurge and all his megalomaniacal forces, and through Judas the power of 'that generation' will be triumphant and will be extended over all the world.[99]

What is important here is not whether Judas will ultimately triumph or not. Rather, what matters is the comparison to Sophia in terms of the care of the self. Both Sophia and Judas are subject to their passions and in need of the freedom that Christ can provide.

---

[95]Piovanelli, "Rabbi Yehuda versus Judas Iscariot," 235.

[96]Meyer, "Interpreting Judas," 41–55.

[97]See Dunderberg, *Beyond Gnosticism*, 95–118.

[98]Meyer, "Interpreting Judas," 45–46.

[99]Meyer, "Interpreting Judas," 47.

Meyer also points out that "themes associated with Wisdom, even personified Wisdom, may be disclosed as well in the person of Judas Iscariot as a figure of wisdom and a prototype of a person of knowledge in the *Gospel of Judas*."[100] Then he goes on to say that both Judas and Sophia are associated with the thirteenth aeon. This aeon is mentioned in *Pistis Sophia* and the *Book of Jeu*. In *Pistis Sophia*, it is described as an intermediate dimension between this earthly world and the place of righteousness. The description of Judas as a *daimon* who will end up in the thirteenth aeon may thus parallel the restoration of Sophia to the thirteenth aeon. For Meyer, Judas is

> neither a completely positive character nor a totally demonic being, but rather a figure, like Sophia, and like any gnostic being, who is embroiled in this world of mortality yet is striving for gnosis and enlightenment . . . . Judas, like Sophia, is caught between the worlds of mortality and immortality, looking for liberation.[101]

Ismo Dunderberg has likewise commented extensively on the way in which the restoration of Sophia takes place when Christ is able to heal her of her passions. Such an interpretation nicely parallels Dunderberg's thinking with regard to the *Gospel of Judas*—that Judas is represented neither as a hero nor a villain but as an ambiguous figure who is able to become more morally advanced because Jesus helps him to manage his anger (though not to completely eradicate it). Judas cannot achieve the status of a "perfect human," but he will manage to enter the thirteenth aeon.[102] In effect, these interpretations point to the way that the work serves as a vivid depiction of the human quest for healing.

Elaine Pagels also points to possible ambiguities in the text, pointing out that the moral status of various characters is not necessarily fixed within a narrative framework but often develops within it. She argues that Jesus's teaching on baptism may serve to help the reader understand its transformative and liberating power. In addition, she encourages us to consider

---

[100]Meyer, "When the Sethians were Young," 65–66.

[101]Meyer, "When the Sethians were Young," 73.

[102]Meyer, "When the Sethians were Young," 68–73. For arguments that Meyer is incorrectly applying ideas from fourth century works to the earlier *Gospel of Judas*, see Turner, "Sethian Myth in the *Gospel of Judas*," 132n70; and De Conick, "Apostles as Archons," 255.

the possibility that Judas himself may be transformed by this teaching rather than remaining static throughout the work and questions analyses that see him as incapable of change: "Where, after all, do one-sided interpretations leave us?"[103]

Unfortunately, Jesus's teaching regarding baptism is one of the places where a significant number of lines are missing. However, Lance Jenott has supplied part of the textual puzzle in his translation of the *Gospel of Judas* that incorporates a fragment hitherto missing from the critical edition and other translations. In the passage it contains, Jesus says that baptism in his name "will wipe out the entire race of earthly Adam" (*GJudas* 56, 4–6). Jenott interprets this as a reference to physical, human bodies, suggesting that in baptism, the initiate's human body is liberated from demonic forces and subjugation to astrological and cosmic powers. Jenott refers to Paul's similar belief in such liberation as expressed, for example, in Romans 5. In addition, a connection exists between baptism and Jesus's death. Baptism is a symbolic death that "wipes away" the power of demonic forces in a person's life just as Jesus's death wiped away the power of these forces in the universe as a whole (a *Christus Victor* theory of atonement). Jenott goes on to propose a reconstruction of the text involving the exaltation of "the [fruit] of the great race of Adam" (*GJudas* 57,8–14). Jenott points out that earlier (*GJudas* 43,12–44,2) Jesus has associated "fruit" with the heavenly ascent of the soul. The "fruit" consists of those souls who have been baptized.[104] Moreover, Judas sees this "great race" ascending to a large house which Jenott has argued resembles that in Jewish apocalyptic literature (specifically, the Book of the Watchers in 1 Enoch 14). Judas describes the holy members of this "great race" as "standing" in this heavenly temple which reminds the reader of the connotations associated with "standing" as being in a place of transcendent rest free from the movement in the sensory world. There is additionally the connotation of their becoming more like the angels in Jewish and Christian apocalyptic literature.[105]

---

[103]Pagels, "Baptism in the *Gospel of Judas*," 355. Johanna Brankaer makes a similar point, noting that Judas seems to change, or be transformed from 56, 21 onward, right after the section beginning with 55, 24 where Jesus has started to talk about baptism; Brankaer, "Whose Savior," 409.

[104]Jenott, *Gospel of Judas*, 31–34.

[105]Jenott, *Gospel of Judas*, 35.

In fact, then, according to Jenott, the perspective that Jesus's death allowed for the destruction of demonic forces and that those who follow Christ are themselves saved through baptism is *similar* to that of "proto-orthodox" thinkers.[106] This is not a gnostic work with a Docetic Christology. Overall, Jenott argues that figures such as Irenaeus and Epiphanius harshly condemned this text not for its theology per se but for its critique of certain leaders, a theme to which we now turn.

Critique of Apostolic Succession
John Turner colorfully describes the *Gospel of Judas's* characterization of the successors to the disciples as "ministers of error, doomed angelic lackies of the lord ruling the universe."[107] This phrase aptly describes the scholarly consensus regarding the work's vehement critique of the successors to the disciples. Jenott, for example, extends Dunderberg's emphasis on the theme of anger management by pointing out that the primary error of the disciples is their rage. It is their emotional state of being that constitutes their blasphemy against Jesus and therefore allows Judas to be so starkly contrasted with them. In Stoic terms, the disciples are not healed of passion. While Judas is not "perfect" in this respect, he is clearly not as ill as they are. In this respect, the 12 apostles, who will stone Judas to death out of their anger over his betrayal of Jesus, serve as counterpoints to the ideal of persons able to engage successfully in the cure of the passions.

All of this becomes clear in the following passages. The first is one in which the apostles speak with Jesus, asking him where he had gone after leaving them, and Jesus replies, "I went to another great and holy

---

[106]Bas van Os, Einar Thomassen, and John Turner see the *Gospel of Judas* as *critical* of the practice of baptism. None of these critiques, however, include the fragment to which Jenott refers. Van Os critiques the martyrdom hypothesis, pointing out that the text does not explicitly mention persecution by Roman authorities. He therefore argues that it is the actual sacrament of the Eucharist or, even more likely, baptism, that is being criticized as many early people identifying with Christ conceived of baptism as a kind of death. See van Os, "Stop Sacrificing," 367–386. Einar Thomassen concurs and discusses the idea that Jesus's denunciation of sacrificial acts is an allusion to baptism; Thomassen, "Is Judas Really the Hero of the *Gospel of Judas*," 164. John Turner argues that baptism is a referent as well, but that this is *in addition to* the Eucharist and possibly even martyrdom; Turner, "The Place of the *Gospel of Judas* in Sethian Tradition," 187–237.
[107]Turner, "Sethian Myth in the *Gospel of Judas*," 127.

generation (*GJudas* 36,16–17). The disciples then respond, "Lord, what is the great generation that is superior to us and holy (*GJudas* 36,19–20) and Jesus actually laughs (*GJudas* 36,23) and tells them that "no one born [of] this aeon will see that [generation] . . . and no person of mortal birth will be able to associate with it" (*GJudas* 37,3–8). When they hear this, they are "troubled in [their] spirit" (*GJudas* 37,18–19). Clearly, they are not members of "the strong and holy generation."

Later, the apostles tell Jesus that they have had a vision (*GJudas* 37,22) in which they saw an altar with 12 priests. The priests were engaged in all kinds of immoral sacrifices, including sacrifices of their very own wives and children. They were also engaged in eating the bodies and blood of these sacrifices. Jesus tells them that they themselves are those priests and that they are mistaken in thinking that he comes from the god who is pleased by such sacrifices:

> "We [have] seen a great house [with a] large altar [in it, and] twelve men—
> they are the priests, we would say; and a name <—>; and a crowd of people is
> waiting at that altar, [until] the priests [finished] [presenting] the offerings.
> We [also] kept waiting." [Jesus said], "What are [—] like?" And they [said],
> "Some [— for] two weeks; [others] sacrifice their own children, others their
> wives . . . . still others commit a multitude of sins and deeds of lawlessness.
> [And] the men who stand [before] the altar invoke your [name]. And while
> they are involved in all the deeds of their sacrifice, that [altar] is filled"
> (*GJudas* 38,1–39,3).

After this, the disciples are "quiet" (*GJudas* 39,4) because they are "troubled" (*GJudas* 39,5). Jesus then says to them,

> Why are you troubled? Truly I say to you, all the priests who stand before
> that altar invoke my name. And again I say to you, my name has been written
> on [—] of the generations of the stars by the human generations. [And] they
> have planted trees without fruit, in my name, in a shameful manner (*GJudas*
> 39,6–17).

He then says,

> It is you who are presenting the offerings on the altar you have seen. That
> one is the god you serve, and you are the twelve men you have seen. And the
> cattle that are brought in are the sacrifices you have seen—that is, the many
> people you lead astray before that altar (*GJudas* 39,18–40,1).

He goes on to equate priests with "ministers of error" (*GJudas* 40,22–23) and commands them: "Stop sac[rificing —]" (*GJudas* 41,1–2).

The charges of human sacrifice—that of the priests' own children and wives—are particularly striking. Many scholars have recognized that the charge of human sacrifice was a discursive strategy in the ancient world by which one group could cast another as cultural barbarians associated with a practice deemed crude and barbaric.[108] Jenott emphasizes this fact and in his most recent work, he sees no more in this passage than a stock list of polemics meant to disparage the leaders of proto-orthodox groups.[109]

Philip Tite also expounds on the nature of the use of negative moral exempla (of which the disciples seem to be examples par excellence) and the use of virtue and vice lists in marking the presence of *paraenesis*, or moral exhortation.[110] Such lists derive from the Stoic perspective that linked knowing a particular truth with the ability to act virtuously in a certain respect.[111] Indeed, the list of accusations against the apostles functions much like one of these vice lists. These are clearly not models for imitation or figures of authority to whom one should be submitting.

Tite identifies five features common to *paraenesis*: the use of the imperative or hortative subjunctive, discussion of figures who serve as moral exemplars, vice/virtue lists, two-way schema, and household codes. The *Gospel of Judas* manifests three of these five features: imperatives, moral exempla (the disciples serving as negative exempla and Judas as an ambiguous one), and vice lists. Overall, Tite argues that paraenetic texts function as "discursive voices" that attempt to persuade their readers regarding morality.[112] Indeed, it is with this type of argument—that works categorized as gnostic have much to say about morality—that Dunderberg also concurs when he describes the *Gospel of Judas* as a reflection on anger management in a manner reminiscent of Stoic thought.[113] Thus, although Tite's insightful work was published prior to the *Gospel of Judas*, it could

---

[108]J. Rives, "Human Sacrifices Among Pagans and Christians," 65–85.

[109]Jenott, *Gospel of Judas*, 58–60.

[110]Tite, "Valentinian Ethics and Paraenetic Discourse," 133–144. Tite analyzes Valentinian works, but his analysis seems applicable to the Sethian text of the *Gospel of Judas* as well.

[111]Tite, "Valentinian Ethics and Paraenetic Discourse," 137.

[112]Tite, "Valentinian Ethics and Paraenetic Discourse," 300.

[113]This is also a primary argument of Dunderberg's *Beyond Gnosticism*.

well be argued that its narrative framework functions as moral exhortation. Such *paraenesis* functions as a call to engage in the therapy of the emotions and the care of the self.

For Jenott, the argument is not so much over the practice of Eucharist itself as over who has the right to conduct it and the moral character of those who are claiming the exclusive right of officiating:

> The author of *Judas* responded by writing the equivalent of a modern political attack ad: a smear campaign against the twelve disciples that cut at the very root of the clergy's authority. The target of the *Gospel of Judas*'s criticism is neither the Eucharist, nor the ideology of sacrifice, nor the sacrificial interpretation of Jesus' death, but the twelve disciples and their corrupt moral character. The author takes issue with the form of church leadership which established itself upon the doctrine of apostolic succession. Thus he carefully develops a portrayal of the Twelve as men who were confused about the true identity of Jesus and the god they served. Although they believed they worshipped the true God and father of Jesus, in actually their god is nothing more than an apostate angel *who afflicted their souls with bitter passion*. As a consequence of their devotion to such a god, the disciples themselves became enflamed with anger and contention, were morally debased, and ultimately led their followers into sin and error. By telling the story of the twelve disciples this way, *Judas* challenges the foundational myth held by many Christians who maintained that the 12 were the authoritative group to whom Jesus entrusted his teaching, commissioned to evangelize the world, and who established the only legitimate, apostolic churches to which all true Christians must belong.[114]

Certainly, many other scholars have discussed the negative depiction of the apostles and the critique of apostolic authority. Einar Thomassen does so at length, arguing that the *Gospel of Judas* portrays the disciples with even less intelligence or understanding than other texts such as the four New Testament gospels, the *Gospel of Mary*, and the *Gospel of Thomas*. In the *Gospel of Judas*, the apostles are completely beyond redemption in failing to worship the right God, in committing terrible crimes, and in leading others astray.[115] Later, he comments:

---

[114]Jenott, *Gospel of Judas*, 41. Emphasis added.
[115]Thomassen, "Is Judas Really the Hero of the *Gospel of Judas*?," 160.

The *Gospel of Judas* is clearly a very unusual document. It uses a genre, the revelation dialogue of Jesus and the disciples, that is normally used to legitimise certain doctrines as secret apostolic tradition. But it totally subverts this genre by discounting the disciples altogether and by portraying Judas Iscariot as simultaneously the worst and the best of the disciples. Judas receives a revelation, but he is utterly unable to profit from it, because his destiny has already been decided. So who is supposed to profit from the revelation? This is another of the enigmas of the *Gospel of Judas*. Normally in revelation dialogues, the recipient, or recipients, of the revelation are models of identification for the readers. The reader, by identifying with the recipient disciple, himself becomes the recipient of the revelation divulged by the written text. That cannot be the situation here . . . . Jesus is seen as the source of revelation, but every single one of his disciples is rejected as able to receive and transmit his revelation.[116]

April De Conick actually interprets the work as a parody in which even Judas, corrupt as he is, understands who Jesus is better than 12 of his other apostles do, but that fact only underscores the ways in which these 12 greatly lack understanding of Jesus. It does not make Judas a hero. She compares the portrayal of the apostles in the *Gospel of Judas* to that in the *Gospel of Mark* where the 12 repeatedly fail to "get" who Jesus is and what he is about.[117]

In fact, De Conick and virtually all scholars regardless of their position with respect to Judas's moral character agree in seeing the text as a critique of what she refers to as "apostolic," "catholic," or "mainstream" Christianity (also termed "proto-orthodox" Christianity by many scholars).[118] She argues that the work bitterly lampoons the notion of apostolic succession and the ecclesiastical structure based on that hierarchy, as well as the practice of sacrifice and the doctrine of the atonement as a sacrifice pleasing to and even willed by God.[119] Thus, while scholars vigorously debate the nature of Judas's character, most concur in seeing the text

---

[116]Thomassen, "Is Judas Really the Hero of the *Gospel of Judas*?," 168–170.

[117]De Conick, *Thirteenth Apostle*, 103–108.

[118]De Conick, *Thirteenth Apostle*, 6.

[119]De Conick, *Thirteenth Apostle*, 169, 180–182. Lance Jenott refers to this specifically when he says that the focus on the critique of sacrifice has been too far entwined with the discussion surrounding the moral character of Judas; Jenott, *Gospel of Judas*, 23.

serving as a critique of practices and theological beliefs centered on sacrifice.[120] In fact, for those who see Judas as represented unfavorably, Judas's very act of sacrificing Jesus serves to epitomize and underscore the negative representation of sacrifice in the work. Einar Thomassen, for example, contends:

> The *Gospel of Judas* generally holds a very negative opinion of sacrifice . . . .
> When the author chooses to describe Judas' handing over of Jesus as an act of
> sacrifice, that can hardly, therefore, be intended as a positive characterization.
> The phrase 'you will exceed all of them' may even be taken to imply the
> opposite: by performing his particular sacrifice, Judas is even worse than the
> others.[121]

Louis Painchaud shares this opinion as well, stating that in no way does this text rehabilitate Judas.[122] Rather, Judas "is the ruling 'archon' presiding over this sacrificial ideology and governing those who adhere to it and curse him."[123] He commits "the worst of inequities" in sacrificing Jesus and is worse even than the other 12 apostles.[124]

De Conick has also described the work as one in which "[a] harsher treatment of the doctrine of apostolic authority could not be had!"[125] She goes on to say that "[t]he twelve disciples are little more than puppets of the archons." For her, the genre is that of a tragedy:

---

[120]The dissenting voice is that of Lance Jenott who, as discussed above, argues the text reflects a vision of a *Christus Victor* theory of atonement. His argument is well made and does much to dispel the notion that gnostic works are "anti-atonement." However, it is quite plausible that the author of the *Gospel of Judas* is at odds with the conception of a substitutionary atonement, which is a major theme in some early writers such as Ignatius of Antioch. In these texts, martyrdom is linked to this particular interpretation of Jesus's death as well.

[121]Einar Thomassen, "Is Judas Really the Hero of the *Gospel of Judas*?," 166. Thomassen does go on to say that there is a certain ambiguity even here as Judas is represented as better than the others in certain ways.

[122]Painchaud, "Polemical Aspects of the *Gospel of Judas*," 177. See also Louis Painchaud, "'You will sacrifice the man who bears me.'"

[123]Painchaud, "Polemical Aspects of the *Gospel of Judas*," 178.

[124]Painchaud, "Polemical Aspects of the *Gospel of Judas*," 183–184.

[125]De Conick, "Mystery of Betrayal," 254.

By betraying Jesus, Judas has offered Jesus' body as a sacrifice to Ialdabaoth, a sacrifice more evil than any the other apostles would ever make (56, 17–21) . . . . By framing Judas' sacrifice of Jesus alongside that of the other apostles who sin by also offering Ialdabaoth evil sacrifices (c.f. *Gospel of Judas* 56,11–13; 39,18–40,1), the gospel goes a long way to critique and mock mainstream interpretations of Jesus' death in sacrificial terms. This criticism and mockery includes a strong condemnation of eucharist theology.[126]

Further Critique of Sacrifice and Martyrdom

Anna Van den Kerchove most clearly points out the details that help us to see how the *Gospel of Judas* may indeed be offering incisive critique of the glorification of sacrifice and both the Eucharist and martyrdom conceived of as symbolizing or imitating sacrifices of substitutionary atonement desired by God. She clearly points out the ways in which the author of the *Gospel of Judas* seems to be inscribing himself (or herself) into debates among various groups of Christ followers regarding specific interpretations of the Eucharist and martyrdom that were prevalent in their thinking during the second and third centuries. She argues that the author most certainly belongs to a social context in which accusing a group of making human sacrifices is a general way of accusing them of social deviance, but it is important not to overlook the possibility that this critique may well be referring to specific practices involving particular interpretations of the Eucharist and martyrdom. She argues that the author specifically uses two discursive strategies to do this: (1) attributing a literal meaning to phrases commonly used metaphorically in these communities, and (2) amalgamating the ritual practices of the Jewish temple with the discourses of communities in which both the Eucharist and martyrdom were associated with sacrifice.[127] Lance Jenott has also written about the way that the description of the temple in Judas's vision (as a temple encircled by "lightning" or

---

[126]De Conick, "Mystery of Betrayal," 261. Franklin Trammell notes a similar critique of the apostles but in the *Apocalypse of James* that immediately precedes the *Gospel of Judas* in the Codex Tchacos; Trammell, "God of Jerusalem as the Pole Dragon," 337–349.

[127]Van den Kerchove, "Maison, l'Autel et les Sacrifices," 311–329. Van den Kerchove also argues that the conflation of associations regarding Jewish temple practices and practices of early Christ movements is a critique of both. See also Jenott, "*Gospel of Judas* 45,6–7 and Enoch's Heavenly Temple," 476.

"fire" corresponds to parallels of the description of the Jewish temple in the Book of the Watchers, 1 Enoch, and 3 Enoch. He argues that the earthly temple and the heavenly temple are being contrasted in order to criticize the way that the Eucharist—and martyrdom conceived of as a Eucharist sacrifice—are being conceived.[128]

Specifically, Van den Kerchove refers to the passage in which the male disciples tell Jesus of their vision, a vision in which 12 priests are making sacrifices of children and women in a house with an altar before which a crowd of people is waiting. She points out that the specific Coptic words used for "house" and "altar" conjure up associations both with the temple in Jerusalem and the altar where sacrifices had been made prior to its destruction as well as with the homes in which Christ people met and the table they used for the celebration of the Eucharist. Likewise, the crowd is said to be "waiting before the altar." (*GJudas* 38,6–8). The phrase is one that is not found commonly in Greek literature or the Hebrew Bible but that occurs eleven times in the New Testament as well as in texts by Clement of Alexandria, Origen, and Cyprian, and in the *Acts of Peter*. The verb has the sense of "persevering" before the altar and is associated with activity that is accomplished near the Eucharist table. The use of this phrase may serve to invoke connotations with the point of view in which some saw Christ's sacrifice (and the Eucharist that commemorates it) as a replacement for the kinds of sacrifices made in the Jerusalem temple. Of course, at the time the *Gospel of Judas* is being written, the temple has almost certainly been destroyed, but by alluding to temple worship and conflating it with celebration of the Eucharist, the author critiques those groups who interpret the Eucharist as a sacrifice or the imitation or commemoration of a sacrifice.[129] More specifically, I would add that it may well be directed to those who see this practice as a commemoration of a substitutionary atonement (as opposed to the kind of sacrifice envisioned in a *Christus Victor* theory of atonement). Van den Kerchove also points out that in the *Gospel of Judas* 40,22, the priests are described as "ministers of error." The term for "minister" is *diakonos*, the word commonly used for deacons, persons authorized to serve the Eucharist. In other words, the author of the *Gospel of Judas* is using the very terms and phrases that other authors use to speak about the Eucharist in a variety of works, leading one to

---

[128]Jenott, "*Gospel of Judas* 45,6–7 and Enoch's Heavenly Temple," 476.

[129]Van den Kerchove, "Maison, l'Autel et les Sacrifices," 320–321.

believe that possible critique on the part of the author with regard to the interpretations of these practices cannot be excluded. Van den Kerchove also explains that while references to the sacrificing of children have several classical precedents, accusations of sacrificing women are less common. She refers to the fact that both Polycarp and Tertullian talk about the bodies of women as altars and sites of intercessory prayer that is efficacious for others. While the sacrifice of women could be relevant in some way to the evolving discussion about purity, chastity, and asceticism, she goes on to say that the joint charge of sacrificing both children and women may well have associations with the practice of martyrdom conceived of as a sacrifice. Citing numerous examples of martyrdom interpreted in this way (in the *Recognitions of Pseudo-Clement*, the *Martyrdom of Polycarp*, a letter of Cyprian, Ignatius of Antioch's *Letter to the Romans*, and Irenaeus's *Against Heresies*), she argues that the author of the *Gospel of Judas* may be referring to and critiquing the practice of martyrdom (or, more accurately, the interpretation of it as a sacrifice) in mentioning the sacrifice of children and women. She goes on to say that it is not the practice itself that is being questioned so much as the particular interpretation of it and any glorification of it within an ecclesiological context. Thus, in summary, she argues that in associating the altar and the house with human sacrifice, the author critiques his adversaries, probably those belonging to another "rival" community, and their manner of living and accomplishing certain ritual acts. Though she does not discuss the fact that Jesus specifically states that these male disciples are "leading people astray," this, too, fits with the overall argument as does his injunction to "Stop sacrificing!"[130]

These details mesh well with the argument of a review appearing shortly after the publication of the critical edition of the *Gospel of Judas's*. This article discusses the *Gospel of Judas's* portrait of the male disciples as reflecting the author's critique of certain leaders for endorsing or encouraging martyrdom and leading others toward accepting it uncritically. For this author, sacrifice is in vain, and such leaders are no better than those who would lead innocent sheep to slaughter.[131]

Karen King and Elaine Pagels also provide extensive support for the idea that a critique of martyrdom exists in the *Gospel of Judas*. They argue that fierce disagreements over the value and significance of martyrdom are at

---

[130]Van den Kerchove, "Maison, l'Autel et les Sacrifices," 311–329.

[131]Iricinschi, Jenott, and Townsend, "Betrayer's Gospel."

the heart of it. They point out that a variety of texts existed that glorified martyrdom and encouraged or exhorted people toward this path. Certainly some Biblical passages represent Jesus's death as a substitutionary atonement. I Corinthians 5:7 calls Christ a "paschal lamb." First- and second-century writers such as Ignatius of Antioch (and others discussed in Chap. 3) think of their impending martyrdom in these terms—as the imitation of Jesus's sacrifice. Other treatises (Tertullian's *Scorpiace* being a notable example) also glorify martyrdom. Other sermons, accounts (Polycarp's and Justin's being particularly notable), and histories (especially that of Eusebius) also did so.[132] Robin Darling Young's work on the way in which martyrdom functioned and was represented as a "public liturgical sacrifice" complements Pagel's and King's well.[133]

Noting the strident anger of the tone in the *Gospel of Judas*, which Pagels and King insist must be viewed within the context of its time and place in an era of frightening persecution when perspectives on martyrdom had very concrete consequences for believers, they discuss the apparent conflict within the mind of the author: how could a good and loving God possibly wish for the death of Jesus and all his followers—a view espoused by other contemporary Jesus followers?[134] The only answer for the author of the *Gospel of Judas* was that leaders who encouraged others to offer themselves up for death were, in effect, murderers mistaking the obtaining of martyrdom at all costs for what Jesus had actually taught. In effect, they were engaging in the worship of a "false god."[135]

King and Pagels carefully explain that the author does not denigrate the actual martyrs or denounce martyrdom itself, but the writer does detest the inference made by some Christians that God wanted Jesus to die and even required such a death (understood as a sacrifice) from Jesus and his followers. In other words, the author challenges the particular meaning attributed to martyrdom rather than martyrdom in and of itself.[136]

These scholars also point out the irony of a certain contradiction in that some Christians were once again making sacrifice central to Christian worship by interpreting the death of Jesus as one that served as a sacrifice

---

[132]Pagels and King, *Reading Judas*, 49–57.

[133]Young, *In Procession Before the World*, 12.

[134]Pagels and King, *Reading Judas*, 100.

[135]Pagels and King, *Reading Judas*, xvi.

[136]Pagels and King, *Reading Judas*, 59.

for the sin of human beings and by also asserting that the deaths of martyrs gratified God even though they would not otherwise participate in making sacrifices at the temple in Jerusalem or at sites of pagan veneration.[137] They go on to say that it is of course impossible to know if the author had seen any leaders encouraging martyrdom. However, the strong language and tone of the text indicate the author's serious attempts to expose the absurd and foolish ideas of those leaders who promoted dying a martyr's death by implying that it would assure a heavenly life filled with rewards.[138] King and Pagels acknowledge that the author believes that Jesus's death and those of his followers (including Judas himself) should be thought of as sacrifices, but they nuance this by discussing the idea that conceiving of such an act as sacrifice does not translate into the notion promulgated by leaders such as Ignatius and Irenaeus that such a death ensures a physical and permanent fleshly resurrection from the dead.[139] Finally, they go on to present some of the questions the author seems to be raising:

> What does such teaching make of God? Is God, then, unwilling or unable to forgive human transgression without violent bloodshed—from either the cut throats of goats and bulls, or—worse—human sacrifice? Are Christians to worship a God who demands what the Hebrew Bible says that the God of Abraham refused—child sacrifice, even that of his own son? What kind of God would require anyone—much less his own son—to die in agony before he accepts his followers?[140]

Of course, as discussed in Chap. 3, it is crucial to realize that there were multiple points of view within the early Christ movements, not just two. Regarding the issue of sacrifice itself, as noted above, Victor Aulén has pointed to the fact that many saw Christ's death in terms of a *Christus Victor* theory of atonement, not in terms of the kind of substitutionary atonement that the questions above presuppose. Lance Jenott has done a remarkable job of pointing out that an author such as that of the *Gospel of Judas* may have actually embraced the *Christus Victor* perspective. Thus, it is not even the case that such an author fails to see Jesus's death as a

---

[137]Pagels and King, *Reading Judas*, 68.

[138]Pagels and King, *Reading Judas*, 59.

[139]Pagels and King, *Reading Judas*, 60.

[140]Pagels and King, *Reading Judas*, 66.

sacrifice but rather that he or she vehemently opposes a substitutionary atonement perspective.

Certainly, many scholars have recently been at pains to point out alternatives to substitutionary atonement in the thinking of the early movements as well. Marcus Borg, for example, discusses the fact that a view of Christ's death as a substitutionary atonement did not become entrenched and gain dominance until the Middle Ages under the influence of Anselm.[141] Rita Nakashima Brock and Rebecca Ann Parker have written at length about the plenitude of images of paradise in the first centuries of the Common Era versus the scarcity of crucifixion images.[142] While such discussion is very helpful in illuminating the diverse perspectives and opinions circulating in the second and third centuries when the *Gospel of Judas* was probably written, the presence of a substitutionary atonement perspective in some works (those discussed in the previous chapter) cannot be denied, and the *Gospel of Judas* provides a clear critique of such.

King and Pagels point out that a diversity of viewpoints regarding sacrifice had existed within the various forms of Judaism as well. Prophets such as Amos, Hosea, and Isaiah emphasized loving God and doing justice over mere rituals and insisted that the latter could never substitute for the former. Greek and Roman philosophers, too, argued for the care of the self rather than bloody rituals. Porphyry, for example, said, "The best sacrifice to the gods is a pure mind and a soul free from passions."[143] The *Gospel of Judas* adds greatly to our understanding of the fact that such perspectives existed within early Christ movements as well.[144]

For writers such as Irenaeus, a refusal to accept the doctrine of a fleshly resurrection "offended their sense of justice."[145] Irenaeus believed that those who suffered in the body "should be rewarded in the body."[146] For the author of the *Gospel of Judas*, however, to suggest that God desires or even wills sacrifice is wrong. The immortal life of the soul is a very real

---

[141]Borg, *Speaking Christian*, 97–106.

[142]Brock and Parker, *Saving Paradise*.

[143]Pagels and King cite Eusebius's *The Preparation for the Gospel 4.14d* as the source for this quotation. See Pagels and King, *Reading Judas*, 70n10.

[144]Pagels and King, *Reading Judas*, 69–71.

[145]Pagels and King, *Reading Judas*, 84.

[146]Pagels and King, *Reading Judas*, 84. Joyce Salisbury has also developed this idea extensively in Salisbury, *Blood of Martyrs*.

thing, but spiritual transformation is the goal rather than a fleshly resurrection. Encouraging belief in the latter

> makes people complicit in murder. By teaching that Jesus died in agony "for
> the sins of the world" and encouraging his followers to die as he did, certain
> leaders send them on a path toward destruction—while encouraging them
> with the false promise that they will be resurrected from death to eternal life
> in the flesh.[147]

King and Pagels note the "alternating tones of hope and fear" within the
New Testament itself.[148] Texts such as the *Gospel of Judas* complement and
add to our understanding of the array of perspectives within the second and
third centuries as well.

While scholars are fiercely divided over the character of Judas himself
and many disagree with King, Pagels, and others who have portrayed Judas
in a positive light, many acknowledge King's and Pagels's point regarding
the critique of martyrdom within this work. Marvin Meyer, for example,
explains as follows:

> Elsewhere in the *Gospel of Judas*, Jesus is made to be very critical of sacrifice,
> and that criticism may be interpreted as celebrations of the Christian
> eucharist, sacrificial interpretations of the crucifixion story, and as Karen L.
> King and Elaine H. Pagels propose, the sacrifices that take place in acts of
> martyrdom. Those who advocate such sacrifice, as in acts of martyrdom, may
> be the 'slayers of children' referred to at 40,10–11 and in other passages of
> the *Gospel of Judas*.[149]

Preparation for Martyrdom
Another possibility for fresh, creative ways of interpreting texts such as the
Gospel of Judas is to think of them as focused on "preparation for mar-
tyrdom." This is a compelling argument given that a variety of attitudes

---

[147]Pagels and King, *Reading Judas*, 74.

[148]Pagels and King, *Reading Judas*, 101.

[149]Meyer, "Interpreting Judas," 52. See also Meyer, "When the Sethians were
Young," 61; Painchaud, "Polemical Aspects of the *Gospel of Judas*," 171–186;
Piovanelli, "Rabbi Yehuda versus Judas Iscariot," 238; Robinson, "*Gospel of Judas*,"
91; and Lewis, "Fate and the Wandering Stars," 54–55.

toward the care of the self and more specifically, toward martyrdom, existed in the early centuries of the Common Era. This range of attitudes can be seen by examining the full spectrum of early writings associated with followers of Christ. Karen King takes this approach.[150] Her argument helps us begin to think in terms of a variety of ways in which self-formation was being conceived rather than a distinct binary opposition between orthodox and heretical (or gnostic) views. King is careful to note that it is the *meaning* of martyrdom that is at stake for various groups rather than a simple dichotomy of embracing or shying away from it. In conceiving of these works as part of a new kind of genre that could be thought of as "preparation for martyrdom" texts, King points out that it is not only the actual content of a particular work but also its grouping as well as the order of texts within a codex that participate in the elaboration and nuancing of certain themes in relation to each other. She explains that not only the *Gospel of Judas* but the two works that precede it, the *Letter of Peter to Philip* and the *First Apocalypse of James*, articulate views about the meaning of martyrdom.[151] Thus, the codex as a whole reflects a range of perspectives regarding martyrdom for the readers to consider. In the *Gospel of Judas*, the idea that sacrifice is pleasing to God is angrily challenged. Both Jesus and Judas suffer and die at the hands of others. However, for King, their deaths are not portrayed as meaningful sacrifices. She mentions that an actual reason for even Jesus's suffering is not explicitly given. In the *Letter of Peter to Philip* and the *First Apocalypse of James*, encouragement is given to those who are facing martyrs' deaths. In short, if one is able to understand and accept Jesus's true teaching, one will be freed from fear, able to act and to preach the gospel, and able to accept death with equanimity. In the *Letter of Peter to Philip*, it is the apostles themselves who are given this message. By contrast, in the *Gospel of Judas*, "the twelve" are severely admonished for participating in evil acts and abominable sacrifices to a false god. In a sense, then, this text, poses a strong counterpoint not only to others in the Tchacos Codex but to one such as Ignatius's *Letter to the Romans*. King remarks: "What sets these Christians apart is not that they sought to avoid martyrdom nor were not put to death as Christians, but rather that the meaning they gave to their suffering and deaths was

---

[150]King, "Martyrdom and Its Discontents," 23–42.
[151]King, "Martyrdom and Its Discontents," 24.

distinctive."[152] In all three works, however, Jesus reveals to one or more of his apostles that the true and immortal self is not the same as the body. Even if the body suffers, this is not necessarily the ultimate fate of the soul. King's overall thesis—that understanding the *Gospel of Judas* as one of a number of texts that provide insight into the array of attitudes regarding martyrdom and a variety of responses as to how to face it—is most helpful for the larger project of elucidating attitudes toward the care of the self. Moreover, her insight into the fact that a number of authors emphasize the importance of receiving, understanding, and accepting the teaching of Jesus is likewise crucial for conceptualizing early notions in Christ-related groups regarding the care of the self. Such an insight resonates with those of Dunderberg regarding Jesus's teaching about the therapy of emotions.

Marvin Meyer, too, notes an insight similar to King's. Citing a private conversation with Rodolphe Kasser, he comments that all the works in Codex Tchacos are similar in that they relate discussions and revelations that Jesus has with various people before his crucifixion. They also "are unified in their common concern for death and life in this world and beyond."[153]

Alistair Logan likewise discusses the other documents included with the *Gospel of Judas* and reflects on the choice of these particular texts and what significance their order in the codex as a whole could have had for those that wrote and read them. He, too, mentions that all of the works involve revelations to disciples and that those works in which Peter and James figure prominently come first in the codex. These two were well known for having suffered persecution and martyrdom. The dominant themes seem to center around how one overcomes suffering and how one deals with persecution. Whether one should seek it, avoid it, or merely endure what comes are all questions for discussion.[154]

In short, numerous scholars agree that the *Gospel of Judas* provides new and valuable insights into the controversies prevailing among various Christ movements in the second and third centuries of the Common Era. Simultaneously, the work provides insight into conversations regarding themes of anger management and other issues related to the care of the self. Therefore, it is important not to dismiss it as "heretical" but rather to

---

[152]King, "Martyrdom and Its Discontents," 41.
[153]Meyer, "Interpreting Judas," 43n6.
[154]Logan, "Tchacos Codex," 3–21.

mine it for the understandings it provides for retelling history in terms of varying attitudes toward the care of the self.

THE RESURRECTION OF THE FLESH

All of the texts mentioned above also should be considered in the context of debates over whether the resurrection of the body is a fleshly one, one involving the reconstitution of the very same material parts one had before dying. Indeed, fierce controversies over the nature of the resurrection are prevalent in this period. Carolyn Walker Bynum gives a lengthy exposition of what is at stake in these debates. She helps us to see that the insistence on a fleshly resurrection—and, indeed, the resurrection of exactly the same particles of flesh (or *sarx*) that constituted one's body prior to death—is a theological development of the second century rather than the first. In fact, the doctrine of a fleshly resurrection emerges in the context of persecution. She points out that there existed (and, indeed, exists) a horror of decay and putrefaction. Those facing martyrdom wished for reassurance that even if they were devoured by beasts, burned, or improperly buried, all would be well. Theologians such as Irenaeus and Tertullian spoke to these fears in a very pastoral way, assuring members of early Christ movements that God could raise them intact, so to speak.[155] Such teaching actually contrasts with that found in the oldest writings of the New Testament, those of the Apostle Paul. Paul clearly lays out a belief in a bodily resurrection in 1 Corinthians 15, but he characterizes the body prior to death as the "seed" of the transformed, resurrected body. The English translation for this latter body is "spiritual body," but scholars such as Dale Martin and Troels Engberg-Pedersen explain that such a translation is misleading. The actual phrase is *pneumatic body*. They feel that Paul was influenced by Stoicism, and for the Stoics, *pneuma* was real, tangible matter. Thus, Paul is not saying that the resurrected body is merely spiritual; rather, he feels it is of a

---

[155]Bynum, *Resurrection of the Body*. Joyce Salisbury develops this matter further when she discusses the development of the theology of the resurrection of the flesh in the context of persecution. She writes that conceiving of the resurrection in this way resonated with a sense of justice for those facing persecution. See Salisbury, *The Blood of Martyrs*.

different caliber altogether—still altogether material but of a different quality than the fleshly body one has prior to death.[156]

The works examined earlier—the *Apocalypse of Peter*, the *Testimony of Truth*, the fragments of Basilides and Valentinus, and the *Gospel of Judas* are in many respects different from each other. However, none of them affirm a fleshly resurrection. The *Apocalypse of Peter* criticizes those who believe in a "restored Christ" (*Apoc. Pet.* 74,10) or "cleave to the name of a dead man" (*Apoc. Pet.* 74,14–15). Moreover, the text asserts the triumph of the immortal soul rather than the resurrection of the earthly body, which is ruled by a soul filled with passion: "For every soul of these ages has death assigned to it . . . . because it is always a slave, since it is created for its desires" (*Apoc. Pet.* 75,16–20). In the *Testimony of Truth*, the author exhorts the readers/hearers: "Do not expect the carnal resurrection" (*TTruth* 36,31). Basilides believes in the transmigration of souls, not a fleshly resurrection. In the fragment of Valentinus, there is not enough context to be sure of the author's views, but the phrase "have been immortal" implies a belief in a preexistent soul that will live eternally rather than the resurrection of a fleshly body. In the *Gospel of Judas*, Jesus teaches that human bodies perish. Salvation lies in his own ascent to the heavenly realm and that of those who understand his teaching—those who belong to the "great and holy race" (*GJudas* 8.3–4).[157]

Others, like Jenott, whose views are discussed earlier in this chapter, do not see Judas as filled with understanding. His sacrifice of Jesus is an evil act. However, in accordance with a two-natures Christology, it is only the human nature of Jesus that perishes, not the divine spirit. The divine spirit triumphs over death and demons. There is no fleshly resurrection.

It is important to recognize that to speak of the resurrection of the flesh is to reflect a particular theological choice. It may be that those who believed in Jesus as the healer of the emotions but who did not believe in a

---

[156]I am particularly indebted to Dale Martin for delineating the Stoic understanding of *pneuma* in his lecture entitled "Epistemologies of the Body in the New Testament" at the Rocky Mountains Great Plains SBL/AAR/ASOR luncheon at the Iliff School of Theology, March 19, 2011. For discussions of the various beliefs regarding resurrection in the New Testament, see Engberg-Pedersen, *Cosmology and Self in the Apostle Paul*. For a helpful exposition of distinctions in the various conceptions of the resurrection, see also Riley, *Resurrection Considered*.

[157]Pagels and King, *Reading Judas*, 77, 131.

fleshly resurrection simply could not accept the development of the kinds of theology reflected in the writings of Irenaeus, Tertullian, and others, and indeed, in the passages of *1 Clement*, the *Letters of Ignatius*, and the *Martyrdom of Polycarp* discussed in Chap. 3. However, in voicing their concerns and presenting alternative views, allying themselves with the Pauline conception of the resurrection, they disrupted the discourse of martyrdom and the suffering self that was gaining enormous momentum—as Judith Perkins traces in her own seminal work. Such debates have come down to us as doctrinally-based, but indeed, they may well have been rooted in different practices and conceptions regarding the best way to care for the self. One important caveat is in order. Groups that tended to place their emphasis on a kind of spiritual transformation emphasizing the therapy of the emotions were not necessarily disloyal to the faith or lacking in courage or a willingness to endure martyrdom. Indeed, as we have seen, the reader/hearer is exhorted in various ways not to be afraid of anything, including death. Rather, these groups simply may not have seen such practices as most conducive to the practice of their faith. Indeed, the emotional theatrics and drama associated with the practices of voluntary martyrdom may have seemed to be in direct conflict with the disassociation from the emotions advocated in philosophical circles.[158] Dunderberg himself notes that the opponents were not balanced or neutral in presenting the views of those with whom they disagreed, completely failing to mention the presence of moral exhortation and focusing instead on issues of difference.[159]

Furthermore, Moss comments that the discursive strategies of both Clement and Irenaeus have been unwittingly assumed as factual and used as evidence of a binary opposition between supposedly orthodox Christians and so-called Gnostics, the former dying as martyrs and the latter avoiding it. Such thinking hides the complexity of the "thickly braided" ancient

---

[158]Certainly this was an issue for the Stoics, and perhaps the Valentinians felt similarly. As mentioned above, the Stoic emperor Marcus Aurelius remarks in *Meditations* 11.3, "What a soul that is which is ready, if at any moment it must be separated from the body, and ready either to be extinguished or dispersed or continue to exist; but so that this readiness comes from a man's own judgment, not from mere obstinacy, as with the Christians, but considerately and with dignity and in a way to persuade another, without tragic show." See Marcus Aurelius, *Meditations of Marcus Aurelius*, 285.

[159]Dunderberg, *Beyond Gnosticism*, 8–10.

discourse regarding martyrdom. It serves only as a reification of polemics disparaging Gnostics and their writings.[160]

In conclusion, one has to ask why the disagreements are so fierce. Ultimately, all the groups involved in the debates believe in Jesus—he is represented as *alive*—and none of the texts discussed here portray him as merely a good man who was put to death and remained in his grave. They all depict him as their leader, model, redeemer, or revealer of the divine. However, not all of those identifying themselves with Christ buy into the discourse of the glorification of martyrdom and suffering that was often linked to the idea that Christ was transformed in the flesh. Pheme Perkins comments insightfully that both the Gnostics and the orthodox saw Jesus as sinless. However, the former associated sin with entrapment in a body filled with passions. Thus, they (or, I would qualify, at least some of those labeled as Gnostics) minimalized the idea of the necessity of the Savior fully assuming a body. Some even said he never took on a body at all—that he used a psychic one (cf. *Haer* I 6.1). Perkins notes that

> Though people today are uncomfortable with the picture of an impassible savior that resulted from this division, it corresponds to a widespread ascetic ideal in Gnostic, Christian, and philosophical circles. The perfected soul represents the *apatheia* of God.[161]

Perkins's insight regarding "the perfected soul" as representing "the *apatheia* of God" is most illuminating. This passage is also helpful in seeing the difficulty of escaping interpretation of gnostic texts through presuppositions such as their inherent Docetism even by scholars as astute as Perkins, whose work has been foundational in paving the way for appreciation of these works. Whether Gnostics were actually Docetists or whether they ascribed to a two-natures Christology has been discussed above. They may have been minimalizing the need for a body no more or less than proto-orthodox figures who held the latter position.

In a classic article about differing views of Christ's passion among various early Christ movements, Elaine Pagels poignantly asks why some interpretations were so vigorously denounced and then says:

---

[160]Moss, *Ancient Christian Martyrdom*, 157–158.
[161]Perkins, *Gnostic Dialogue*, 185–186.

I am convinced that we cannot find the answer to this question as long as we consider controversies between orthodoxy and heresy, as scholars tradition- ally have, exclusively in terms of the history of dogma. When we investigate the writings of the "fathers of the church" and of their gnostic contempo- raries to see how Christology actually functions in each type of literature, we may see that it involves specific practical issues—often social and political ones—as well. Specifically, controversy over the interpretation of Christ's passion and death involves, for Christians of the first and second centuries, an urgent practical question: how are believers to respond to persecution, which raises the imminent possibility of their [?] *own* suffering and death?[162]

Irenaeus's defense of martyrdom is precisely the context of his attack on gnostic views of Christ's passion (*Haer.* 3.16.1–3.18.5). Thus, such a comment brings us full circle to the thesis of Chap. 2: that in focusing on practices regarding the care of the self rather than the history of doctrine, many useful insights can be gleaned regarding the competing visions of these groups and the falsely simplistic opposition between Gnosticism and orthodoxy can be exposed. Debates about who Christ was and what he was like, what those who pursue his way can expect, and how to be loyal in identifying with him would continue in the centuries to come. Such debates reflect not a binary opposition between heresy or Gnosticism on the one hand and orthodoxy on the other but rather a variety of thoughtful responses to that which transcends full human comprehension and thus will always remain subject to a certain degree of speculation.

References

Ancient Works

Ante-Nicene Fathers

Roberts, Alexander, and James Donaldson, eds. *The Ante-Nicene Fathers: The Writings of the Fathers down to A.D. 325*. American Reprint of the Edinburgh Edition. 10 vols. Edited by A. Cleveland Coxe. New York: Charles Scribner's Sons, 1903.

---

[162]Pagels, "Gnostic and Orthodox Views of Christ's Passion," 265.

Apocalypse of Peter

Brashler, James, trans. *Apocalypse of Peter (NHC VII, 3)*. Pages 201–47 in the *Coptic Gnostic Library: Nag Hammadi Codex VII*. Edited by Birger A. Pearson. Nag Hammadi and Manichaean Studies 30. Leiden: Brill, 1996.

Werner, Andreas. "Die Apokalypse des Petrus: Die dritte Schrift aus Nag Hammadi-Codex VII eingeleitet und übersetzt vom Berliner Arbeitskreis für koptisch-gnostische Schriften." *Theologische Literaturzeitung* 99 (1974): 575–84.

Clement of Alexandria

John Ferguson, trans. *Stromateis: Books One to Three*. Vol. 85 of *The Fathers of the Church: A New Translation*. 2d ed. Washington, D.C.: Catholic University of America Press, 1991.

Gnostic Texts

Foerster, Werner. *Gnosis: A Selection of Gnostic Texts*. Vol. 1. Patristic Evidence. Edited and translated by R. McL. Wilson; London: Oxford at the Clarendon Press, 1972.

Layton, Bentley. *Gnostic Scriptures: Ancient Wisdom for the New Age*. New York: Doubleday, 1987.

Gospel of Judas

Jenott, Lance. *The "Gospel of Judas": Coptic Text, Translation and Historical Interpretation of the "Betrayer's Gospel."* Edited by Christoph Markschies et al. Studien und Texte zu Antike und Christentum 64. Tübingen: Mohr Siebeck, 2011.

Kasser, Rodolphe, Gregor Wurst, Marvin Meyer, and François Gaudard. *The Gospel of Judas Together with the Letter of Peter to Philip, James, and a Book of Allogenes from Codex Tchacos: Critical Edition*. Washington, D.C.: National Geographic, 2007.

Gnostic Texts

Layton, Bentley. *Gnostic Scriptures: Ancient Wisdom for the New Age*. New York: Doubleday, 1987.

Marcus Aurelius

Eliot, Charles W., ed. *Meditations of Marcus Aurelius*. Translated by George Lang. New York: P. F. Collier and Son, 1937.

New Testament Apocrypha

Schneemelcher, Wilhelm, ed. *New Testament Apocrypha*. English translation edited by Robert McLachlan Wilson. 2 vols. Cambridge: James Clarke; Louisville: Westminster/John Knox, 1991–92.

Origen

O'Meara, John J. *Prayer: Exhortation to Martyrdom*. Westminster, Maryland: Newman, 1954.

Testimony of Truth

Birger A. Pearson, trans. *Testimony of Truth* Pages 617–628 in *The Nag Hammadi Scriptures: The International Edition*. Edited by Marvin Meyer. New York: HarperOne, 2007.

Birger A. Pearson, ed., *Testimony of Truth (NHC IX, 3)*. Pages 122–203 in the *Coptic Gnostic Library: Nag Hammadi Codices IX and X*. Translated by Birger A. Pearson and Søren Giversen. Nag Hammadi Studies 25. Leiden: Brill, 1981.

Valentinus

Markschies, Christoph. *Valentinus Gnosticus? Untersuchungen zur valentinianischen Gnosis mit einem Kommentar zu den Fragmenten Valentins*. Tübingen: J. C. B. Mohr (Paul Siebeck), 1992.

Modern Works

Aulén, Gustaf. *Christus Victor: An Historical Study of the Three Main Types of the Idea of Atonement*. New York: Macmillan, 1966.

Bauer, Walter. *Orthodoxy and Heresy in Earliest Christianity*. Philadelphia: Fortress, 1971.

Borg, Marcus. *Speaking Christian: Why Christian Words Have Lost Their Meaning and Power—and How They Can Be Restored*. New York: Harper One, 2011.

Boyarin, Daniel. *Dying for God: Martyrdom and the Making of Christianity and Judaism*. Figurae. Stanford: Stanford University Press, 1999.

Brankaer, Johanna. "Whose Savior? Salvation, Damnation, and the Race of Adam in the *Gospel of Judas*." Pages 387–412 in *The Codex Judas Papers: Proceedings of the International Congress on the Tchacos Codex held at Rice University, Houston, Texas, March 13–16, 2008*. Edited by April D. De Conick. Nag Hammadi Manichaean Studies 71. Edited by Johannes van Oort and Einar Thomassen. Leiden: Brill, 2009.

Brock, Rita Nakashima, and Rebecca A. Parker. *Saving Paradise: How Christianity Traded Love of this World for Crucifixion and Empire*. Boston: Beacon, 2008.

Burns, Dylan M. "Sethian Crowns, Sethian Martyrs? Jewish Apocalyptic and Christian Martyrology in a Gnostic Literary Tradition." Paper presented at the annual meeting of the SBL, Chicago, 17 November 2012.

Bynum, Caroline Walker. *The Resurrection of the Body in Western Christianity, 200–1336*. New York: Columbia University Press, 1995.

Church, F. Forrester. "Sex and Salvation in Tertullian." *Harvard Theological Review* 68 (1975): 83–101. Repr. pages 199–217 in *Women in Early Christianity*. Edited by David M. Scholer. Vol. 14 of *Studies in Early Christianity: A Collection of Scholarly Essays*. Edited by Everett Ferguson, David M. Scholer, and Paul C. Finney. New York: Garland, 1993.

De Conick, April. "Apostles as Archons: The Fight for Authority and the Emergence of Gnosticism in the Codex Tchacos and Other Early Christian Literature." Pages 243–88 in *The Codex Judas Papers: Proceedings of the International Congress on the Tchacos Codex held at Rice University, Houston, Texas, March 13–16, 2008.* Edited by April D. De Conick. Nag Hammadi Manichaean Studies 71. Edited by Johannes van Oort and Einar Thomassen. Leiden: Brill, 2009.

De Conick, April. "The Mystery of Betrayal. What does the *Gospel of Judas* Really Say?" Pages 239–64 in *The Gospel of Judas in Context: Proceedings of the First International Conference on the Gospel of Judas, Paris, Sorbonne, October 27th–28th, 2006.* Edited by Madeleine Scopello. Nag Hammadi Manichaean Studies 26. Edited by Stephen Emmel and Johannes van Oort. Leiden: Brill, 2008.

De Conick, April. *The Thirteenth Apostle: What the Gospel of Judas Really Says.* New York: Continuum, 2007.

Desjardins, Michael. "Introduction to *Apocalypse of Peter (NHC VII, 3)*." Pages 201–16 in *Nag Hammadi Codex VII.* Edited by Birger A. Pearson. Translated by James Brasher. Nag Hammadi and Manichaean Studies 30. Leiden: Brill, 1996.

Dubois, Jean-Daniel. "L'Évangile de Judas et la Tradition Basilidienne." Pages 145–54 in *The Gospel of Judas in Context: Proceedings of the First International Conference on the Gospel of Judas, Paris, Sorbonne, October 27th–28th, 2006.* Edited by Madeleine Scopello. Nag Hammadi Manichaean Studies 26. Edited by Stephen Emmel and Johannes van Oort. Leiden: Brill, 2008.

Dunderberg, Ismo. *Beyond Gnosticism: Myth, Lifestyle, and Society in the School of Valentinus.* New York: Columbia University Press, 2008.

Dunderberg, Ismo. "Judas' Anger and the Perfect Human." Pages 201–221 in *The Codex Judas Papers: Proceedings of the International Congress on the Tchacos Codex held at Rice University, Houston, Texas, March 13–16, 2008.* Edited by April D. De Conick. Nag Hammadi Manichaean Studies 71. Edited by Johannes van Oort and Einar Thomassen. Leiden: Brill, 2009.

Ehrman, Bart D. *The Lost Gospel of Judas Iscariot: A New Look at Betrayer and Betrayed.* New York: Oxford University Press, 2006.

Emmel, Stephen. "The Presuppositions and the Purpose of the *Gospel of Judas*." Pages 33–39 in *The Gospel of Judas in Context: Proceedings of the First International Conference on the Gospel of Judas, Paris, Sorbonne, October 27th–28th, 2006.* Edited by Madeleine Scopello. Nag Hammadi Manichaean Studies 26. Edited by Stephen Emmel and Johannes van Oort. Leiden: Brill, 2008.

Engberg-Pedersen, Troels. *Cosmology and Self in the Apostle Paul: The Material Spirit.* Oxford: Oxford University Press, 2010.

Hadot, Pierre. *Philosophy as a Way of Life: Spiritual Exercises from Socrates to Foucault.* Edited by Arnold I. Davidson. Translated by Michael Chase. Oxford: Blackwell, 1995.

Holzhausen, Jens. "Gnosis und Martyrium: Zu Valentins viertem Fragment." *Zeitschrift für die neutestamentliche Wissenschaft und die Kunde der älteren Kirche* 85 (1994): 116–131.

Holzhausen, Jens. "Valentinus and Valentinians." Pages 1144–57 in *Dictionary of Gnosis and Western Esotericism*. Vol. 2. Edited by. J. Hanegraaff et al. Leiden: Brill, 2005.

Iricinschi, Eduard, Lance Jenott, and Philippa Townsend. "The Betrayer's Gospel" (review of Rodolphe Kasser and Gregor Wurst, eds., *The Gospel of Judas Together with the Letter of Peter to Philip, James, and a Book of Allogenes from Codex Tchacos: Critical Edition*), *New York Review of Books*, June 8, 2006.

Jeanes, Gordon. "Baptism Portrayed as Martyrdom in the Early Church." *SL* 23 (1993): 158–76. Repr. pages 62–80 in *Forms of Devotion: Conversion, Worship, Spirituality, Asceticism*. Edited by Everett Ferguson. Vol. 5 of *Recent Studies in Early Christianity: A Collection of Scholarly Essays*. Edited by Everett Ferguson. New York: Garland, 1999.

Jenott, Lance. "The *Gospel of Judas* 45, 6–7 and Enoch's Heavenly Temple." Pages 471–77 in *The Codex Judas Papers: Proceedings of the International Congress on the Tchacos Codex held at Rice University, Houston, Texas, March 13–16, 2008*. Edited by April D. De Conick. Nag Hammadi Manichaean Studies 71. Edited by Johannes van Oort and Einar Thomassen. Leiden: Brill, 2009.

Kelly, J. N. D. *Early Christian Doctrines*. Rev. ed. San Francisco: Harper, 1978.

King, Karen L. "Martyrdom and Its Discontents in the Tchacos Codex." Pages 23–42 in *The Codex Judas Papers: Proceedings of the International Congress on the Tchacos Codex held at Rice University, Houston, Texas, March 13–16, 2008*. Edited by April D. De Conick. Nag Hammadi Manichaean Studies 71. Edited by Johannes van Oort and Einar Thomassen. Leiden: Brill, 2009.

King, Karen L. and Elaine H. Pagels. *Reading Judas: The Gospel of Judas and the Shaping of Christianity*. New York: Viking Penguin, 2007.

Koschorke, Klaus. "Die Polemik der Petrusapokalypse (*NHC VII, 3*) gegen das Kirchliche Christentum." Pages 11–90 in *Die Polemik der Gnostiker gegen das Kirchliche Christentum*. Leiden: Brill, 1978.

Koschorke, Klaus. "Die Polemik von Testimonium Veritatis (*NHC IX, 3*) gegen die 'Häresien' der Katholiken und Gnostiker." Pages 91–174 in *Die Polemik der Gnostiker gegen das Kirchliche Christentum*. Leiden: Brill, 1978.

Kasser, Rodolphe. "Introduction: Lost and Found: The History of Codex Tchacos." Pages 1–25 in *The Gospel of Judas Together with the Letter of Peter to Philip, James, and a Book of Allogenes from Codex Tchacos: Critical Edition*. Edited by Rodolphe Kasser et al. Washington, D.C.: National Geographic, 2007.

Le Boulluec, Alain. *La notion d'hérésie dans la littérature grecque*. 2 tomes. Paris: Etudes Augustiniennes, 1985.

Lewis, Nicola Denzey. "Fate and the Wandering Stars: The Jewish Apocalyptic Roots of the *Gospel of Judas*." Pages 289–304 in *The Codex Judas Papers:*

Proceedings of the International Congress on the Tchacos Codex held at Rice University, Houston, Texas, March 13–16, 2008. Edited by April D. De Conick. Nag Hammadi Manichaean Studies 71. Edited by Johannes van Oort and Einar Thomassen. Leiden: Brill, 2009.

Logan, Alastair. "The Tchacos Codex: Another Document of the Gnostics?" Pages 3–21 in *The Codex Judas Papers: Proceedings of the International Congress on the Tchacos Codex held at Rice University, Houston, Texas, March 13–16, 2008.* Edited by April D. De Conick. Nag Hammadi Manichaean Studies 71. Edited by Johannes van Oort and Einar Thomassen. Leiden: Brill, 2009.

Löhr, Winrich A. *Basilides und seine Schule: Eine Studie zur Theologie-und Kirchengeschichte des zweiten Jahrhunderts.* Wissenschaftliche Untersuchungen zum Neuen Testament 83. Edited by Martin Hengel und Otfried Hofius. Tübingen: J. C. B. Mohr (Paul Siebeck), 1996.

Markschies, Christoph. *Gnosis: An Introduction.* Translated by John Bowden. London: T&T Clark, 2003.

Martin, Dale B. "Epistemologies of the Body in the New Testament." Lecture presented at the Rocky Mountains Great Plains SBL/AAR/ASOR luncheon at the Iliff School of Theology, March 19, 2011.

Matthews, Shelly. *Perfect Martyr: The Stoning of Stephen and the Construction of Christian Identity.* Oxford: Oxford University Press, 2010.

Meyer, Marvin. "Interpreting Judas: Ten Passages in the *Gospel of Judas.*" Pages 41–55 in *The Gospel of Judas in Context: Proceedings of the First International Conference on the Gospel of Judas, Paris, Sorbonne, October 27th–28th, 2006.* Edited by Madeleine Scopello. Nag Hammadi Manichaean Studies 26. Edited by Stephen Emmel and Johannes van Oort. Leiden: Brill, 2008.

Meyer, Marvin. "When the Sethians were Young: The *Gospel of Judas* in the Second Century." Pages 57–73 in *The Codex Judas Papers: Proceedings of the International Congress on the Tchacos Codex held at Rice University, Houston, Texas, March 13–16, 2008.* Edited by April D. De Conick. Nag Hammadi Manichaean Studies 71. Edited by Johannes van Oort and Einar Thomassen. Leiden: Brill, 2009.

Moss, Candida R. *Ancient Christian Martyrdom: Diverse Practices, Theologies, and Traditions.* New Haven, Conn.: Yale University Press, 2012.

Moss, Candida R. *The Other Christs: Imitating Jesus in Ancient Christian Ideologies of Martyrdom.* New York: Oxford University Press, 2010.

Nussbaum, Martha. *The Therapy of Desire: Theory and Practice in Hellenistic Ethics.* Princeton: Princeton University Press, 1994.

Pagels, Elaine H. "Baptism in the *Gospel of Judas:* A Preliminary Inquiry." Pages 353–66 in *The Codex Judas Papers: Proceedings of the International Congress on the Tchacos Codex held at Rice University, Houston, Texas, March 13–16, 2008.* Edited by April D. De Conick. Nag Hammadi Manichaean Studies 71. Edited by Johannes van Oort and Einar Thomassen. Leiden: Brill, 2009.

Pagels, Elaine H. "Gnostic and Orthodox Views of Christ's Passion: Paradigms for the Christian's Response to Persecution?" Pages 262–88 in *The Rediscovery of Gnosticism: Proceedings of the International Conference on Gnosticism at Yale, New Haven, Connecticut, March 28–31, 1978.* Vol 1. Edited by Bentley Layton. Studies in the History of Religions. Supplements to Numen 41. Leiden: Brill, 1980–1981.

Painchaud, Louis. "Polemical Aspects of the *Gospel of Judas.*" Pages 171–86 in *The Gospel of Judas in Context: Proceedings of the First International Conference on the Gospel of Judas, Paris, Sorbonne, October 27th–28th, 2006.* Edited by Madeleine Scopello. Nag Hammadi Manichaean Studies 26. Edited by Stephen Emmel and Johannes van Oort. Leiden: Brill, 2008.

Painchaud, Louis. 'You will sacrifice the man who bears me.' (*Gos. Jud.* 56.19–20). Paper presented at the annual meeting of the SBL, Chicago, 17 November 2012.

Pearson, Birger A. "Anti-Heretical Warnings in Codex IX from Nag Hammadi." Pages 183–93 in *Gnosticism, Judaism, and Egyptian Christianity.* Studies in Antiquity and Christianity. New York: Clark International, 2004.

Pearson, Birger A. "Gnostic Interpretation of the Old Testament in the *Testimony of Truth* from Nag Hammadi (CG IX, 3)." *Harvard Theological Review* 71 (1980): 311–19.

Pearson, Birger A. "Introduction to IX:3: The *Testimony of Truth.*" Pages 101–20 in *Testimony of Truth (NHC IX, 3).* Edited by Birger A. Pearson. Pages 122–203 in the *Coptic Gnostic Library: Nag Hammadi Codices IX and X.* Translated by Birger A. Pearson and Søren Giversen. Nag Hammadi Studies 25. Leiden: Brill, 1981.

Pearson, Birger A. "Jewish Haggadic Traditions in *The Testimony of Truth* from Nag Hammadi." Pages 39–51 in *Gnosticism, Judaism, and Egyptian Christianity.* Studies in Antiquity and Christianity. New York: Clark International, 2004.

Perkins, Pheme. *The Gnostic Dialogue: The Early Church and the Crisis of Gnosticism.* New York: Paulist Press, 1980.

Piovanelli, Pierluigi. "Rabbi Yehuda versus Judas Iscariot: The *Gospel of Judas* and Apocryphal Passion Stories." Pages 223–39 in *The Codex Judas Papers: Proceedings of the International Congress on the Tchacos Codex held at Rice University, Houston, Texas, March 13–16, 2008.* Edited by April D. De Conick. Nag Hammadi Manichaean Studies 71. Edited by Johannes van Oort and Einar Thomassen. Leiden: Brill, 2009.

Riley, Gregory J. *Resurrection Considered: Thomas and John in Controversy.* Minneapolis: Fortress Press, 1995.

Rives, J. "Human Sacrifices Among Pagans and Christians." *Journal of Religious Studies* 85 (1995): 65–85.

Robinson, Gesine Schenke. "The *Gospel of Judas*: Its Protagonist, Its Composition, and Its Community." Pages 75–94 in *The Codex Judas Papers: Proceedings of the International Congress on the Tchacos Codex held at Rice University, Houston, Texas, March 13–16, 2008*. Edited by April D. De Conick. Nag Hammadi Manichaean Studies 71. Edited by Johannes van Oort and Einar Thomassen. Leiden: Brill, 2009.

Salisbury, Joyce E. *The Blood of Martyrs: Unintended Consequences of Ancient Violence*. New York: Routledge, 2004.

Thomassen, Einar. "Is Judas Really the Hero of the *Gospel of Judas*?" Pages 157–70 in *The Gospel of Judas in Context: Proceedings of the First International Conference on the Gospel of Judas, Paris, Sorbonne, October 27th–28th, 2006*. Edited by Madeleine Scopello. Nag Hammadi Manichaean Studies 26. Edited by Stephen Emmel and Johannes van Oort. Leiden: Brill, 2008.

Tite, Philip L. "*Valentinian Ethics and Paraenetic Discourse: Determining the Social Function of Moral Exhortation in Valentinian Christianity*." Ph.D. diss., McGill University, 2005.

Turner, John D. "The Place of the *Gospel of Judas* in Sethian Tradition." Pages 187–237 in *The Gospel of Judas in Context: Proceedings of the First International Conference on the Gospel of Judas, Paris, Sorbonne, October 27th–28th, 2006*. Edited by Madeleine Scopello. Nag Hammadi Manichaean Studies 26. Edited by Stephen Emmel and Johannes van Oort. Leiden: Brill, 2008.

Turner, John D. "The Sethian Myth in the *Gospel of Judas*: Soteriology or Demonology?" Pages 95–133 in *The Codex Judas Papers: Proceedings of the International Congress on the Tchacos Codex held at Rice University, Houston, Texas, March 13–16, 2008*. Edited by April D. De Conick. Nag Hammadi Manichaean Studies 71. Edited by Johannes van Oort and Einar Thomassen. Leiden: Brill, 2009.

Van den Kerchove, Anna. "La Maison, l'Autel et les Sacrifices: Quelque Remarques sur la Polémique dans *l'Évangile des Judas*." Pages 311–29 in *The Gospel of Judas in Context: Proceedings of the First International Conference on the Gospel of Judas, Paris, Sorbonne, October 27th–28th, 2006*. Edited by Madeleine Scopello. Nag Hammadi Manichaean Studies 26. Edited by Stephen Emmel and Johannes van Oort. Leiden: Brill, 2008.

Van Oort, Johannes. "Irenaeus on the *Gospel of Judas*: An Analysis of the Evidence in Context." Pages 43–56 in *The Codex Judas Papers: Proceedings of the International Congress on the Tchacos Codex held at Rice University, Houston, Texas, March 13–16, 2008*. Edited by April D. De Conick. Nag Hammadi Manichaean Studies 71. Edited by Johannes van Oort and Einar Thomassen. Leiden: Brill, 2009.

Van Os, Bas. "The *Testimony of Truth* Reconsidered." Paper presented at the annual meeting of the SBL, Chicago, November 17, 2012.

Williams, Michael A. *The Immovable Race: A Gnostic Designation and the Theme of Stability in Late Antiquity.* Nag Hammadi Studies 29. Leiden: Brill, 1985.

Williams, Michael A. "Stability as a Soteriological Theme in Gnosticism." Pages 819–29 in *The Rediscovery of Gnosticism. Vol 2: Sethian Gnosticism.* Edited by Bentley Layton. Studies in the History of Religions (supplement to *Numen*) 41. Leiden: Brill, 1981.

Young, Robin Darling. *In Procession Before the World: Martyrdom as Public Liturgy in Early Christianity.* Milwaukee: Marquette University Press, 2001.

CHAPTER 5

Complementary Representations of the Care of the Self in the *Gospel of Mary* and the *Martyrdom of Perpetua and Felicity*

Thus far, we have explored the significance of the care of the self in Greco-Roman antiquity. Michel Foucault has articulated the way in which this practice is the focal point around which ancient Greco-Roman philosophical thought circulates. In particular, as scholars continue to analyze its influence on the early Christ movements, its pervasiveness becomes clearer. In the Greco-Roman world and especially in the Stoic perspectives that influenced the writers of the New Testament and newly discovered Christian texts of the first three centuries C.E. to at least some degree, the care of the self entailed engaging in "technologies of the self" that included the therapy of emotions.[1] In this social milieu, the discourse of the suffering self and a discourse of martyrdom emerged and proved crucial in the formation of "proto-orthodox Christian identity," as Judith Perkins and Daniel Boyarin have persuasively argued in work now foundational to the study of the early Christ movements (as discussed in Chap. 2). Elizabeth Castelli has highlighted the way in which the letters of those facing martyrdom or the accounts of martyrdoms functioned as what Foucault would call technologies of self-writing. Eventually, many scholars argue that martyrdom was glorified to such a degree that some even desired it (as discussed in Chap. 3). In addition, we have seen how such glorification was disrupted by writings of those in some early Christ movements who argued that such exaltation was

---

[1] An excellent reference for exploring Stoic influence on early Christian texts is Rasimus, Engberg-Pedersen, and Dunderberg, ed., *Stoicism in Early Christianity*.

© The Author(s) 2017
D. Niederer Saxon, *The Care of the Self in Early Christian Texts*,
The Bible and Cultural Studies, DOI 10.1007/978-3-319-64750-0_5

misleading. They, too, focused on the care of the self, seeing the Christ as the master teacher who explained and modeled how to go about self-care, including the extirpation of passions, such as fear and anger, and effected it in their own lives (as discussed in Chap. 4). Moreover, with Caroline Walker Bynum, we have also briefly explored the way in which care of the self morphed into the care of the body and became associated with an emphasis on a fleshly resurrection in the context of persecution and martyrdom.

Once we understand and acknowledge the significant role that the care of the self played during this era, we are able to recognize these themes in many works written by and for followers of Christ. In this chapter, we explore the representation of women in terms of the care of the self and the implications of the varying attitudes toward this set of practices for women. We do this with two texts probably written within roughly a century of each other.[2] The first is the *Gospel of Mary*.[3] One or more women named Mary are is

---

[2] The dating is not possible to determine conclusively. Perpetua's martyrdom is usually dated to 203 C.E., and the text recounting it traditionally has been thought to date to about this time; see Musurillo, *Acts of the Christian Martyrs*, xxvi–xxvii; Barnes, "Pre-Decian *Acta Martyrum*," 521–525; and Moss, *Ancient Christian Martyrdom*, 130–132. Dating the *Gospel of Mary* is also difficult. Most scholars date it to the second century C.E. Karen King dates it to the first half of the second century because debates about women's authority in the early Christ movements were particularly heated then; King, *Gospel of Mary of Magdala*, 184; King, "Gospel of Mary Magdalene," 628. Anne Pasquier dates it to the second half of the second century, which would place its composition closer to that of the *Martyrdom of Perpetua and Felicity*, Pasquier, *Évangile selon Marie*, 3–4.

[3] Carl Reinhardt bought the Coptic manuscript that contains the most complete version of the text, Papyrus Berolinensis, from a Cairo antiquities dealer in 1896, but it was not published until 1955, when the Coptic appeared alongside a German translation in Till, *Gnostischen Schriften des koptischen Papyrus Berolinensis 8502*. It was published in English with the Nag Hammadi Library, even though it was not found at Nag Hammadi, in Wilson and MacRae, "Gospel according to Mary." There are two other short fragments of the text, Oxyrhynchus Papyrus (POxy) 3525 and the Rylands Papyrus (PRyl) 463. The first of these two was published in Parsons, "3525: *Gospel of Mary*," and the latter is in "463: The *Gospel of Mary*" in the *Catalogue of the Greek Papyri in the John Rylands Library*, 3:18–23. The most recent critical edition of the text is Tuckett, *Gospel of Mary*, 86–118. Karen King provides a careful and inclusive English translation in King, *Gospel of Mary of Magdala*, 13–18. Esther A. de Boer's English translation is also very helpful, in de Boer, *Gospel of Mary*, 8–21.

mentioned in many early Christian writings.[4] The *Gospel of Mary*, however, is the only surviving gospel whose main message is attributed to a woman. The colophon at the end clearly reads, "The gospel according to Mary."[5] The second work is the *Martyrdom of Perpetua and Felicity*.[6] It is an early example of a first-person account that was both widely used by early Christ groups and represents itself as written, or narrated, at least in part by a woman.[7]

In the New Testament, Mary Magdalene is the first witness to the resurrection, a woman who functions as the apostle to the apostles by being the one whom Jesus commissions to share the good news.[8] However, later

---

[4]In addition to the *Gospel of Mary*, texts with a Mary include the Gospel of Mark, the Gospel of Matthew, the Gospel of Luke, the Gospel of John, the Acts of the Apostles, the *Epistula Apostolorum*, the *Gospel of Peter*, the *Secret Gospel of Mark*, the *Gospel of Thomas*, the *Sophia of Jesus Christ*, *Eugnostos the Blessed*, the last part of the *Codex Askewianus*, the *Pistis Sophia*, the *Dialogue of the Savior*, the *Gospel of Philip*, the *Manichaean Psalms*, the *Acts of Philip*, the *Statutes of the Apostles*, the *Protevangelium*, the Dormition narratives, and the *Gospel (Questions) of Bartholomew*. For a brief summary of issues around this name, see Bovon, "Privilège pascal de Marie-Madeleine," 147–57, 228–35.

[5]For a discussion of what the term *gospel* actually means, see Koester, *Ancient Christian Gospels*, 1–48.

[6]This *passio*, or martyrdom account, was most likely composed in Latin, but survives in both Latin and Greek. Lucas Holstenius discovered the most complete Latin version in 1661 at the Benedictine Monastery at Monte Cassino; see discussion in Jacqueline Amat's critical edition, the most recent; Amat, *Passion de Perpétue et de Félicité suivi de Actes*, 84–88. Two shorter versions of the text are included in Amat's critical edition, and contain some textual variants, such as Perpetua depicted as less sympathetic to her father's pleas and more willing to reject her son; these may reflect a later attempt to make her transgression of existing gender norms less palatable to readers in a post-Constantinian world, where Roman social norms regarding the family were still firmly ensconced. The standard English translation is in Musurillo, *Acts of the Christian Martyrs*, 106–31.

[7]Most likely women in various Christ movements were writing long before 200 c. e., but many early texts have been lost or suppressed. Christoph Markschies notes that Theodor Mommsen, the renowned nineteenth-century classicist, once estimated that 85% of second-century texts *that were known* had not survived; Markschies, "Lehrer, Schüler, Schule," 98.

[8]John 20:17–18. The *Gospel of Mary* does not actually use the term "Magdalene" or "Magdala" to identify this Mary, and there has been vigorous debate regarding which Mary this gospel is actually representing. To think that it is Mary Magdalene is a very

theologians with a patriarchal bias distorted her role in the New Testament gospels and other texts.[9] Over the centuries, her character has been both extolled and maligned.[10] Over the past three decades, however, contemporary scholars have rediscovered and reexamined works that represent her as a strong leader, bringing her role as the apostle to the apostles into sharper focus.[11] Likewise, Perpetua's story of courageous resistance and bravery in facing martyrdom has been a source of inspiration through the centuries.[12] Her portrayal also, however, contains certain troubling ambiguities discussed below.

---

reasonable conclusion given the fact that Mary Magdalene is either the first or one of the first resurrection witnesses in the New Testament gospels. Moreover, in John 20, Jesus speaks to Mary and commissions her to tell the other disciples that he is alive. For a compelling argument regarding Mary's apostleship that underscores her essential role as a witness, see Ann Graham Brock, *Mary Magdalene*. Brock also argues that the presence of conflict between Peter and Mary indicates that Mary Magdalene is the one being depicted in the *Gospel of Mary* because friction between these two is depicted in other texts as well. For an extended discussion, see Brock, *Mary Magdalene*, 73–104. Stephen J. Shoemaker, however, argues that ancient readers could just as easily have understood the Mary in the *Gospel of Mary* as Mary of Nazareth; see Shoemaker, *Mary in Early Christian Faith*, 72–87. Mary Ann Beavis argues that consideration should also be given to Mary of Bethany as a "significant component" in this text and others. See Beavis, "Reconsidering Mary of Bethany," 297.

[9]The foundational work that provides an overview of patriarchal bias is Elisabeth Schüssler Fiorenza, *In Memory of Her*.

[10]Susan Haskins details the varying representations of Mary Magdalene through the centuries in Haskins, *Mary Magdalene*. See also Jane Schaberg's analyses in Schaberg, "How Mary Magdalene Became a Whore," 30–37, 51–52, and Schaberg, *The Resurrection of Mary Magdalene*, 65–120. It is important to note that she is never depicted as a prostitute anywhere in the New Testament.

[11]While it is hard to date the resurgence of her apostolic role precisely, François Bovon's article listing the texts in which she is mentioned seems to have been extremely important in this regard. Certainly, questioning the legitimacy of conflating her with the woman in Luke 7:37–50 begins much earlier, notably in the Reformation with John Calvin as well as in the Counter Reformation with a French priest, Jacques Lefèvre d'Etaples; see Haskins, *Mary Magdalen: Myth and Metaphor*, 26, 248–51.

[12]Theologians in the early church including Tertullian, Augustine, and Quodvulteus remark favorably on Perpetua's courage, although, at the same time, they carefully qualify her leadership role. For the reception history of Perpetua, see Joyce Salisbury, *Perpetua's Passion*, 149–79, 204–08; and Streete, *Redeemed Bodies*, 49–72, 132–36.

These texts remarkably represent women as examples par excellence of such a cure and the spiritual maturity it connotes.[13] There was, of course, a cultural predisposition to depict women as weaker than men in the ancient Greco-Roman culture. An early Christian writer, Clement of Alexandria (ca. 150–ca. 215) firmly expresses the belief that men are more active and superior to women (*Paed.* 3.3.19,1); in particular, he comments that a man full of vice is still superior to even a virtuous woman (*Strom.* 4.8).[14]

However, the *Gospel of Mary* and the *Martyrdom of Perpetua and Felicity* represent their main figures as those who have successfully engaged in the care of the self (the therapy of emotions) and have been "healed," or "cured," of their passions, particularly, the emotions of fear and anger. Both of them also engage in a specific practice of the care of the self, *parrhēsia*, or bold speech. Foucault focuses almost exclusively on this concept in the last two years of his lectures. I would argue that it is both a practice of the care of the self and a result of it.[15] The bold proclamations of Mary and Perpetua are also is related to the contemplation of death, another practice of the care of the self that is described at length by Foucault and Hadot.[16]

In addition, both works have a vision of ascent. Mary describes what may well be a practice of the care of the self involving an ascent of the soul, an exercise in mental concentration related to developing a bird's eye perspective or the view from above—a view that strengthens one's ability to put things into their proper perspective regardless of how difficult one's

---

[13]Of course, one can never make sweeping, general statements regarding the status of women but must carefully nuance such discussions. Erika Mohri makes this case well with regard to Mary Magdalene in *Maria Magdalena*, 11. Assessing the roles of women in early texts often categorized as gnostic has been the subject of considerable discussion; see Goehring, "Libertine or Liberated," 183–98; Boughton, "From Pious Legend to Feminist Fantasy," 362–83; McNamara, "Sexual Equality and the Cult of Virginity," 219–32; Clark, Elizabeth, A., "Holy Women, Holy Words," 413–30.

[14]All citations of Clement of Alexandria are from Roberts, *Ante-Nicene Fathers*.

[15]For extended discussion, see Foucault, *Government of Self and Others* and Foucault, *Courage of Truth*.

[16]Foucault discusses this succinctly at the end of the *Hermeneutics of the Self*. See Foucault, *Hermeneutics of the Self*, 477–80. Also see Hadot, *Philosophy as a Way of Life*, 68–69.

current circumstances may seem (*GMary* 9.1–29).[17] Likewise, Perpetua has a vision in which she ascends to heaven on a ladder and awakes strengthened in her resolve to act courageously (*Mart. Perpet.* 8.4).[18]

In fact, Perpetua has several dream-like experiences that she discusses and reflects on in a diary as she grapples with the meaning and purpose of her impending earthly demise. This writing down and thinking about the meaning of dreams or visions as well as meditation on death are both practices associated with the care of the self. Mary engages in thinking about the possibility of persecution and death when she boldly exhorts the disciples at the beginning of her gospel. Her speech is short, but it reflects the attitude of someone who has thought through how life is to be lived and what attitude toward suffering is appropriate for those who have been engaged in a relationship with a master teacher, the one they call "the Savior" (*GMary* 5.4–8).

As we use feminist theology, postmodern critical theory, and historiography to pay attention to the discursive strategies used to represent Mary and Perpetua, we see that the depictions in both texts provide rich, complex opportunities for reflecting on the ways in which they function as models of those who have achieved a goal much admired in their Greco-Roman cultural context—a "cure" from their enslavement to passions such as anger and fear. Of course, postmodern historiography helps us to understand the difficulty of recovering a historical Mary or a historical Perpetua fully. We read with the understanding that these works are literarily crafted representations and that power dynamics influence these portrayals and how each generation interprets them. Reading these texts through the lens of the care of the self, however, lets powerful new understandings emerge regarding the way in which Mary and Perpetua function as model disciples: steadfast, loyal, courageous, fearless, and lacking in anger toward those who demean or persecute them.

The Representation of Mary

The foremost example of a woman who demonstrates emotional stability is Mary in the *Gospel of Mary*. Most scholars judge its genre to be a post-resurrection dialogue. Judith Hartenstein, however, has astutely

---

[17] All citations and translations for the *Gospel of Mary* come from Karen King's inclusive translation in King, *The Gospel of Mary of Magdala*.

[18] All citations and translations for the *Martyrdom of Perpetua and Felicity* come from Musurillo, *Acts of the Christian Martyrs*.

observed that the actual experience Mary is describing could have happened prior to the resurrection even if it is being described in a post-resurrection context; nothing in the material available to us at this point indicates when it actually happened.[19]

With one exception, commentators agree that the author of the *Gospel of Mary* represents Mary as steadfast, resolute, and calm.[20] This exception is Mary's weeping near the end of the text (*GMary* 10.5), which some commentators argue somewhat mitigates this contrast and her overall strength of character. Christopher Tuckett, in particular, interprets her weeping as a sign of weakness. He also notes, however, that

> the weeping could be explained psychologically . . . as a natural human reaction to an unjustified attack on her integrity and/or her status by someone she might have expected support from; or as sorrow at Peter's and Andrew's failure to understand properly.[21]

De Boer, too, points out that Mary's weeping reflects a momentary condition and does not necessarily reflect poorly on her character as a whole, noting, "Whereas the (male) disciples do not waver all the time, Mary is likewise not stable all the time."[22] No more than Jesus's weeping detracted from his strong role when he wept for Lazarus in John 11:35, Mary's weeping does not detract from the strong role she has played in comforting and exhorting the other disciples—the practice of *parrhēsia*—and in remaining unwavering and able to receive a vision.

The literary elements that are the keys to seeing that the author of the *Gospel of Mary* represents Mary as one who has successfully engaged in the therapy of emotions are noticing (a) the vocabulary the writer chooses in representing her as one who did not *waver*, (b) the parrhesiastic role the writer ascribes to her as a courageous disciple who stands, faces the male disciples, and boldly exhorts them to preach the gospel in spite of their fear

---

[19]See Hartenstein, *Zweite Lehre*, 128–30, 152–55. For the argument that Mary's experience occurs *after* the resurrection, see King, *Gospel of Mary of Magdala*, 29–34; and Tuckett, *Gospel of Mary*, 31–41.

[20]Toward the end of the account, Mary weeps (*GMary* 10.5), but this does not necessarily undermine the strength of her depiction as a whole, a point discussed at more length below.

[21]Tuckett, *Gospel of Mary*, 188–89.

[22]De Boer, *Gospel of Mary*, 77–78.

of possible persecution, (c) the fact that she is either considered worthy of receiving a vision, which is characteristic of one who is "healed" of her passions, or of participating in an ancient contemplative practice engaged in by those actively involved in the therapy of emotions and (d) the particular content of that vision—a description of the ascent of the soul that accords well with a Stoic contemplative practice sometimes described as cultivating *a bird's eye view* or *a view from above.*

THE POSITIVE CONNOTATION OF NOT WAVERING

In the text, the Savior praises Mary "for not wavering" when she saw him in a vision (*GMary* 7.3). The Coptic phrase is ATKIM and in Greek would be *asaleutos.*[23] This short phrase had significant, positive philosophical connotations. Ancient Greco-Roman writers applied the designation of being unwavering or immovable to objects, races, and as in this case, to individual persons.[24] To be unwavering had the connotation of being emotionally stable and free of the volatile, shifting sensations caused by the passions. As discussed above, the very term *passion* had strongly negative associations. As Long and Sedley explain, passion represented "the source of unhappiness, wrong-doing and the flaws of character which issue in wrong-doing." Writers of the time described fear, distress, appetite, and pleasure as the four primary ones.[25] Long and Sedley go on to explain that the passion of appetite included anger, and those of fear and distress included hesitancy and confusion as well as jealousy, grief, worry, and annoyance. A quote from Philo of Alexandria captures the negative view of passion well: "For the soul faints and

---

[23]De Boer, *Gospel of Mary*, 75–76.

[24]Michael A. Williams has traced the concept of immovability and its relationship to being free of passion extensively in Williams, *Immovable Race*, 8–9, 27–28, 55, 77, 114–15, 128, and 178–79. His main focus is the illumination of the term *immovable race* in Sethian writings, but he provides extensive support for the positive connotation that being motionless, or *asaleutos*, had in a wide variety of both Jewish and Greco-Roman philosophical contexts. For an insightful discussion of the influence of Stoicism and Stoic notions of *apatheia* on the *Gospel of Mary*, see King, *Gospel of Mary of Magdala*, 43–47. Esther de Boer discusses Stoic influences on the *Gospel of Mary* in de Boer, *Gospel of Mary*, 35–59, 71, 76–78; de Boer also discusses these issues in "A Stoic Reading of the *Gospel of Mary*," 199–219.

[25]Long and Sedley, *Hellenistic Philosophers*, 1:419. See also Nussbaum, "Stoics on the Extirpation of the Passions," 129–77.

loses all power through passion when it receives from the body the flood of tossing surge caused by the storm wind which sweeps down in its fury, driven on by unbridled appetite" (*Prelim. Studies* 60).[26] Michael Williams describes the beliefs of ancient thinkers this way:

> The instability excited by the archons and demons takes its characteristic form in the churning nausea of deep-seated passions (grief, fear, desire, anger, etc.)—as difficult to root out as ingested bacteria. These turbulent passions, aroused deep within the individual, had to be eradicated in order for one to be perfect and therefore "immovable."[27]

In fact, God himself was thought to be perfect and thus completely immovable in this sense. Philo of Alexandria says that "so vast in its excess is the *stability* of the Deity that he imparts to chosen natures a share of his steadfastness to be their richest possession" (*Dreams* 2.223).[28] Later, Clement of Alexandria discusses the pillar of fire that led the Hebrews in the wilderness (mentioned in Exodus 13:21) as a reflection of "God's *stable permanence* and his unchanging light, which no form can catch" (*Strom.* 1.163.6).[29] Thus, humans who exhibited this kind of stability were also admired greatly.

In addition, Greco-Roman works contain portrayals of various male heroes described in terms of their immovability (with physical stability symbolizing their emotional strength of character). The followers of Socrates, for example, described him as standing immovable in contemplation for 24 hours at a time. Later, Iamblichus, a third-century Syrian Neoplatonist, describes Pythagoras as making a voyage in which he remained in the same position without moving for three nights without eating or sleeping.[30]

---

[26]Citations and translations of Philo taken from Colson and Whitaker, Loeb Classical Library.

[27]Williams, *Immovable Race*, 152. Here Williams is discussing the representation of the passions in the *Apocryphon of John*, but Christopher Tuckett notes possible parallels between the *Apocryphon of John* and the *Gospel of Mary* in Tuckett, *Gospel of Mary*, 175–80.

[28]Emphasis added.

[29]All citations and translations of Clement of Alexandria in this chapter are from Ferguson, *Clement of Alexandria*. Emphasis added.

[30]*Vit. Pythag.* 16; see discussion in Williams, *Immovable Race*, 6, 28.

Jewish texts also describe heroes in this way. For example, Philo of Alexandria portrays Abraham and Moses in terms of their standing fixed and immovable before God. In Genesis 18:22 Abraham stands before the Lord while the guests he has just hosted turn toward Sodom in order to destroy it; in Deuteronomy 5:31 Moses continues to stand beside the Lord on Mount Sinai to receive the commandments.[31] Philo says of Abraham:

> For when should we expect a mind to stand and no longer sway as on the balance save when it is opposite God, seeing and being seen. For it gets its equipoise from these two sources: from seeing, because when it sees the Incomparable it does not yield to the counter pull of things like itself; from being seen, because the mind which the Ruler judges worthy to come within His sight He claims for the solely best, that is for Himself. (*Dreams* 2.226–27)

With regard to Moses, Philo says, "For that which draws near to God enters into affinity with what is, and through that immutability becomes self-standing" (*Dreams* 2.228). Williams summarizes Philo's position well:

> Persons such as Moses, wise men, filled with virtue, belong to a group whom God draws to himself and grants participation in his own stability. They belong to a group which God has firmly fixed near himself—like Moses to whom he said, "Stand here by me" (Deut. 5:31, *SAC* 8). Philo is particularly interested in the ethical dimensions of this—the instability of the fool tossed by passions vs. the immovability of virtue and the wise men who possess it. But the achievement of ethical excellence is portrayed by Philo as an *ascent* to the Olympian realm of virtue (*Post.* 31) where divine stability is to be found. Those who follow virtue are set above everything that is earthly and mortal (*Det. pot. ins.* 114). Like Moses, they "stand at rest, firm and unwaveringly, in God alone." (*Ques. Exod.* frag 11).[32]

Philo was, of course, writing in the first century of the Common Era. However, at the end of the third century, many of the apologists in various

---

[31] See also discussion in Williams, *Immovable Race*, 27; de Boer, *Gospel of Mary*, 76–77; Brown, *Body and Society*, 31–32. I find it interesting that Philo chooses Moses despite the fact that Moses was not allowed to enter the Promised Land because he struck a rock in anger and, in this sense, did not demonstrate control over passion in Numbers 20:11.

[32] Williams, *Immovable Race*, 76.

Christ-related groups continued to appropriate the thought of Philo. Clement of Alexandria, for example, makes the same point that Philo did with regard to Abraham and Moses.[33]

In some of the writings of early Christ movements, the ability to "not be moved" is an ideal as well. In Psalms 15:5, those who live righteously "shall never be moved."[34] Likewise, Psalms 21:7 says that the king who "trusts in the Lord" and experiences "the steadfast love of the Most High . . . shall not be moved." In the New Testament, too, one also finds references to immovability. Second Thessalonians 2:2 contains an exhortation "not to be quickly shaken in mind or alarmed, either by spirit or by word or by letter." Likewise, the writer of James 1:6–8 admonishes the readers in terms reminiscent of Philo's: "But ask in faith, never doubting, for the one who doubts is like a wave of the sea, driven and tossed by the wind; for the doubter, being double-minded and unstable in every way, must not expect to receive anything from the Lord."[35]

As we move into works of the first centuries of the Common Era, we find a continuation of this theme. Ignatius of Antioch, for example, commends the followers of Christ in Smyrna as "wise" by saying, "I observed that you are established in an *unshakeable* faith, having been nailed, as it were, to the cross of the Lord Jesus Christ in both body and spirit, and *firmly established* in love by the blood of Christ (*Smyrn.* 1.1).[36] Likewise, the narrator of the *Martyrdom of Polycarp* carefully notes that Polycarp does not need to be nailed down when the Romans light the fires that will consume his body. He is completely immovable even without physical constraints:

> Then the materials prepared for the pyre were placed around him; and as they were also about to nail him, he said, "Leave me as I am; for the one who enables me to endure the fire will also enable me to remain on the pyre without moving" (*Mart. Pol.*13.3).[37]

---

[33]Williams, *Immovable Race*, 55.

[34]All Bible quotes are from the NRSV.

[35]Emphasis added. See discussion in de Boer, *Gospel of Mary*, 76.

[36]All citations and translations of Ignatius's letters are from Holmes, *Apostolic Fathers*. Emphasis added. Regarding this point, see the discussion in Williams, *Immovable Race*, 149.

[37]All citations and translations of the *Martyrdom of Polycarp* are from Musurillo, *Acts of the Christian Martyrs*.

Clement of Alexandria also writes about one transformed by perfect knowledge who ascends mystically into a state of stability: "into the chamber of the Father, to the abode which is truly the Lord's, to be, as it were, an eternally standing and abiding light, totally immutable" (*Strom.* 7.57.5). Clement also discusses the Son of God's lack of passion in his form as the perfect Logos, or "impassible Human" (*Strom.* 7.5.5). Clement says, "He was quite completely without passion, and into him slipped no passionate movement at all, neither pleasure nor grief (*Strom.* 6.71.2). For Clement, perfection lies in becoming like Christ in this way. In fact, he describes the apostles as those who were completely free from passion, remaining in a state of complete self-control after the resurrection of their Savior (*Strom.* 6.71.3).

MALE DISCIPLES' FEAR VERSUS MARY'S LACK OF FEAR

In the *Gospel of Mary*, however, we do not find the male disciples represented in these glowing terms. Jesus has just appeared to them and told them to go and preach the gospel (*GMary* 8.21–22). After he departs, the text says:

> But they were distressed and wept greatly. "How are we going to go out to the rest of the world to announce the good news about the Realm of the child of true Humanity?" they said. "If they did not spare him, how will they spare us?" (*GMary* 5.1–3)[38]

As Esther de Boer notes, "the disciples … bring forth passion, which arises from their despair, which is a result of focusing on the suffering of Man."[39] In short, the text depicts them in precisely the terms noted above—as fearful, hesitant, confused, and worried.

It is at this point that Mary exhorts the men to be steadfast rather than afraid:

---

[38]Despite the *Gospel of Mary* being labeled "Gnostic," the text contains no hint of Docetism, that is, the belief that Christ did not actually suffer and die, which was a common accusation against supposed Gnostics. See Silke Petersen in Petersen, *"Zerstört die Werke der Weiblichkeit*, 135 note 197; de Boer, *Gospel of Mary*, 6; and Tuckett, *Gospel of Mary*, 14.

[39]De Boer, *Gospel of Mary*, 89.

Then Mary stood up. She greeted them all, addressing her brothers and sisters, "Do not weep and be distressed nor let your hearts be irresolute. For his grace will be with you all and will shelter you. Rather, we should praise his greatness, for he has prepared us and made us true Human beings." When Mary had said these things, she turned their heart [to]ward the Good, and they began to deba[t]e about the wor[d]s of [the Savior]. (*GMary* 5.4–9)

As Karen King explains, in this context, it is clear that the one who embodies a lack of fear and the emotional stability associated with advanced spiritual status is Mary:

> Throughout the Gospel, Mary is clearly portrayed as an exemplary disciple. She doesn't falter when the Savior departs. She steps into his place after his departure, comforting, strengthening, and instructing the others. Her spiritual comprehension and maturity are demonstrated in her calm behavior and especially in her visionary experience. These at once provide evidence of her spiritual maturity and form the basis for her legitimate exercise of authority in instructing the other disciples. She does not teach in her own name, but passes on the words of the Savior, calming the disciples and turning their hearts toward the Good. Her character proves the truth of her revelation and by extension authorizes the teaching of the *Gospel of Mary*.[40]

Therefore, it is, in fact, the content of Mary's character that qualifies her as a leader of the disciples.

Indeed, Mary's spiritual status in many ways parallels that of the Savior himself. Esther de Boer notes the similarity of the beginning of the *Gospel of Mary*, in which Jesus speaks and then departs, to the departure of Jesus in Luke 24:50–51; Acts 1:9, and John 14 and 16:16–23, but whereas Jesus himself encourages the disciples to rejoice in the Gospel of John, it is Mary

---

[40]King, *Gospel of Mary of Magdala*, 90 and also 30–31, where King discusses Mary's position as "parallel to that of the Savior." King sees the role Mary plays in this first part of the text as that in the first of three dialogues that are embedded within each other in order to draw the reader into increasingly deeper understanding. In this first dialogue, the conversation is between Mary and other disciples, and Mary *instructs* the others. The second layer is one in which Mary models the way a true disciple *acts*, while the third layer describes the triumph of the soul as it moves upward into joy and rest. King remarks: "Both the content and the configuration [of these three layers] lead the reader *inward* toward the stability, power and freedom of the true self, the soul set free from the false powers of ignorance, passion, and death."

who takes on the role of the encourager in the *Gospel of Mary*.[41] Erika Mohri notes that "Mary replaces the sovereign position of the Savior, who has left the disciples."[42] Christopher Tuckett also draws attention to Mary's taking over character attributes and activities of Jesus.[43] In this sense, Mary is like Christ. However, the *Gospel of Mary* portrays this Christ-likeness in an entirely different manner than the *imitatio Christi* of the martyr accounts (discussed in Chap. 3). In those cases, the focus is on freedom from passions such as fear and anger and on patient endurance, but it is the patient endurance of torture, suffering, and death. In the *Gospel of Mary*, Mary acknowledges those possibilities and advocates for facing them courageously, but the emphasis is on *living* with freedom from passion and refusing enslavement to any of the fears that would constrain one in pursuing a life that fully reflects Christ.

The idea that the Savior has "made us into human beings" is also an important part of this passage (*GMary* 9.12–24). Using this particular phrase evokes the idea of being cured or healed. Philo of Alexandria, for example, comments that Gen 6:9 describes Noah as a

> righteous human being . . . not according to the common form of speech, to the mortal animal endowed with reason, but to the one, who pre-eminently verifies the name by having expelled from the soul the untamed and frantic passions and the truly beast-like vices (*Abraham* 32).

---

[41]De Boer, *Gospel of Mary*, 24, 89.

[42]Mohri, *Maria Magdalena*, 265: "Tritt Maria souverän an die Stelle des Erlösers, der die Jüngerinnen und Jünger verlassen hat." In conversation, Ann Graham Brock has pointed out a similar parallel representation of Mary in her depiction as a shepherdess in the *Manichaean Psalms* as stepping into the role of the Savior. In the *Manichaean Psalms*, Mary is charged with leading eleven male disciples back. In the New Testament and early Christian art, Jesus is frequently depicted as the Good Shepherd.

[43]See Tuckett, *Gospel of Mary*, 68–69: "In general terms too, it is agreed by many that, in the *Gospel of Mary*, the figure of Mary takes over many of the characteristics and/or activities of Jesus himself. Hence it is possible that the note about the 'doubt' of the disciples (a statement by the author of Matthew, but placed on the lips of Mary here) may be a further link connecting these two passages. Hence the motif of Mary bidding the other disciples not to 'doubt' may be a recollection of Matthew's resurrection scene." With reference to this point, also see Tardieu, *Écrits gnostiques*, 78; and Marjanen, *Woman Jesus Loved*, 107 note 53.

Michael Williams argues that works idealizing the ability to become a "perfect human" or to achieve "immovability" are *not* distinctively "gnostic." He discusses the way these themes pervade Greco-Roman texts and writers such as Plotinus and Philo.[44] In these passages of the *Gospel of Mary*, however, the male disciples are depicted as far from perfect humans, and the contrast between them and Mary is considerable.

Mary as a Disciple Who Did not Waver

In the next section, Mary begins to describe a vision in which the soul ascends to a perfect place of rest, and, as just discussed above, she starts by recounting the Savior's saying to her, "How wonderful you are for not wavering at seeing me! For where the mind is, there is the treasure" (*GMary* 7.3–4).[45] The Savior's calling Mary "wonderful," which can also be translated as "blessed," has a certain resonance with other texts.[46] In addition, as Karen King explicates these lines, she emphasizes the Savior's describing Mary as unwavering:

---

[44]See Williams, *Immovable Race*, 5–7, 177–79 for discussion of the significance of the term "immovable" that is connoted by the use of "not wavering."

[45]At 7.1, the work shifts from the initial appearance of Christ and the ensuing conversation among the disciples to Mary's recounting of her vision. Scholars have debated whether or not this shift reflects the joining of two texts into a composite one (or insertion of material into the text); see Till, *Gnostischen Schriften*, 26; Henri-Charles Puech and Beate Blatz, "The *Gospel of Mary*," 391–95; Wilson, "New Testament and the Gnostic *Gospel of Mary*," 236–43; Markschies, *Gnosis*, 42; Pasquier, *Evangile selon Marie*, 7–10, 96–101. Others, however, see a unity of form and content throughout; Michel Tardieu, *Écrits gnostiques*, 22–23; G. P. Luttikhuizen, "Evaluation of the Teaching of Jesus," 626–22; Marjanen, *Woman Jesus Loved*, 100–104; Petersen, *"Zerstört die Werke,"* 59; Mohri, *Maria Magdalena*, 266–72; de Boer, *Gospel of Mary*, 15. Understanding this unity is most relevant to the thesis of this chapter, which emphasizes Mary's representation as a steadfast, emotionally stable character throughout the work, exhorting the other disciples in the first section and being described as "unwavering" in the second.

[46]Although it is Mary, the mother of Jesus (Mary of Nazareth) who is called "blessed" in the Gospel of Luke 1:30, this term is also sometimes used of Mary Magdalene, for example in *Pistis Sophia*; Ann Graham Brock, "Setting the Record Straight," 43–52.

The term "wavering" carries important connotations in ancient thought where it implies instability of character. Mary's stability illustrates her conformity to the unchanging and eternal spiritual Realm, and provides one more indication of her advanced spiritual status . . . . It is because Mary has placed her mind with God that she can direct others to the spiritual treasure of the Good.[47]

The fact that the Savior refers to the mind being the treasure is also significant with regard to Mary's exemplary, steadfast character (*GMary* 10.15–16). Karen King explains that the work seems to posit a human being with a tripartite composition (body, soul, mind) in which the "mind" is

the most divine part of the self, that which links it with God . . . rules and leads the soul, so that when the mind is directed toward God, it purifies and directs the soul toward spiritual attainment.[48]

The mind is that part of a human being which can see a vision. The apologist Justin states: "the vision of God does not occur with the eyes, as with other living beings, but He can be grasped only by the mind . . . ." (*Dial.* 3).[49] Origen, too, makes reference to the mind in this way: "God, moreover, is in our judgment invisible, because He is not a body, while He can be seen by those who see with the heart, that is the mind, no indeed with any kind of heart, but with one which is pure" (*Cels.* 6:69).[50] Esther de Boer explains the significance of the mind with regard to the care of the self in a way that greatly illumines the significance of the *Gospel of Mary*:

Passion and confusion came into the created cosmos because of a power contrary to Nature. Redemption consists in the fact that the Son of Man, the crucified and resurrected Jesus, as God did when creating truly living beings, once again blows the Spirit into the *nous*, the mind, which has the task of ordering the turbulence of the soul. The Son of Man thus re-creates his

---

[47]King, *Gospel of Mary of Magdala*, 63. See also King "Gospel of Mary Magdalene," 612; Perkins, *Gnostic Dialogue*, 135; Marjanen, *Woman Jesus Loved*, 111; Tuckett, *Gospel of Mary*, 171; de Boer, *Gospel of Mary*, 76.

[48]King, *Gospel of Mary of Magdala*, 65.

[49]Also see discussion of the perspectives of Justin and Origen in King, *Gospel of Mary of Magdala*, 66–67.

[50]King, *Gospel of Mary of Magdala*, 67.

followers into (true) Human Beings. Through his living within them they are empowered to bring forth his peace instead of passion and confusion which belong to the power contrary to Nature. They, having been restored to Nature's Root by the Good One can indeed be "fully assured" (*GosMary* 8.7). Opposite nature has no power over them. They are thus prepared to proclaim the gospel of the Kingdom of the Son of Man.[51]

MARY'S VISION

Mary then goes on to share a vision she has had of the Savior. Unfortunately, six pages are missing from the Berlin Codex at this point. The text, however, may well be describing the struggle within the soul of a living human being here and now in trying to become fully human. Hal Taussig, for example, sees the description of the ascent of the soul as a description of authentic engagement in the struggle to become a better human being through successfully negotiating a path through the ignorance, desire, and anger that arise in all human beings and may serve both positive and negative purposes.[52] Hadot describes a contemplative practice common to most of the philosophical schools called "the view from above." He maintains that this type of vision is not a trance, a supernatural experience, or a seizure, but comes about as a consequence of the soul separating from the body, and that at times, when the body is near death, souls may be temporarily divided from their bodies. This moving apart, however, can also occur in dreams.[53]

---

[51]De Boer, *Gospel of Mary*, 72.

[52]Taussig, "Introduction to the *Gospel of Mary*" 220–21.

[53]Hadot discusses the view from above at length. Hadot, *Philosophy as a Way of Life*, 238–248. See 89n79, 94 for remarks on what the view from above is *not*. See also Foucault, *Hermeneutics of the Subject*, 280–85 for a moving description of the view from above. Foucault, too, argues that "there is absolutely no passage to another world here. The world to which we gain access . . . is the world in which we live . . . . We distance ourselves from it, so to speak, by stepping back. And stepping back we see the context in which we are placed opening out, and we grasp again this world as it is, the world in which we exist. So it is not a passage to another world. It is not a movement by which we turn away from this world to look elsewhere. It is the movement by which we are [enabled to] grasp this world here as a whole, without ever losing sight of this world here, or of ourselves within it, or of what we

Most importantly, though, Hadot describes a practice of the separation of the soul while one is very much alive as "a specific conception of the power of thought and the divine nature of the soul, which is able to raise itself above the categories of space and time."[54] He explains that the ancients believed that the soul could separate from the body by strictly spiritual means through the practice of a philosophical exercise.[55] Later he argues that it is not the *repression* of passion that is the point, but rather the ability to see "from above," that is, to see *neutrally* without being influenced by passion.[56] Many of the examples Hadot cites also involve a looking back down after one has ascended and seeing the earth and all the human activities that are going on and realizing that when we are in the midst of them, we do not see things as they truly are:

> To observe the human affairs from above means, at the same time, to see them from the point of death. It is only this perspective which brings about the necessary elevation and loosening of the spirit, which can provide the distance we need in order to see things as they truly are.[57]

Of course, an important part of Stoic and Epicurean teachings and practices was the cultivation of being constantly in the present moment. For the Epicureans, it was the idea that one must fully enjoy and appreciate the wonder of each instant while for Stoics there was a constant vigilance over oneself. Therefore, engaging in the view from above was one exercise grounded firmly in the context of being appreciative of or absorbed in each moment of daily life. Such an exercise allowed one to keep that which arouses the passions in the proper perspective while living in and deeply

---

are within it . . . . it is a matter of placing ourselves at a point that is both so central and elevated that we can see below us the overall order of the world of which we ourselves are parts . . . . below us, we can see the world in its general order, the tiny space we occupy within it, and the short time we remain there . . . . It is the self's view of itself from above which encompasses the world of which we are a part and which thus ensures the subject's freedom within this world itself." See Foucault, *Hermeneutics of the Subject*, 282.

[54]Hadot, *Philosophy as a Way of Life*, 240.

[55]Hadot, *Philosophy as a Way of Life*, 241n17.

[56]Hadot, *Philosophy as a Way of Life*, 284.

[57]Hadot, *Philosophy as a Way of Life*, 247.

attuned to all the strife and turmoil of our lives.[58] In other texts, it was a concentrated meditation in which one participated to strengthen one's ability to put things into their proper perspective. This may have been how the author intended Mary's vision to be understood although too much of the original is missing to be certain.

In fact, as we examine these works more closely, we find that there are similarities with others discussed earlier. For example, in the *Apocalypse of Peter*, Peter has been engaged in a relationship with a teacher, Jesus, and is involved in a dialogue that helps the hearer or reader reflect on the meaning of death. In this case, the Savior is the one who engages in *parrhēsia*. In the *Gospel of Judas*, too, Jesus functions in the role of the one participating in the practice of *frank speech* while Judas is the one who is willing to stand before Jesus and hear his words. In the *Gospel of Mary*, however, Mary engages in thinking about the possibility of persecution and death and steps into the position of boldly exhorting the disciples at the beginning of her gospel. As we unpack the *Gospel of Mary*, we can reflect on how all three of these texts reflect practices of the care of the self and serve as a model for those hearing or reading them to engage in it.

In short, Mary shows those who *are* wavering how to achieve a state of stability through her engagement in the practice of *parrhēsia* with them. This work is not a treatise on systematic theology but rather a narrative that provides an example of the kind of transformation that happens when one fully engages in a relationship with the Savior and comes to understand his teachings, teachings that may involve actual contemplative practices related to an examination of conscience and meditation on one's eventual death.

The text thus indicates that Mary can relate a vision regarding the ascent of the soul because she herself has undergone a transformation—a "healing" from passion. In other words, she is so emotionally stable that she is in a position to access this kind of knowledge or engage in practices of meditation accessible to those who have faithfully engaged in the process of the care of the self and are more spiritually advanced. Moreover, through doing so, she serves as a model to the other disciples for conquering any "wavering" of their own. Mary reveals what it really means to follow Jesus—to allow him to make one into a true human being—and how to live when Jesus renews one's very mind.

---

[58]Hadot, *Philosophy as a Way of Life*, 251–63.

MARY'S EQUANIMITY VERSUS PETER'S PASSION

After Mary relates the vision, Andrew and Peter react defensively to her words:

> Andrew responded, addressing the brothers and sisters, "Say what you will about the things she has said, but I do not believe that the S[a]vior said these things, f[or] indeed these teachings are strange ideas." Peter responded, bringing up similar concerns. He questioned them about the Savior: "Did he, then, speak with a woman in private without our knowing about it? Are we to turn around and listen to her? Did he choose her over us?" (*GMary* 10.1–4)

Levi, however, reacts differently. He defends Mary and rebukes Peter, calling him "hot-tempered." De Boer notes that the text uses this same word for "wrath," the seventh power in Mary's vision. She believes the author of the work is making an analogy between Peter's opposition of Mary and the way in which the adversaries in Mary's vision try to oppose the soul, in other words—"the powers of passion"; therefore, when Levi makes a comparison between Peter's conduct and that of the soul's adversaries, the text is indicating that the adversaries actually exist within the male disciples themselves.[59]

Others have commented extensively on the conflict between Peter and Mary as well. Ann Graham Brock has examined a wide variety of early manuscripts and pointed out the significance of Peter's many challenges to Mary's status.[60] In the *Gospel of Mary* specifically, Karen King has shown the contrast between the two figures with particular attention to the issue of character.[61] Andrew's and Peter's responses reinforce the idea that Mary's engagement in dialogue with them, first by exhorting them to go and preach and then by relating knowledge of an experience in which the soul ascends to God, exemplifies the practice of *parrhēsia*.

In short, then, in and of itself, Mary's initial bold address to the disciples is the practice of *parrhēsia*, and her words to them near the end also

---

[59]De Boer, *Gospel of Mary*, 57, 91. See also Perkins, *Gnostic Dialogue*, 133–37.
[60]Brock, *Mary Magdalene*, 81–86. See also Mohri, *Maria Magdalena*, 278–81.
[61]King, *Gospel of Mary of Magdala*, 67, 177. See also Tuckett, *Gospel of Mary*, 166; Pasquier, *Évangile selon Marie*, 7–10, 96–101; and de Boer, *Gospel of Mary*, 29, 90.

demonstrate her participation in this practice. In the last two years that Foucault lectured, he focused his attention closely on this specific practice of the care of the self. As with the care of the self more generally, Foucault traces the way that this term is used in ancient texts and how its meaning evolves and expands over time. Initially, it refers to frank, direct speech that involves boldness and courage in speaking up and saying what needs to be said. It also comes to involve a vulnerability and risk of one kind or another. In the *Gospel of Mary*, when Mary addresses the men, she repeatedly and deliberately places herself in a position susceptible to ridicule and criticism.

Foucault notes that the term *parrhēsia* appears in the Septuagint (the Greek translation of the Hebrew Scriptures) in the book of Proverbs to describe what Wisdom, the personification of an attribute of God in feminine terms, does when she shouts out in the street in Proverbs 1:20–21, and the author could indeed have intentionally invoked this imagery of *Sophia* with Mary. In the *Gospel of Mary*, Mary exemplifies this practice as she stands up and speaks. She steps into the role of Jesus, the one whose *parrhēsia* led to death at the hands of the Roman Empire. Foucault notes that *parrhēsia* is often linked to a concern with justice, and the two strong admonitions in the *Gospel of Mary* not to lay down any rules other than those given by the Savior seem to accord with such an interest.

Mary's speech can be compared to the strong critiques of those who lead the "little ones" astray in the *Apocalypse of Peter* or even of the critiques of those in the line of apostolic succession in the *Gospel of Judas*. These critiques employ the rhetorical strategies of their time and place; they must not be idealized just as the harsh critiques of Irenaeus or Ignatius or others should not be. They should be acknowledged for what they are, and yet, the way in which they serve as strong exhortations to those whom they feel are misrepresenting the meaning of Jesus and his teachings, the proper way to follow him, and even his death and resurrection, are indeed a kind of *parrhēsia*. Yet in the *Gospel of Mary*, we find none of these heated rhetorical strategies in the speech of Mary, the main protagonist who drives the action forward. Mary stands and encourages the others to have courage without ridiculing or mocking them, and later, she simply responds to Peter's challenge with a plain, clear description of the ascent of the soul.

Finally, Karen King points out the manner in which a work like the *Gospel of Mary* also indirectly offers a means to reflect on resistance to earthly powers:

> The *Gospel of Mary* makes it possible for people to see the struggle against violence in their own situations as part of a necessary and justified resistance against Powers that seek to keep people enslaved to their passions: anger, desire, lust, envy, greed. The mythic framework of the *Gospel Mary* allows the spiritual, the psychological, the social, the political, and the cosmic to be integrated under one guiding principle: resistance to the unjust and illegitimate domination of ignorant and malevolent Powers. It also offers a strategy for that resistance: preaching the gospel and appropriating the teachings of the Savior in one's own life.[62]

Scholars have sometimes conceived of supposedly gnostic texts as less resistant to existing sociocultural norms or forces of domination.[63] King, however, helps us to see that this is not necessarily true, although the critique may be disguised.[64] In this sense, the *Gospel of Mary* reflects the concern for justice that Foucault associates with the practice of *parrhēsia*.

Without Hadot's and Foucault's keen observations regarding the importance of the practice of the care of the self and more specifically, their articulation of *parrhēsia* as one of the most important practices of such self-care, it would be easy to miss the way in which these works portray that practice. All too often texts not written in a form intended to serve as a systematic laying out of theology have been scrutinized for what they seem to say about the beliefs of early Christ followers. Yet, if that is our sole focus, we overlook what these authors were teaching altogether. We fail to recognize the way in which they help us to understand how these early Christ people were articulating their actual relationship to the Savior and how this relationship had transformed their lives and emboldened them to speak up.

---

[62]King, *Gospel of Mary of Magdala*, 79.

[63]Williams, *Rethinking "Gnosticism"*, 96–115.

[64]For those living in a society where critique is punished, this kind of resistance may be the only kind possible. See Scott, *Domination and the Arts of Resistance*, 103–107, 124, 198–99. See also King, *Gospel of Mary of Magdala*, 76–81.

THE END RESULT

Finally, the conflict between the disciples is not the end of the story. The very last phrase declares "they started going out [to] teach and to preach" (*GMary* 10.14).[65] Thus, it is Mary's ability to perceive the true teaching of Jesus in a vision (because of her emotional stability and lack of passion), as well as her steadfastness and perseverance in relating this teaching to the other disciples, serving as a Christ-like figure of encouragement, that results in the preaching of the Gospel.[66]

PARALLELS BETWEEN MARY AND PERPETUA

Examples abound of courage, boldness, and a lack of fear typical of one who has successfully engaged in the therapy of the emotions among other women who were part of Christ-related groups. This chapter focuses on the comparisons and contrasts between the representation of Mary and that of the martyr Perpetua. There is another very popular account of a woman identifying with Christ—a woman who exhibits the courage, boldness, and lack of fear typical of one who has successfully engaged in the therapy of emotions who may have served as a model for Perpetua or those who wrote about her. It is that of Thecla, a woman who heard the teaching of Paul, converted, baptized herself, and then traveled widely with the apostle. Although Thecla was almost martyred several times, she died a natural

---

[65]For de Boer, this is a positive ending; *Gospel of Mary*, 57. Tuckett, however, makes much of the fact that while the Coptic manuscript has "they," the Greek fragment has *he* rather than *they*. Therefore, Tuckett he argues, it may be Levi alone who goes to preach; yet, he notes that this does not necessarily preclude the preaching of the others: Mary, Peter, or Andrew; Tuckett, *Gospel of Mary*, 195–96. For Karen King, the ending is ambiguous; King, *Gospel of Mary of Magdala*, 85–86, 109.

[66]Certainly other extracanonical works confirm a very positive portrait of Mary during this era. I am grateful to Ann Graham Brock for pointing out to me that *Pistis Sophia* also portrays Mary's self-control in particular, saying that "Mary remains strong" (2.94), and in the *Manichaean Psalms*, Mary is the one who rallies the others and strengthens them. She also noted that it would be worthwhile to compare the courageous depiction of "Mariamme" in the fourth-century *Acts of Philip* in this respect.

death.[67] Jan Bremmer discusses the possibility that Perpetua heard or read about Thecla, and it is to Perpetua that we now turn.[68]

Her story is a remarkable illustration of some of the most vivid narratives about women in the early Christ movements in martyr accounts.[69] Indeed, the depiction of Perpetua, a young Roman matron who had been writing in a diary of her desire to suffer and die when she boldly endured the arena in Carthage around 203 C.E., provides a stellar example.[70] The written text

---

[67]For an account of Thecla's life excerpted from the *Acts of Paul and Thecla*, see Lefkowitz and Fant, *Women's Life in Greece and Rome*, 311–13.

[68]Bremmer, "Magic, Martyrdom and Women's Liberation," 44. Indeed, other women martyrs of the same era were reportedly influenced by Thecla. For example, in a single book of narratives about early women martyrs, the narrator of the martyr Eugenia's story said she read "the book of the story of the discipleship of Thecla," and this sparked her new lifestyle, which eventually led to her martyrdom; the martyr Justa struck a man in the face, modeling herself after "her sister Thecla," who had struck Alexander; and two more women martyrs, Drusis and Euphemia, baptized themselves like Thecla; see Smith, *Select Narratives*, 2 (Eugenia), 188–89 (Justa), 75 (Drusis), and 162 (Euphemia).

[69]Agnes Lewis Smith translated a fascinating book of the accounts of women martyrs that had been written over the Old Syriac gospels; Smith, *Select Narratives*. The most often cited standard edition of martyrdom accounts with translation into English is that of Musurillo, *Acts of the Christian Martyrs*, 1972.

[70]Scholars debate whether Perpetua's account is actually her own self-representation. It is impossible to know whether Perpetua herself wrote the account as the editor of the text asserts. What is important for our purposes is the way Perpetua is represented within the work regardless of whether she authored parts of it. Jacqueline Amat carefully examines this issue in Amat, *Passion de Perpétue et de Félicité suivi de Actes*, 5, 8, 83. Elizabeth Castelli cautions against thinking of the account as an autobiography as the very term belongs to the Enlightenment; however, she usefully situates the martyrdom account within Foucault's framework of self-writing as a discursive strategy used in the care of the self; Castelli, *Martyrdom and Memory*, 70–78, 85–92, 233–35, 237–41. Finally, whether or not it is Perpetua who writes parts of the account or someone else claiming that she does, Emanuela Prinzivalli characterizes Perpetua's account as a "rare jewel," noting how few women in this time period have left any written records at all in Prinzivalli, "Perpetua the Martyr," 118–40, 221–25. Some have thought Tertullian was the editor, such as de Labriolle, *Crise montaniste*, 345–53; and Musurillo, *Acts of the Christian Martyrs*, xxvii. That hypothesis currently enjoys less scholarly support; Butler, *New Prophecy and "New Visions,"* 49–57, 156–60.

of her imprisonment and death contains more details than exist in many other cases.[71] As such, her story resonates powerfully on an emotional level with a wide range of readers, and although Perpetua herself may have been a member of the New Prophecy movement, her courage has been much admired by the "orthodox" throughout the centuries.[72] In fact, the popularity of Perpetua has been nothing short of enormous. In addition to modern books and articles devoted solely to her, many writers choose her as a key example in discussions of women in early Christ movements or even of Roman women as a whole.[73]

Perpetua's narrative parallels the representation of Mary in the *Gospel of Mary* in a number of ways. The work strongly frames Perpetua's character in terms of her steadfast endurance, self-control, and courage—that is, in terms characteristic of one who has successfully engaged in the therapy of emotions and become free of passions such as fear and anger. Like Mary

---

[71] Musurillo refers to *The Martyrdom of Perpetua and Felicity* as the "archetype of all later Acts of the Christian martyrs" in Musurillo, *Acts of the Christian Martyrs*, xxv. See also Prinzivalli, "Perpetua the Martyr," 132.

[72] It should be noted that characterizing a work as that of New Prophecy, a.k.a. "Montanist," has been a means of marginalizing it by categorizing it as heretical. Frederick Klawiter argues that the writer of the martyrdom account of Perpetua is Montanist, but he carefully notes, "It is significant that even as late as the fifth century, Perpetua was remembered as a martyr in both the catholic and Montanist communities of North Africa. Very probably, the persecution of 203 happened when the New Prophecy had not yet been rejected by the Carthaginian catholic community" in "Role of Martyrdom," 105–15. Joyce Salisbury argues against necessarily assuming Montanist influence as she feels "the church in Carthage had not yet split into such clear distinctions" in Salisbury, *Perpetua's Passion*, 158.

[73] Yet today Perpetua has some detractors as well. Frend, for example, depicts her as "a fanatic" and sees "a real poignancy in her father's continuous efforts to save her from humiliating death as a result of which the family itself would hardly recover," in Frend, "Blandina and Perpetua," 91, 94. Frend's comments may be a good example of what Mary Lefkowitz calls "the consistent failure of male scholars to acknowledge the positive significance of femininity in the performance of certain heroic acts"; see Lefkowitz, "Motivations for St. Perpetua's Martyrdom," 417–21. For more on this issue, see David Daube, *Civil Disobedience in Antiquity*, 5–6 and Rosemary R. Ruether, "Misogynism and Virginal Feminism in the Early Church," 262–95.

with the male disciples, Perpetua also engages in *parrhēsia*. She speaks boldly to her father as well as to the prison guards, demanding that they provide better food not only for her but also for the others imprisoned with her. Like Mary, Perpetua describes an ascent that occurs in a vision. During this experience, she climbs a narrow ladder and then ascends to paradise, but a dragon rests down at the bottom of the ladder, and along the sides are many sharp things like hooks and spears that can impede one's journey to the top. These seem to parallel the ignorance, desire, and anger that the soul must struggle to get past in Mary's vision. These provide evidence that Perpetua has the emotional fortitude and the ability to encourage others in concrete ways. Indeed, at the beginning of the martyrdom account, the compiler refers to the purpose of recounting such deeds as helpful to others in their "achiev[ing] . . . spiritual strengthening" (*Mart. Perpet.* 8.1), and at the end he mentions that they can be read "for the consolation of the Church" (*Mart. Perpet.* 8.21).[74]

THE REPRESENTATION OF PERPETUA

In understanding Perpetua's narrative, it is helpful to discuss the way in which gladiatorial contests generally served as a means for philosophical reflection because Perpetua's courageous participation in such an event is an important part of her representation. For the Stoics in particular, the emphasis in philosophical discussions was on the idea that how one faces death is extremely important, an indication of one's underlying moral character, given the fact that death is inescapable.[75] A public death, honorably faced, is an opportunity to convey a powerful message to those who witness it. Those who die in the arena can serve as models for how to reflect on and face death. A contest in the arena "was not only a spectacle to amuse and divert the crowd but a . . . ritual designed to affect and transform the witnesses . . . . It was expected that the process of watching

---

[74]All citations and translations of the *Martyrdom of Perpetua and Felicity* come from Musurillo, *Acts of the Christian Martyrs*, 106–31.

[75]Edwards, *Death in Ancient Rome*, 10, and esp. 78–112 on Stoic attitudes toward death, which contains many parallels with Perpetua. See also Moss, *Ancient Christian Martyrdom*, 36–37.

people die in the arena would have an impact on the viewer."[76] Bettina Bergmann comments that the gladiatorial contest is an event discussed by the philosophers in terms of a "professional performance of . . . self-control, the performance of virtue."[77] This is in line with Seneca's discussion of dying willingly and unconquered" (*Ep.* 37.2). Both imagery describing performance in battle and discussion regarding control of the passions are common.[78]

As we turn specifically to Perpetua's representation, it is important to note that the compiler consistently represents Perpetua as "a very strong personality" and leader.[79] He speaks, for example, of "her perseverance and nobility of soul" (8.16) and of the way in which she and the others imprisoned with her speak with "steadfastness" (8.17). Indeed, the *Martyrdom of Perpetua* presents us with human beings who die honorably—as honorably and admirably as any of the Greek, Roman, or Carthaginian heroes or heroines present in the consciousness of those living in the Roman Empire during the second and third centuries c.e.[80] This is also true of the slave Felicity and the men featured in the narrative, but Perpetua is the one whom the editor of the text features in detail. She is every bit as dignified as Lucretia, Polyxena, Dido, or Arria (who, like Perpetua, draws the sword to her own throat and encourages others to

---

[76]Salisbury, *Perpetua's Passion*, 124 for quote, and see also 134. Also relevant is Edwards, *Death in Ancient Rome*, 53.

[77]Bergman, *Art of Ancient Spectacle*, 22.

[78]Edwards, *Death in Ancient Rome*, 46–77, 90–100.

[79]Prinzivalli, "Perpetua the Martyr," 129. Frend comments that the *Passion of Perpetua and Felicity* represents the martyrs as "the true leaders of the Church" in Frend, "Blandina and Perpetua," 92–93. For the way in which groups identifying with Christ linked martyrdom and women's leadership, see Klawiter, "Role of Martyrdom and Persecution," 105–15. See also Brown, *Making of Late Antiquity*, 54–80, for discussion of the ways that the church elevated the status of martyrs as what he terms "the friends of God."

[80]Salisbury discusses the particular Carthaginian admiration of women who give their lives as sacrifices, noting that the Carthaginians were even more steeped in the myths of such women than the Romans. See Salisbury, *Perpetua's Passion*, 33–57.

follow her in death).[81] Mediterranean society considered such a death honorable.[82] When Seneca was forced to commit suicide and his wife wanted to die with him, he encouraged her because it would honor her.[83] Likewise, the mother in 4 Maccabees, a work greatly influenced by Stoic ideals, emboldens each of her seven sons to commit what is represented as a heroic suicide, and then follows them by taking her own life.[84]

Dido, Lucretia, and Cleopatra are all heroines who take their own lives in accordance with the founding of a new political order (the city of Rome, the Roman Republic, and the Roman Principate, respectively).[85] In a sense, Perpetua's death also marks the beginning of a new era, an era in which a collective identity for those in early Christ movements is coalescing under the rubric of the "suffering self" (as Judith Perkins has articulated so well).[86] Indeed, the formation of this new identity transcends existing social norms regarding class. Heroines who are not high-born like Perpetua are represented as equally courageous. Felicity, for example, is a slave who

---

[81]Polyxena stands out because, like Perpetua, she takes an extra step in courage, undoing her clothing and offering her executioner a choice of her breast or her throat. Similarly to Perpetua's covering her thigh with her tunic, Polyxena takes care to fall modestly: Lefkowitz, *Women in Greek Myth*, 100.

[82]Joyce Salisbury focuses on a particular admiration for women's deaths in Carthage in particular due to a long-standing tradition of such deaths occurring there; Dido, for example, came from Carthage; Salisbury, *Perpetua's Passion*, 53–57. For a discussion of women's deaths represented as honorable, see Edwards, *Death in Ancient Rome*, 179–206, with her notable discussion of Lucretia, a noble woman who committed suicide after being raped, on 180–83. Mary Lefkowitz also discusses the tradition of women heroines who commit suicide in various Greek myths, arguing that doing so is the most active role Greek women are given to play; Lefkowitz, *Women in Greek Myth*, 95–111.

[83]See discussion in Streete, *Redeemed Bodies*, 20.

[84]For discussion, see Jensen, *God's Self-Confident Daughters*, 27, 34, 37.

[85]See Edwards, *Death in Ancient Rome*, 186. Mary Lefkowitz interprets Perpetua's resistance in social terms seeing martyrdom as an escape "releasing women from the hierarchical structure imposed by patriarchal society, which the church in its own organization would increasingly incorporate and emulate," in Lefkowitz, "Motivations for St. Perpetua's Martyrdom," 421. Other scholars, however, question an emphasis on Perpetua's resistance in strong political or social terms; Jensen, *God's Self-Confident Daughters*, 104.

[86]Perkins, *Suffering Self*, 104–23.

dies along with Perpetua. At one point, Perpetua helps her to her feet (*Mart. Perpet.* 8.20). Likewise, a slave named Blandina who perishes in the fierce persecutions of Lyons and Vienne, is especially noted for her courage.[87] Thus, while dying for a worthy cause was in keeping with Roman social ideals, it is also important to note that the dignity of women from both high and low social classes serves to distinguish them as part of a new group who owe allegiance to an authority wholly different from that of the Roman Empire.[88] It is truly stories such as these, in which the high-born Perpetua stands hand in hand with the equally valiant slave Felicity (*Mart. Perpet.* 20.6–7), in which the upper class Perpetua's story is read alongside that of a slave such as Blandina, that perpetuate the establishment of a new community to which those who follow Christ belong.[89]

However, although Perpetua belongs to a long lineage of Greco-Roman women who illustrate the idea that there is courage and honor in dying, it is important to note one major difference. Usually, these cases of noble death serve to *reinforce* the existing social norms, not as examples that undermine them. Lucretia, for example, commits suicide after being raped. Her death serves to release her from the shame of living with dishonor.[90] Remarkably, however, Mary and Perpetua are represented as exemplars in spite of the fact that they *transgress* accepted social norms for women.[91]

---

[87]Musurillo, *Acts of the Christian Martyrs*, 78–81.

[88]This issue is discussed above. Nicola Denzey's article is especially helpful; Denzey, "Facing the Beast," 176–98.

[89]See Perkins, *Suffering Self*, esp. 15–40. Streete discusses Perpetua and Blandina in relation to each other, in Streete, *Redeemed Bodies*, 15–16. Jensen comments on the lack of social distinctions among those identifying with Christ, in Jensen, *God's Self-Confident Daughters*, 124. See also Frend, *Martyrdom and Persecution*, 275. Edwards notes the way in which gladiators serve as models for the marginalized, in Edwards, *Death in Ancient Rome*, 68.

[90]D'Ambra, *Roman Women*, 58–59.

[91]Mary R. Lefkowitz notes that women martyrs who identify with Christ are different from other Greek and Roman women martyrs in that they "die courageously but in noticeable isolation from their families in defiance of, rather than in loyalty to, their husbands or fathers," in Lefkowitz, "Motivations," 418. The one caveat is that these portrayals may reflect idealized notions of what women should be rather than actual realities. See Dixon for discussion of this idea as well as discussion regarding the importance of genre in shaping representations; Dixon, *Reading Roman Women*, 16–25.

Women are most vulnerable to being portrayed as lacking in virtue when they speak out.[92] As discussed above, both Mary and Perpetua are vocal figures who engage in *parrhēsia*.

Perpetua's speaking out involves a considerable transgression of existing social norms on several levels. We see this first during her time in prison. She is resolute in the way she deals both with her father and the local authorities—a further indication of her courage. In the Roman world, a father's authority and legal status as the paterfamilias extended to his children and grandchildren from their birth until his death. Fathers literally exercised the power of life and death over their families. Legally, fathers determined whether or not their newborn infants would be accepted or exposed to the elements. Society demanded an attitude of unquestioning obedience to fathers. Perpetua, however, unceasingly resists the repeated pleas of her father to recant her faith and escape punishment and death.[93] She is determined that he will not "shake" her "resolution" (*Mart. Perpet.* 8.3).

Moreover, Perpetua is depicted bravely transgressing Roman gender norms when she gives up her infant son. In the eyes of Roman society, "Perpetua's willingness to abandon her child made her . . . absolutely deviant from the ideal of the self-effacing woman, nourisher, and keeper of

---

[92]Determining norms is, of course, difficult, as ancient depictions of women are sparse, but Origen argues against women prophesying in his commentary on 1 Corinthians; see Coyle, "Fathers on Women and Women's Ordination," 139. Karen King also comments on negative social evaluation of women who did not keep silent in "Prophetic Power and Women's Authority," 29. For more on the idea that silence was expected in public spaces, see Karen Torjesen and Virginia Burrus, "Household Management and Women's Authority," 53–87.

[93]The representation of Perpetua is that of a mature woman, not a young one. The compiler gives her age as 22. Girls often married around 13 years of age, and it was common for people to die in their 20s and 30s. See Shelton, *As the Romans Did*, 20–21, 93. The text does not reveal whether the child she is weaning is actually her first, but for an ancient reader, Perpetua would not necessarily have seemed young or immature even though the work does refer to her as "a delicate young girl" when she is standing in the arena (*Mart. Perpet.* 8.20). In fact, such a depiction may serve to re-feminize Perpetua and mitigate the "manly" courage she has shown rather than to describe her accurately as discussed below.

the house."[94] Yet Perpetua's action calls to mind a saying recorded by Tertullian quoting the prophetess Priscilla, one of the leaders of the New Prophecy movement: "Do not wish to die in bed, in miscarriage, or with debilitating fever, but in martyrdom, in order to glorify the one who suffered for you."[95]

In addition, Perpetua is not afraid of her Roman jailers, and she leads the way in negotiating with them for her group with remarkable poise. During her stay in prison, she demands better food for herself and her fellow prisoners, speaking of them and herself as "the most distinguished of the condemned prisoners" (*Mart. Perpet.* 8.16) and advocating for proper treatment in terms so strong that the official in charge of their care actually blushes (*Mart. Perpet.* 8.16). Likewise, when the authorities try to make her and the others dress as priests and priestesses of Saturn and Ceres during their ordeal in the arena, she asserts their right not to do so according to previous negotiations: "We came to this of our own free will, that our freedom should not be violated. We agreed to pledge our lives provided that we would do no such thing. You agreed with us to do this" (*Mart. Perpet.* 8.18). This is an important detail because the idea of death as a sacrifice to the gods was present in the minds of the Romans, but Perpetua refuses to accede to attempts to portray her death in this way. She staunchly refuses to be arrayed in the robes of priestesses of Saturn or Ceres. Wearing these garments would have allowed the spectators in the arena to conceive of her death as a pagan sacrifice instead of what she, Perpetua, wanted it to signify.[96]

Given our discussion in previous chapters regarding the meaning of martyrdom, it is also important to understand that the language ascribed to Perpetua is not that of imitating Christ in terms of substitutionary

---

[94]Prinzivalli, "Perpetua the Martyr," 126. See also Frend, *Martyrdom and Persecution*, 283, 321–22, 364–65. Francine Cardman notes that "conversion to Christianity, especially by women, begins the dismantling of the patriarchal household; impending martyrdom hastens its disintegration." See Cardman, "Acts of the Women Martyrs," 101, and see also 98–104, esp. 104, where Cardman argues, "In their passage from death to life, women martyrs profoundly unsettled the social and familial relationships on which their world had depended for its coherence."

[95]Jensen, *God's Self-Confident Daughters*, 160.

[96]See Aline Rouselle, *Porneia*, 116; Salisbury, *Perpetua's Passion*, 138–39; Coleman, "Fatal Charades," 66.

atonement. Rather, her representation is one of her triumph over cosmic forces of evil—the devil himself—in her visions. This is in accord with a *Christus Victor* theory of atonement (as discussed in Chap. 4). In both the *Gospel of Mary* and the *Martyrdom of Perpetua and Felicity*, the emphasis is the risen Christ rather than the suffering Savior. It is the former that Perpetua sees in her visions.[97]

Perpetua's Representation in the Arena Itself

In going into and enduring the ordeal in the amphitheater itself, Perpetua's representation emerges as that of one completely free of the passion of fear, one who exercises remarkable courage and self-control and acts with composed dignity. This is consistent with a philosophical emphasis on the idea that death is better than slavery—enslavement to one's passions.[98] Above all, she is not a victim but rather an active agent who refuses to allow others control over her life but instead takes charge of her death and makes it a "noble" one.[99] It is perhaps in this sense, if any, that her death is voluntary.[100] Greco-Roman philosophers, particularly Stoics, do not conceive of this kind of willingness to die as negative or immoral. In fact, quite

---

[97]See King, "Prophetic Power," 41 note 87; Moss, *Ancient Christian Martyrdom*, 123–25; Moss, *Other Christs*, 97–102.

[98]See Edwards, *Death in Ancient Rome*, 70–72.

[99]For an overview of the meaning of the term *noble death* in Greco-Roman antiquity, see Droge and Tabor, *Noble Death*, 1972.

[100]The text clearly presents one of the other martyrs, Saturus, as voluntarily turning himself in for arrest. One of the first to emphasize the sometimes voluntary nature of martyrdom among those in early Christ movements was de Ste. Croix, *Christian Persecution, Martyrdom, and Orthodoxy*, 2006. See also Bowersock, *Martyrdom and Rome*; Middleton, *Radical Martyrdom*; and Tite, "Voluntary Martyrdom and Gnosticism." Also noteworthy is that Perpetua's facing death without fear parallels the representation of Thecla, the popular figure mentioned above, for Thecla demonstrates bravery by voluntarily climbing up on a pyre to be burned (though God puts out the fire with a thunderstorm). See Bremmer, "Magic, Martyrdom and Women's Liberation," 49.

the opposite is true.[101] Death is "an act of heroism, something to be celebrated."[102]

Even on the day of sentencing, Perpetua writes that she and her companions "returned to prison in high spirits" (*Mart. Perpet.* 8.6), and on the day itself, they enter the arena calmly, joyfully, and free of fear. It is as if they are "joyful collaborators" in their death.[103] Perpetua in particular marches "with shining countenance and calm step . . . putting down everyone's stare by her own intense gaze" (*Mart. Perpet.* 8.18). Spectators considered a steady gaze on the part of a gladiator a sign of invincibility; thus, the inclusion of such a detail is not necessarily arbitrary on the part of the compiler of the text.[104]

During their ordeal, the writer notes that they are in complete control of their own deaths as Christ answers their previous prayers "by giving each one the death he had asked for," and when Felicity is knocked to the ground, Perpetua retains the composure to help Felicity back to her feet and stands with her "side by side" (*Mart. Perpet.* 8.19). Perpetua also encourages the others in terms reminiscent of Mary's call to be courageous: "You must all stand fast in the faith" (8.20). In addition, three gestures specifically point to Perpetua's self-control, courage, and dignity. Demonstrating remarkable composure in the face of torture, she pulls her tunic back over her legs when the "mad heifer" attacking her rips it (*Mart. Perpet.* 8.20). Likewise, she smooths out her hair and even has the composure to ask for a pin so that she can tie it up neatly (*Mart. Perpet.* 8.20)![105]

---

[101] Catharine Edwards gives an excellent overview of this belief, in Edwards, *Death in Ancient Rome*, 1–18. Droge and Tabor's *A Noble Death* provides a multitude of examples.

[102] Edwards, *Death in Ancient Rome*, 1.

[103] Edwards, *Death in Ancient Rome*, 210. Rita Nakashima Brock and Rebecca A. Parker, too, speak of Perpetua's death as represented in terms that emphasize her empowerment and moral agency, in Brock and Parker, *Saving Paradise*, 56–83.

[104] Edwards, *Death in Ancient Rome*, 61; Salisbury, *Perpetua's Passion*, 138.

[105] Some interpreters see these gestures as part of a representation that re-feminizes Perpetua, mitigating any unseemly "manly" courage. See Streete, *Redeemed Bodies*, 71. Salisbury comments that the insertions of these gestures into the work reflect the male perspective of the narrator, as Perpetua would hardly have had the time to think of such things, in Salibury, *Perpetua's Passion*, 143. However, I would argue that these gestures are not unambiguously feminine. They also express a sense of

Finally, most strikingly, she and the others approach their final dispatch at the hands of a gladiator with a sword by going under their own volition to the spot where he stands. Prisoners or defeated gladiators were often required to meet their final demise in a spot where the crowd could easily see them and note how they indeed behaved in their very final moments. Then, Perpetua herself guides the gladiator's sword to her throat. The text states, "It was as though so great a woman, feared as she was by the unclean spirit, could not be dispatched unless she herself were willing" (*Mart. Perpet.* 8.21).[106] This comment, in particular, seems in keeping with a *Christus Victor* theory of atonement rather than a theory of penal substitution, a theory also consistent with Perpetua's fourth vision, where she fights with and overcomes an Egyptian whom she feels symbolizes the devil. In other words, the narrator represents Perpetua's struggle in terms of the overcoming of the cosmic forces of evil rather than in terms of the imitation of a blood sacrifice needed in order to propitiate a bloodthirsty god.

Moreover, spectators generally approved the gladiator who did not flinch and actually offered his neck to his opponent's blade when vanquished. Such a valiant action is specifically commended by Seneca for gladiators generally.[107] Even outside the arena, bravely offering one's neck was seen as a mark of courage. Cicero, for example, leaned out of the litter he was traveling in and offered his neck for his head to be cut off by soldiers sent to execute him when he was condemned by Mark Antony.[108] Carlin Barton sees parallels in Cicero's action with that of a gladiator's "defiant complicity."[109] Perpetua, however, goes one step farther. She not only offers her neck; she also guides the sword.

---

remarkable composure and the ability to attend to the details that allow a woman to feel she is dying with her dignity intact. For an excellent analysis of how texts represent women martyrs ambiguously in both masculine and feminine terms, see Cobb, *Dying to Be Men*. Carly Daniel-Hughes's work regarding Perpetua's dream in which she sees herself stripped naked and turned into a man is also insightful, in Daniel-Hughes, *Salvation of the Flesh*, 102–07.

[106]See Edwards, *Death in Ancient Rome*, 62; also King, "Prophetic Power," 41n87.

[107]Edwards, *Death in Ancient Rome*, 73.

[108]Edwards, *Death in Ancient Rome*, 61–74.

[109]Barton, *Sorrows of the Ancient Romans*, 39.

PERPETUA'S CONTEMPLATION OF DEATH

Even before she approaches the arena, Perpetua perceives of her death as a victory.[110] She is represented as successfully imbuing her earthly demise with that meaning by communicating the content of those visions—her ascent into paradise, her conquest of the Egyptian—in writing. She clearly seems to be employing what Foucault calls "the technology of self-writing."[111]

The fact that Perpetua not only dies but also *contemplates* her death is an important part of the way she is represented.[112] This activity is one of the practices of the care of the self. When her brother asks her to request a dream, or vision, in order that they may know whether or not she will face martyrdom (*Mart. Perpet.* 8.4), Perpetua has one. During its beginning, she steps on a dragon, or serpent, who is beneath the bottom rung of a ladder ascending into heaven: "Slowly, as though he were afraid of me, the dragon stuck his head out from underneath the ladder. Then, using it as my first step, I trod on his head and went up" (*Mart. Perpet.* 8.4). Such action symbolizes her courageous vanquishing of Satan.[113]

In her fourth vision, she is actually transformed into a male gladiator who successfully defeats an Egyptian one by stepping on his head. Upon awaking, Perpetua states her belief that she has been given a foreshadowing of her ability to fight and overcome the devil in the arena (*Mart. Perpet.* 8.10). She will be successful not only in dying but also in doing so like a

---

[110]Joyce Salisbury discusses the representation of the visions articulately in Salisbury, *Perpetua's Passion*, 31, 84–90. For the respect accorded to visionaries in early Christ movements in this period generally, see Fox, *Pagans and Christians*, 440–41; Brown, *Body and Society*, 65–82.

[111]See Foucault, "Écriture de soi," 207–22. Elizabeth Castelli elaborates on the way in which Perpetua engages in this activity as a means of identity formation, in Castelli, *Martyrdom and Memory*, 70–78, 85–92, 233–35, 237–41.

[112]Edwards, *Death in Ancient Rome*, 18, 131–34. Maureen A. Tilley discusses the way Perpetua expresses a sense of taking control of her body in her writing; see Tilley, "Passion of Perpetua and Felicity," 829–58.

[113]Stepping on the head of the dragon may be an allusion to Gen 3:15. Frend points out parallels with Jacob's vision of a ladder in Gen 28:12 as well as in the *Shepherd of Hermas*; Frend, *Martyrdom and Persecution*, 363. Salisbury points out parallels with pagan concepts of ladders and the role they play in symbolizing an ascent to another world; Salisbury, *Perpetua's Passion*, 101.

strong and courageous gladiator rather than a lowly criminal.[114] Indeed, later in the account, the editor emphasizes the significance of this event by referring back to it, explaining that Perpetua starts to sing a psalm as "she was already treading on the head of the Egyptian" (*Mart. Perpet.* 8.18).[115] She is contemplating her death.

TROUBLING ASPECTS OF PERPETUA'S REPRESENTATION

For all of the ways in which Perpetua is affirmed as a courageous witness of the faith, however, there are several troubling aspects in her representation. First of all, Perpetua literally becomes a man in her fourth vision. She becomes a male gladiator in the arena, a gladiator who defeats the Egyptian he/she faces and conquers him by stepping on him with her foot. Some modern commentators find the idea that Perpetua might need to be represented as "manly" in order to be deemed courageous is troubling; however, in the cultural context of that time, it is important to recognize, it was a declaration of admiration. Designating an especially courageous woman as "manly," is not uncommon in Greco-Roman texts.[116] At the same time, Seneca clearly thinks women themselves are capable of moral virtue:

> But who has claimed that nature has dealt grudgingly with women's natures and has restricted their virtues to a narrow field? Believe me they have as much force, as much capacity, if they choose, for virtuous action: they are just as capable of enduring pain and trouble when they are used to them (*Marc.* 16.1).[117]

---

[114]Prinzivalli, "Perpetua the Martyr," 128; Frend, "Blandina and Perpetua," 93; and Salisbury, *Perpetua's Passion*, 99–104.

[115]Salisbury, *Perpetua's Passion*, 106–12.

[116]See Edwards's discussion of the representation of Lucretia in *Death in Ancient Rome*, 187. Mary Lefkowitz, too, notes Augustine's emphasis on this: *Women in Greek Myths*, 105. Gail Streete's discussion in *Redeemed Bodies* is also helpful: 21, 26, 130. See also Moss, *Ancient Christian Martyrdom*, 28–33. Another Christian example is in the *Gospel of Thomas*, when Peter questions Mary's worth because she is a woman, Jesus is portrayed saying that he himself will make Mary male (logion114); see Meyer, *Nag Hammadi Scriptures*, 153.

[117]Edwards, *Death in Ancient Rome*, 189–90.

His statement is indeed a defense of women in light given that many did not think of women in this way. Such a statement may seem chauvinistic to contemporary readers, and it behooves us to recognize the inherent sexism. Nonetheless, in the cultural context of the times, referring to a woman as exercising "manly" courage would have been a positive designation.[118]

The second troubling aspect of Perpetua's representation is that she is an exemplar for those writers who make it clear that women should exercise such boldness primarily in the context of submitting their bodies to violence in the arena. As Gail Streete notes:

> When women laid claim to institutional rather than spiritual or moral authority in the church in accord with these same virtues, they were censured for appropriating "male" roles. Ironically, these pioneering women often made such claims with reference to heroines like Perpetua and Thecla, seeing their stories as more evidence of the power and divine sanction of their antisocial behavior.[119]

On a more positive note, women could be praised for their philosophic studies, scholarship, and learning;[120] Jewish scripture praises various women of power, including prophetesses and judges. Some gospels and letters of the New Testament likewise portray women in leadership roles,

---

[118]In fact, Perpetua's courage is represented so positively that later interpreters of her martyrdom are at pains to minimize or carefully qualify it; see Shaw, "The Passion of Perpetua," 3–45. As Shaw notes, Augustine, for example, makes clear to emphasize that the courage of Perpetua and Felicity can be *celebrated*, but it cannot be *imitated* in "Sermon 280—On the Birthday of the Martyrs Perpetua and Felicity." Prinzivalli also notes Augustine's focus on the socially acceptable values of piety and chastity rather than courage per se in his sermons where he cleverly makes a pun on the "perpetual felicity" of these martyrs: Prinzivalli, "Perpetua the Martyr," 139–40. Lefkowitz wryly notes that while Christianity offered Perpetua a chance to separate from the patriarchal values in the Roman Empire, such values also existed in the Christian church, in Lefkowitz, *Women in Greek Myth*, 104. See also Streete, *Redeemed Bodies*, 59; Salisbury, *Perpetua's Passion*, 163–79; Edwards, *Death in Ancient Rome*, 212.

[119]Streete, *Redeemed Bodies*, 11, 10–11, 21, 30, 41, 53–54. For discussion of the parallels between Perpetua and Thecla, see Bremmer, "Magic, Martyrdom and Women's Liberation," 42–44.

[120]McNamara, "Sexual Equality and the Cult of Virginity in Early Christian Thought," 230n14.

depicting them as disciples, apostles, leaders of Christ groups meeting in homes, deaconesses, workers, and prophets.[121] But in some communities, women were criticized or prevented from occupying other positions as role models, leaders, preachers, or bishops.[122] Tertullian, for example, declared:

> It is not permitted for a woman to speak in the church, nor is it permitted for her to teach, nor to baptize, nor to offer [the Eucharist], nor to claim for herself a share in any masculine function—least of all, in priestly office (*Virg.* 9).[123]

Tertullian, of course, elsewhere in his writings complained about women in what he called "heretic" communities who did not follow his rules about sharing manly functions (*Prescript.* 41), including against Thecla, whom he claimed was an example for women to baptize (*de Bap.* 17). Even earlier Irenaeus had complained about a woman in a competing community who participated in the Eucharistic ritual with Irenaeus's opponent Marcos (*adv. Haer 1* 13.2). The scribe of the Coptic *Gospel of Mary* depicted Mary teaching the men and then setting out to preach with them. In fact, both activities are indicators of Mary's apostolic authority, and both are teaching activities that Tertullian opposed in women, as seen in his quote above. Other examples abound. According to the second-century author of the *Acts of Thecla* that is embedded in the *Acts of Paul*, Paul himself told Thecla to go teach (*Acts of Paul* 3.41). According to the author of the *Acts of Philip*, Miriamne broke the communion bread (*APhil* 8.2), was made an evangelist by Jesus (*APhil* 8.3), helped exorcize a demon (*APhil* 9.1–5), and baptized women (*APhil* 14.9); this author also listed male and female priests and male and female deacons in parallel (*APhil* 1.12).[124] The author of the Six Books Dormition narrative about the end of Mary of Nazareth's

---

[121]See discussion in King, *Gospel of Mary of Magdala*, 186.

[122]Gail P. Corrington suggests that there are three main models for women's empowerment in the Greco-Roman and early Christian worlds: that of being possessed by a male deity, martyrdom, and asceticism. She cites Perpetua as an example of the way in which martyrdom could actually have been perceived as empowerment, a means of resisting control, the battleground being the woman's body; Corrington, "The 'Divine Woman'?", 172–74.

[123]All citations and translations of Tertullian are taken from Roberts, *Ante-Nicene Fathers*.

[124]Citations are from Bovon, *Acts of Philip*.

life—a work some scholars suggest may be as early as the second century like the *Protevangelium of James*—which was about the beginning of her life—depicted the mother of Jesus healing, exorcising, sealing, sprinkling water, preaching the gospel, and sending women with writings around the Mediterranean.[125] These authors described these women performing the activities associated with Tertullian's "priestly office" without comment or explanation, suggesting that their readers were familiar with these female activities and needed no explanation. In *Ordained Women in the Early Church*, Kevin Madigan and Carolyn Osiek provide documentary evidence, both positive and adverse reports, that women served as deacons and priests.[126] Suggesting that indeed such female leadership was not out of the ordinary for women in some communities, Ally Kateusz has demonstrated that the two very oldest surviving carvings to depict people inside a real church depicted men and women in parallel on either side of the altar, scenes that suggest gender parity in the ancient performance of the liturgy.[127] This gender parity at the altar has a certain resonance with the parallel synagogue titles for women that Bernadette Brooten has documented in the Second Temple era and the centuries directly afterwards.[128] In some early communities, at least, women appear to have had multiple approved paths through which to engage in and express their care of the self.

Martyrdom, however, appears to have been the most certain means of approval for women in communities such as Tertullian's. In a passage praising the strength of the martyrs, Tertullian uses women for half of his examples (*Mart.* 4). Jo Ann McNamara notes that certain "reservations were nullified when the physical courage of the battlefield was transformed into that of the martyrs."[129]

---

[125]Kateusz, "Collyridian Déjà vu," 80–86.

[126]Madigan and Osiek, *Ordained Women in the Early Church*, 163–202.

[127]Kateusz, "'She sacrificed herself as the priest,'" 54–63, figs. 1 and 2.

[128]Brooten, *Women Leaders in the Ancient Synagogue*, 5–99.

[129]McNamara, "Sexual Equality and the Cult of Virginity in Early Christian Thought," 221. Frederick Klawiter suggests that "in the 'catholic' church woman was 'liberated' to become a minister as long as she participated in the suffering of Christ. The moment she was set free from the suffering of prison, she was placed back into the 'imprisoning' role of female subordinate to male"; Klawiter, "Role of Martyrdom and Persecution," 115.

In the final analysis, therefore, Perpetua achieves high status in her community only through willingly subjecting her body to violence and literally dying. As Peter Brown says,

> In Christian circles direct intimacy with God was so drastic as to incapacitate the recipient. Put bluntly, the "power" of the martyr was unambiguous: but the life expectancy of such a wielder of power was, by definition, severely limited. We touch on a very savage streak in the Roman world—exaltation by violence.[130]

Indeed, "exaltation by violence" is the most effective means to make Perpetua's voice heard among the clamor of patriarchal voices. Religious conflicts were played out on the very bodies of martyrs, many of whom were women.[131]

An admiration for Christian women's patiently enduring or even subjecting themselves to suffering has been evident throughout history. One of the texts of late antiquity regarding the life of Mary of Nazareth, the *Life of the Virgin*, represented even Mary Magdalene as eventually having become a martyr, although we have no reason to believe this portrayal is rooted in any kind of fact (*Life of the Virgin* 71).[132] Some of the women who embodied the best of the medieval Christian mystical tradition—Catherine of Siena, Teresa of Avila, Margery Kempe (known for her emotional weeping), and Julian of Norwich—have also been represented as sufferers par excellence.[133] In modern contexts as well, counseling for Christian women has all too often encouraged enduring abuse silently and patiently.[134] In short, Christian tradition has commonly implied that virtue walks hand in hand with suffering.

---

[130]Brown, *Making of Late Antiquity*, 66.

[131]This is no less true today, although the bodies are often those of Muslim women rather than Christian ones. For parallels between Christian and Islamic women martyrs, see Streete, *Redeemed Bodies*, 7–8, 112–122; Castelli, *Martyrdom and Memory*, 200–201; Fox, *Pagans and Christians*, 420.

[132]Citation from Shoemaker, *Life of the Virgin*.

[133]Discussion of these figures at length exceeds the scope of this chapter, but for an excellent introduction, see McGinn, *Essential Writings of Christian Mysticism*.

[134]The large number of books recently published on this topic with an autobiographical or biographical focus is sobering. They include Andersen, *Woman Submit!*; Hegstrom, *Angry Men*; Heitritter and Vought, *Helping Victims of Sexual*

Furthermore, compilers of martyrdom accounts have often been unable to resist the temptation to eroticize the deaths of the women. The compiler of Perpetua's martyrdom draws attention to the vulnerable nakedness of both Perpetua and Felicity (*Mart. Perpet.* 8.20). In addition, as they enter the arena, they are re-feminized in certain respects. "A mad heifer" is chosen to attack them in order, the editor notes, "that their sex might be matched with that of the beast" (*Mart. Perpet.* 8.20). Feminine modesty returns as Perpetua covers her body (naked just moments before), and smooths her hair. For some, her representation is as much in terms of her propriety as her courage at this point. Notably, in Perpetua's fourth vision, even just after the moment of her ultimate conquest, her defeat of the Egyptian, the trainer who rewards her with the branch granted to the victor refers to her not as a male but as "daughter." Evidently, she is a man no more (*Mart. Perpet.* 8.10).[135] Overall, there is a certain malleability in the representations of women martyrs to which men are simply not subject.[136]

Notably, both *The Gospel of Mary and The Passion of Perpetua and Felicity* represent women in terms of the care of the self as those who have successfully engaged in the therapy of emotions through their relationship with Christ and have received complete healing from fear and anger. In fact, both works portray their main figures as actually participating in practices of the care of the self. Thus, both of the works reflect an emphasis on a larger cultural value informing the social context of the Roman Empire. In the case of Perpetua, however, such courage surfaces primarily in the context of her subjecting her body to violence through facing and

---

Abuse; Madden, *Stolen Beauty*; Maltby, *Confessions of a Good Christian Girl*; and Nason-Clark and Kroeger, *Refuge from Abuse.*

[135]See discussion in Streete, *Redeemed Bodies*, 39.

[136]See Sebastian Brock and Susan Ashbrook Harvey, *Holy Women of the Syrian Orient* (2d ed.; Berkeley: University of California Press, 1998); Streete, *Redeemed Bodies*, 13, 31–32, 38–47, 70–72; Tilley, "Passion of Perpetua and Felicity," 829–58. Edwards also delineates multiple ways in which women's deaths are frequently represented differently than men's, *Death in Ancient Rome*, 179–206. See also Virginia Burrus, "Torture and Travail: Producing the Christian Martyr," in *A Feminist Companion to Patristic Literature* (ed. Amy-Jill Levine and Maria Mayo Robbins; Feminist Companion to the New Testament and Early Christian Writings 12; New York: T&T Clark, 2008).

enduring martyrdom. In the end, admiration for Perpetua must be held in tension with an acknowledgment of the ambivalence in her representation.

The *Gospel of Mary* counters this portrayal strongly by representing Mary as a steadfast apostle who is able to share the words of the Savior and encourage others to face any possible persecution fearlessly but without necessarily subjecting her body to such violence or glorifying it in and of itself. As Karen King summarizes,

> for the *Gospel of Mary* bodily distinctions are irrelevant to spiritual character since the body is not the true self. Even as God is non-gendered, immaterial, and transcendent, so too is the true Human self . . . . *Rejecting the body as the self* opened up the possibility of an ungendered space within the Christian community in which leadership functions were based on spiritual maturity.[137]

Just as our recovery of the texts discussed in Chap. 4 allows us to see the way in which some groups challenged the discourse of a suffering self (both individually and collectively), our recovery of the way in which the author of the *Gospel of Mary* represents Mary disrupts the monolithic focus on the glorification primarily of women who willingly subject their bodies to violence. It provides a refreshing contrast to works implying that suffering must accompany virtue as in the *Martyrdom of Perpetua and Felicity*. This chapter does not seek to minimize or dismiss the courage of Perpetua and other martyrs. However, it is important to put representations such as that of Mary alongside those of the martyrs so that it is possible for us to understand that there can be a fuller range of possibilities for faithful witness.[138] The *Gospel of Mary* advocates courage in the face of persecution; it does not glorify suffering in and of itself. Karen King notes that the work does "not ascribe any redemptive value to suffering . . . . Believing the

---

[137]King, *Gospel of Mary of Magdala*, 88–89. Emphasis added. See also King, "Prophetic Power," 32–33, where King does not necessarily see this phenomenon in positive terms.

[138]François Bovon argues that texts should not be divided into merely two categories—canonical and apocryphal. In so doing, he argues that "an unfortunate polarization among evangelical and liberal scholars occurs." He reminds us that in antiquity, while certain books were considered to be "disputed," they were nonetheless considered "profitable" and "useful for the soul"; see Bovon, "Beyond the Canonical and the Apocryphal Books," 125–26, 128.

truth of the gospel leads people away from suffering by teaching them to overcome the passions and defeat the powers by putting on the perfect Human," and further, "The *Gospel of Mary* does not teach that people need to suffer in order to gain salvation . . . There is no intrinsic value in the atoning death of Christ or the martyrdom of believers or the punishment of souls."[139] The *Martyrdom of Perpetua and Felicity*, however, despite how courageously it depicts these two women, at the same time exalts them as martyrs and makes them female exemplars for other women for centuries.

Reading across the spectrum of early texts allows us to see that there are various ways to interpret the teachings of Christian tradition. By analogy, readers can reflect on the possibility that there are diverse possibilities for faithful interpretations of spiritual traditions and religious practices in a pluralistic world. It is imperative that those engaging with Christian narratives today examine a wide range of possible ways to witness to the faith— by reading the *Martyrdom of Perpetua* along with the *Gospel of Mary* and many other works in order that the kind of understanding needed in a pluralistic world may emerge.

Unpacking "Gnosticism"

The categorization of texts such as the *Gospel of Mary* as "gnostic" has been unhelpful.[140] In particular, it has been virtually impossible to see the full range of attitudes regarding the care of the self in works coming from various groups identifying themselves with Christ. Instead, the discourse has promoted a false dichotomy (or binary opposition) between "orthodoxy" and "heresy." These categories have been inaccurately characterized as consisting merely of doctrinal differences. As discussed throughout this book, the group who emphasized the kind of care of the self (conflating body and soul) that merged with a glorification of martyrdom and morphed into doctrines emphasizing the fleshly resurrection of the body within the framework of an apocalyptic world view triumphed. However, for those in a wide range of Christ movements, the resurrected Jesus was the

---

[139]King, *Gospel of Mary of Magdala*, 127.
[140]Esther A. de Boer's discussion in *The Gospel of Mary* (82–83) is especially helpful. The term "Gnosticism" itself has been called into question. Many references surrounding this issue are provided in Chap. 1.

great physician, the one who could effect healing of the soul in both this life and the next.

If we fail to recognize the importance of the care of the self in antiquity and in the early thought of these groups, it is difficult to recognize the significance of the way ancient writers represent women such as Mary Magdalene and Perpetua. Moreover, if we dichotomize orthodoxy and heresy, we may well fail to see the way in which texts coming from a wide range of groups portray women who identified themselves with Christ as steadfast, self-controlled witnesses for their faith. By using a discursive approach, the past comes into sharper focus, and the voices of bold and courageous witnesses from diverse communities begin to emerge.

Indeed, when we view Mary and Perpetua in terms of this Greco-Roman philosophical emphasis, particularly the Stoic emphasis on the therapy of the emotions, we understand the very positive manner in which the authors of the *Gospel of Mary* and the *Martyrdom of Perpetua and Felicity* represent these figures.[141] By examining the history of early Christ-related groups with respect to the practice of the care of the self rather than in terms of doctrinal debates regarding the resurrection of the body or the supposed value of "orthodoxy" over and against "Montanism," new understandings of the value of these women as role models in the twenty-first century surface.

In texts that have until recently been dismissed, Mary emerges as a disciple and leader due to her steadfast courage, one who exhibits the characteristics of a person completely healed of the passions of fear and anger. In these works, her character often functions as a contrast to that of Peter, one still struggling to overcome these emotions. Just as the rediscovery of the manuscripts discussed in Chap. 4 allows us to see the way in which certain early groups identifying themselves with Christ interrupted and challenged the discourse of the "suffering self" (including the glorification of martyrdom), so the rediscovery of manuscripts that were unknown in the world until they came to light in the late nineteenth and mid-twentieth centuries allows us to see the significance of the way that these writings represent Mary. They completely disrupt a monolithic discourse in which the only heroines of Christ-related groups are those who

---

[141]Esther A. de Boer has argued persuasively that The *Gospel of Mary* reflects the influence of Stoicism rather than any Gnosticism per se. The *Gospel of Mary* should perhaps be seen as *a testimony of creative mission*; de Boer, *Gospel of Mary*, 59.

willingly subject their bodies to violence and in this way, they undermine an ideal in which virtue and suffering must go hand in hand.

REFERENCES

Ancient Works

Acts of the Christian Martyrs
Musurillo, Herbert. *The Acts of the Christian Martyrs*. London: Oxford University Press, 1972.
Smith, Agnes Lewis. *Select Narratives of Holy Women from the Syro-Antiochene or Sinai Palimpsest as Written above the Old Syriac Gospels by John the Stylite, of Beth-Mari-Qanūn in A.D. 778*. Studia Sinaitica 10. London: C. J. Clay & Sons/Cambridge University Press, 1900. Repr. Nabu.

Acts of Philip

Bovon, François and Christopher R. Matthews, translators. *The Acts of Philip*. Waco, TX: Baylor University Press, 2012.

Ante-Nicene Fathers

Roberts, Alexander, and James Donaldson, eds. *The Ante-Nicene Fathers: The Writings of the Fathers down to A.D. 325*. American Reprint of the Edinburgh Edition. 10 vols. Edited by A. Cleveland Coxe. New York: Charles Scribner's Sons, 1903.

Apostolic Fathers

Holmes, Michael W., ed. and trans. *The Apostolic Fathers: Greek Text and English Translations*. 3d ed.; Grand Rapids: Baker Academic, 2007.

Clement of Alexandria

John Ferguson, trans. *Stromateis: Books One to Three*. Vol. 85 of *The Fathers of the Church: A New Translation*. 2d ed. Washington, D.C.: Catholic University of America Press, 1991.

Gospel of Mary

C. H. Rylands Library. "463: The *Gospel of Mary*." Pages 18–23 in *Catalogue of the Greek Papyri in the John Rylands Library*. Manchester: Manchester University Press, 1938.

King, Karen. *The Gospel of Mary of Magdala: Jesus and the First Woman Apostle*. Santa Rosa: Polebridge, 2003.

Parsons, P. J. "3525: *Gospel of Mary*." Pages 12–14 in *The Oxyrhynchus Papyri*. Vol. 50. London: Egypt Exploration Society, 1983.

Wilson, R. McL., and G. W. MacRae. "*The Gospel according to Mary* BG, I:7, I–19,5." Pages 453–471 in *Nag Hammadi Codices V,2–5 and VI with Papyrus Berolinensis 8502,1 and 4*. Edited by Douglas M. Parrott. Nag Hammadi Studies 11. Leiden: Brill, 1979.

Tuckett, Christopher M. *The Gospel of Mary*. Oxford: Oxford University Press, 2007.

Passion of Perpetua and Felicity

Amat, Jacqueline. *Passion de Perpétue et de Félicité suivi de Actes*. Sources Chrétiennes 417. Paris: Les Éditions du Cerf, 1996.

Philo

Colson, F. H., and G. H. Whitaker, trans. 10 vols. Loeb Classical Library. Cambridge: Harvard University Press, 1958.

Modern Works

Andersen, Jocelyn E. *Woman Submit! Christians and Domestic Violence*. Auburndale, Fla.: One Way Café, 2007.

Barnes, Timothy D. "Pre-Decian *Acta Martyrum*." *Journal of Theological Studies* 19 (1968): 509–31.

Barton, Carlin. *The Sorrows of the Ancient Romans*. Princeton, N.J.: Princeton University Press, 1993.

Bergman, Bettina. Introduction to *The Art of Ancient Spectacle*. Edited by Bettina Bergman and C. Kondoleon. New Haven, Conn.: Yale University Press, 1999.

Beavis, Mary Ann. "Reconsidering Mary of Bethany." *Catholic Biblical Quarterly* 74 (2012): 281–97.

Bovon, François. "Beyond the Canonical and the Apocryphal Books, the Presence of a Third Category: The Books Useful for the Soul." *Harvard Theological Review* 105. 2 (2012): 125–37.

Bovon, Francois. "Le privilège pascal de Marie-Madeleine." *New Testament Studies* 30 (1984): 50–62. Translated as "Mary Magdalene's Paschal Privilege." Pages 147–57, 228–35 in *New Testament Traditions and Apocryphal Narratives.* Translated by Jane Haapiseva-Hunter. Pittsburgh Theological Monograph Series 36. Allison Park, Pa.: Pickwick, 1995.

Bowersock, G. W. *Martyrdom and Rome.* Cambridge: Cambridge University Press, 1995.

Boughton, Lynne C. "From Pious Legend to Feminist Fantasy." *Journal of Religion* 71 (1991): 362–83.

Bremmer, Jan N. "Magic, Martyrdom and Women's Liberation in the Acts of Paul and Thecla." Pages 36–59 in *The Apocryphal Acts of Paul and Thecla.* Edited by Jan N. Bremmer. Kampen, Netherlands: Kok Pharos, 1996.

Brock, Ann Graham. *Mary Magdalene, The First Apostle: The Struggle for Authority.* Cambridge: Harvard University Press, 2003.

Brock, Ann Graham. "Setting the Record Straight—The Politics of Identification: Mary Magdalene and Mary the Mother in *Pistis Sophia.*" Pages 43–52 in *Which Mary? The Marys of Early Christian Tradition.* Edited by F. Stanley Jones. SBL Symposium 19. Atlanta: Society of Biblical Literature, 2002.

Brock, Rita Nakashima, and Rebecca A. Parker. *Saving Paradise: How Christianity Traded Love of this World for Crucifixion and Empire.* Boston: Beacon, 2008.

Brock, Sebastian, and Susan Ashbrook Harvey. *Holy Women of the Syrian Orient.* 2d ed. Berkeley: University of California Press, 1998.

Brooten, Bernadette J. *Women Leaders in the Ancient Synagogue: Inscriptional Evidence and Background Issues.* Brown Judaic Studies 36. Chico, CA: Scholars Press, 1982.

Brown, Peter. *The Body and Society: Men, Women, and Sexual Renunciation in Early Christianity.* Twentieth-anniversary edition. New York: Columbia University Press, 2008.

Brown, Peter. *The Making of Late Antiquity.* Cambridge: Harvard University Press, 1978.

Burrus, Virginia. "Torture and Travail: Producing the Christian Martyr." Pages 56–71 in *A Feminist Companion to Patristic Literature.* Edited by Amy-Jill Levine and Maria Mayo Robbins. Feminist Companion to the New Testament and Early Christian Writings 12. New York: T&T Clark, 2008.

Butler, Rex D. *The New Prophecy and "New Visions": Evidence of Montanism in The Passion of Perpetua and Felicity.* Washington, D.C.: Catholic University of America Press, 2006.

Cardman, Francine. "Acts of the Women Martyrs." Pages 98–104 in *Women in Early Christianity.* Edited by David M. Scholer. Vol. 14 of *Studies in Early Christianity: A Collection of Scholarly Essays.* Edited by Everett Ferguson, David M. Scholer, and Paul C. Finney. New York: Garland, 1993.

Castelli, Elizabeth A. *Martyrdom and Memory: Early Christian Culture-Making.* New York: Columbia University Press, 2004.

Clark, Elizabeth A. "Holy Women, Holy Words: Early Christian Women, Social History, and the 'Linguistic Turn.'" *Journal of Early Christian Studies* 6 (1998): 413–30.

Cobb, Stephanie L. *Dying to Be Men: Gender and Language in Early Christian Martyr Texts.* New York: Columbia, 2008.

Corrington, Gail P. "The 'Divine Woman'? Propaganda and the Power of Celibacy in the New Testament Apocrypha: A Reconsideration." Pages 169–82 in *Women in Early Christianity.* Edited by David M. Scholer. Vol. 14 of *Studies in Early Christianity: A Collection of Scholarly Essays.* Edited by Everett Ferguson, David M. Scholer, and Paul C. Finney. New York: Garland, 1993.

Coyle, J. Kevin. "The Fathers on Women and Women's Ordination." Pages 117–67 in *Women in Early Christianity.* Edited by David M. Scholer. Vol. 14 of *Studies in Early Christianity: A Collection of Scholarly Essays.* Edited by Everett Ferguson, David M. Scholer, and Paul C. Finney. New York: Garland, 1993.

D'Ambra, Eve. *Roman Women.* Cambridge: Cambridge University Press, 2007.

Daniel-Hughes, Carly. *The Salvation of the Flesh in Tertullian of Carthage: Dressing for the Resurrection.* New York: Palgrave MacMillan, 2011.

Daube, David. *Civil Disobedience in Antiquity.* Edinburgh: University of Edinburgh Press, 1972.

De Boer, Esther A. *The Gospel of Mary: Listening to the Beloved Disciple.* London: Continuum, 2005.

De Boer, Esther A. "A Stoic Reading of the *Gospel of Mary:* The Meaning of 'Matter' and 'Nature' in *Gospel of Mary* 7.1–8.11." Pages 199–219 in *Stoicism in Early Christianity.* Edited by Tuomas Rasimus, Troels Engberg-Pedersen, and Ismo Dunderberg. Grand Rapids: Baker Academic, 2010.

De Labriolle, P. *La crise montaniste.* Paris, 1913.

De Ste. Croix, G. E. M. *Papers by De Ste. Croix: Christian Persecution, Martyrdom, and Orthodoxy.* Edited by Michael Whitby and Joseph Streeter. Oxford: Oxford University Press, 2006.

Denzey, Nicola. "Facing the Beast: Justin, Christian Martyrdom, and Freedom of the Will." Pages 176–198 in *Stoicism in Early Christianity.* Edited by Tuomas Rasimus, Troels Engberg-Pedersen, and Ismo Dunderberg. Grand Rapids: Baker Academic, 2010.

Dixon, Sandra. *Reading Roman Women: Sources, Genres, and Real Life.* London: Duckworth, 2001.

Droge, Arthur J., and James D. Tabor, *A Noble Death: Suicide and Martyrdom among Christians and Jews in Antiquity.* San Francisco: HarperSanFrancisco, 1972.

Edwards, Catharine. *Death in Ancient Rome.* New Haven, Conn.: Yale University Press, 2007.

Foucault, Michel. *The Courage of Truth. Lectures at the Collège de France 1983–84.* Edited by Frédéric Gros. Translated by Graham Burchell. New York: Picador, 2011.

Foucault, Michel. "L'écriture de soi." *Corps écrit* 5, "L'autoportrait" (February 1983): 3–23. Translated as "Self Writing" by Paul Rabinow in Foucault, *Ethics, Subjectivity and Truth.* Vol. 1 of *Essential Works of Foucault, 1954–1984,* 207–22. New York: New Press, 1994.

Foucault, Michel. *The Government of Self and Others: Lectures at the Collège de France 1982–83.* Edited by Frédéric Gros. Translated by Graham Burchell. New York: Picador, 2008.

Foucault, Michel. *The Hermeneutics of the Subject: Lectures at the Collège de France 1981–82.* Edited by Frédéric Gros. Translated by Graham Burchell. New York: Picador, 2005.

Fox, Robin Lane. *Pagans and Christians.* New York: Knopf, 1987.

Frend, W. H. C. "Blandina and Perpetua: Two Early Christian Heroines." Pages 87–97 in *Women in Early Christianity.* Edited by David M. Scholer. Vol. 14 of *Studies in Early Christianity: A Collection of Scholarly Essays.* Edited by Everett Ferguson, David M. Scholer, and Paul C. Finney. New York: Garland, 1993.

Frend, W. H. C. *Martyrdom and Persecution in the Early Church: A Study of a Conflict from the Maccabees to Donatus. 1965.* Repr., Cambridge: James Clarke, 2008.

Goehring, James E. "Libertine or Liberated: Women in the So-Called Libertine Gnostic Communities." Pages 329–44 in *Images of the Feminine in Gnosticism.* Edited by Karen L. King. Philadelphia: Fortress, 1988. Repr. pages 183–98 in *Women in Early Christianity.* Edited by David M. Scholer. Vol. 14 of *Studies in Early Christianity: A Collection of Scholarly Essays.* Edited by Everett Ferguson, David M. Scholer, and Paul C. Finney. New York: Garland, 1993.

Hadot, Pierre. *Philosophy as a Way of Life: Spiritual Exercises from Socrates to Foucault.* Edited by Arnold I. Davidson. Translated by Michael Chase. Oxford: Blackwell, 1995.

Hartenstein, Judith. *Die Zweite Lehre: Erscheinungen des Auferstandenen als Rahmenerzählungen frühchristlicher Dialog.* Texte und Untersuchungen zur Geschichte der altchristlichen Literatur 146. Berlin: Akademie, 2000.

Haskins, Susan. *Mary Magdalene: Myth and Metaphor.* New York: Harcourt Brace, 1993.

Hegstrom, Paul. *Angry Men and the Women Who Love Them: Breaking the Cycle of Physical and Emotional Abuse.* Kansas City: Beacon Hill, 2004.

Heitritter, Lynn, and Jeannette Vought. *Helping Victims of Sexual Abuse: A Sensitive Biblical Guide for Counselors, Victims, and Families.* Minneapolis: Bethany House, 2006.

Jensen, Anne. *God's Self-Confident Daughters: Early Christianity and the Liberation of Women.* Translated by O. C. Dean. Louisville, Westminster John Knox, 1996.

Kateusz, Ally. "Collyridian Déjà Vu: The Trajectory of Redaction of the Markers of Mary's Liturgical Leadership." *Journal of Feminist Studies in Religion* 29.2 (Fall 2013): 75–92.

Kateusz, Ally. "'She sacrificed herself as the priest': Early Christian Female and Male Co-Priests." *Journal of Feminist Studies in Religion* 33.1 (Spring 2017): 45–67.

King, Karen L. "Gospel of Mary Magdalene." Pages 601–34 in *A Feminist Commentary*. Vol. 2 of *Searching the Scriptures*. Edited by Elisabeth Schüssler Fiorenza. New York: Crossroad, 1994.

King, Karen L. "Prophetic Power and Women's Authority: The Case of the *Gospel of Mary* Magdalene." Pages 21–41 in *Women Preachers and Prophets through Two Millennia of Christianity*. Edited by Beverly M. Kienzle and Pamela J. Walker. Berkeley: University of California Press, 1998.

King, Karen L. *What Is Gnosticism?* Cambridge: Belknap Press of Harvard University, 2003.

Klawiter, Frederick C. "The Role of Martyrdom and Persecution in Developing the Priestly Authority of Women in Early Christianity: A Case Study of Montanism." *Church History* 49 (1980): 251–61. Repr. pages 105–15 in *Women in Early Christianity*. Edited by David M. Scholer. Vol. 14 of *Studies in Early Christianity: A Collection of Scholarly Essays*. Edited by Everett Ferguson, David M. Scholer, and Paul C. Finney. New York: Garland, 1993.

Koester, Helmut. *Ancient Christian Gospels: Their History and Development*. Philadelphia: Trinity, 1990.

Lefkowitz, Mary R. "The Motivations for St. Perpetua's Martyrdom." *Journal of the American Academy of Religion* 44.3 (1976): 417–21.

Lefkowitz, Mary R. *Women in Greek Myth*. Baltimore, Md.: Johns Hopkins University Press, 1986.

Lefkowitz, Mary R. and Maureen B. Fant. *Women's Life in Greece and Rome: A Source Book in Translation*. 2d ed. Baltimore, Md.: Johns Hopkins University Press, 1992.

Long, A. A., and D. N. Sedley. *The Hellenistic Philosophers*. Vol. 1. Cambridge: Cambridge University Press, 1987.

Luttikhuizen, G. P. "The Evaluation of the Teaching of Jesus in Christian Gnostic Revelation Dialogues." *Novum Testamentum* 30 (1988): 158–68.

Madden, Amy. *Stolen Beauty: Healing the Scars of Childhood Abuse*. Minneapolis: Syren Book, 2007.

Madigan, Kevin and Carolyn Osiek, translators. *Ordained Women in the Early Church: A Documentary* History. Baltimore, MD: John Hopkins University Press, 2011.

Maltby, Tammy. *Confessions of a Good Christian Girl: The Secrets Women Keep and the Grace That Saves Them*. Nashville: Thomas Nelson, 2007.

Marjanen, Antti. *The Woman Jesus Loved: Mary Magdalene in the Nag Hammadi and Related Documents*. Nag Hammadi Manichaean Studies 40. Leiden: Brill, 1996.

Markschies, Christoph. *Gnosis: An Introduction*. Translated by John Bowden. London: T&T Clark, 2003.

Markschies, Christoph. "Lehrer, Schüler, Schule: Zur Bedeutung einer Institution für das antike Christentum." Pages 97–120 in *Religiöse Vereine in der römischen Antike. Untersuchungen zu Organization, Ritual und Raumordnung*. Edited by Ulrike Egelhaaf-Gaiser and Alfred Schäfer. Tübingen: Mohr Siebeck, 2002.

McGinn, Bernard, ed. *The Essential Writings of Christian Mysticism*. New York: Random House, 2006.

McNamara, Jo Ann. "Sexual Equality and the Cult of Virginity in Early Christian Thought." Pages 219–32 in *Women in Early Christianity*. Edited by David M. Scholer. Vol. 14 of *Studies in Early Christianity: A Collection of Scholarly Essays*. Edited by Everett Ferguson, David M. Scholer, and Paul C. Finney. New York: Garland, 1993.

Middleton, Paul. *Radical Martyrdom and Cosmic Conflict in Early Christianity*. Edited by Mark Goodacre. Library of New Testament Studies 307. London: T&T Clark, 2006.

Mohri, Erika. *Maria Magdalena: Frauenbilder in Evangelientexten des 1. bis 3. Jahrhunderts*. Marburg: N. G. Elwert, 2000.

Moss, Candida R. *The Other Christs: Imitating Jesus in Ancient Christian Ideologies of Martyrdom*. New York: Oxford University Press, 2010.

Moss, Candida R. *Ancient Christian Martyrdom: Diverse Practices, Theologies, and Traditions*. New Haven, Conn.: Yale University Press, 2012.

Nason-Clark, Nancy, and Catherine Clark Kroeger. *Refuge from Abuse: Healing and Hope for Abused Christian Women*. Downers Grove, Ill.: Intervarsity Press, 2004.

Nussbaum, Martha. "The Stoics on the Extirpation of the Passions." *Apeiron* 20 (1987): 129–77.

Pasquier, Anne. *L'Évangile selon Marie*. Bibliothèque copte de Nag Hammadi, Section "Textes" 10. Québec: Les Presses de Université Laval, 1983.

Rasimus, Tuomas, Troels Engberg-Pedersen and Ismo Dunderberg, eds. *Stoicism in Early Christianity*. Grand Rapids: Baker Academic, 2010.

Rouselle, Aline. *Porneia: On Desire and the Body in Antiquity*. Translated by Felicia Pheasant. New York: Basil Blackwell, 1988.

Ruether, Rosemary R. "Misogynism and Virginal Feminism in the Early Church." Pages 150–83 in *Religion and Sexism*. New York: Simon and Schuster, 1974. Repr. 262–95 in *Women in Early Christianity*. Edited by David M. Scholer. Vol. 14 of *Studies in Early Christianity: A Collection of Scholarly Essays*. Edited by Everett Ferguson, David M. Scholer, and Paul C. Finney. New York: Garland, 1993.

Perkins, Judith. *The Suffering Self: Pain and Narrative Representation in the Early Christian Era*. New York: Routledge, 1995.

Perkins, Pheme. *The Gnostic Dialogue: The Early Church and the Crisis of Gnosticism.* New York: Paulist Press, 1980.

Petersen, Silke. *"Zerstört die Werke der Weiblichkeit!": Maria Magdalena, Salome und andere Jüngerinnen Jesu in christlich-gnostischen Schriften.* Nag Hammadi Manichaean Studies 48. Edited by S. Emmel and H. J. Klimkeit. Leiden: Brill, 1999.

Prinzivalli, Emanuela. "Perpetua the Martyr." Pages 118–40, 221–25 in *Roman Women.* Edited by Augusto Fraschetti. Translated by Linda Lappin. Chicago: University of Chicago Press, 2001.

Puech, Henri-Charles, and Beate Blatz. "The Gospel of Mary." Pages 391–95 in *Gospels and Related Writings.* Vol. 1 of *New Testament Apocrypha.* Rev. ed. Edited by Wilhelm Schneemelcher. Translated and edited by R. McL. Wilson. Cambridge: James Clarke, 1991.

Salisbury, Joyce. *Perpetua's Passion: The Death and Memory of a Young Roman Woman.* New York: Routledge, 1997.

Schaberg, Jane. "How Mary Magdalene Became a Whore: Mary Magdalene Is in Fact the Primary Witness to the Fundamental Data of Early Christian Faith." *Bible Review* 8 (1992): 30–37, 51–52.

Schaberg, Jane. *The Resurrection of Mary Magdalene: Legends, Apocrypha, and the Christian Testament.* New York: Continuum, 2002.

Schüssler Fiorenza, Elisabeth. *In Memory of Her: A Feminist Theological Reconstruction of Christian Origins.* Tenth-anniversary edition. New York: Crossroad, 2004.

Scott, James. *Domination and the Arts of Resistance: Hidden Transcripts.* New Haven, Conn.: Yale University Press, 1990.

Shaw, Brent D. "The *Passion of Perpetua*—Christian Women Martyred in Carthage in A.D. 203." *Past and Present* 139 (May 1993): 3–45.

Shelton, Jo-Ann. *As the Romans Did: A Sourcebook in Roman Social History.* Oxford: Oxford University Press, 1988.

Shoemaker, Stephen J. *Mary in Early Christian Faith and Devotion.* New Haven: Yale University Press, 2016.

Shoemaker, Stephen J. *The Life of the Virgin.* New Haven: Yale University Press, 2012.

Streete, Gail P. C. *Redeemed Bodies: Women Martyrs in Early Christianity.* Louisville, Ky.: Westminster John Knox, 2009.

Tardieu, Michel. *Écrits gnostiques: Codex de Berlin.* Paris: Les Éditions du Cerf, 1984.

Taussig, Hal, ed. "An Introduction to the Gospel of Mary." Pages 217–223 in *A New New Testament: A Bible for the Twenty-First Century Combining Traditional and Newly Discovered Texts.* Boston: Houghton Mifflin Harcourt, 2013.

Tite, Philip L. "Voluntary Martyrdom and Gnosticism." Paper presented at the annual meeting of the SBL, Chicago, November 17, 2012.

Till, W. C. *Die gnostischen Schriften des koptischen Papyrus Berolinensis 8502: Zweite, erweiterte Auflage bearbeitet von Hans-Martin Schenke.* Texte und Untersuchungen 60. Berlin: Akademie Verlag, 1972.

Tilley, Maureen A. "The Passion of Perpetua and Felicity." Pages 829–58 in *A Feminist Commentary.* Vol. 2 of *Searching the Scriptures.* Edited by Elisabeth Schüssler Fiorenza. New York: Crossroad, 1994.

Torjesen, Karen, and Virginia Burrus. "Household Management and Women's Authority." Pages 53–87 of *When Women Were Priests.* Edited by Karen Torjesen. San Francisco: HarperSanFrancisco, 1993.

Tuckett, Christopher M. *The Gospel of Mary.* Oxford: Oxford University Press, 2007.

Williams, Michael A. *The Immovable Race: A Gnostic Designation and the Theme of Stability in Late Antiquity.* Nag Hammadi Studies 29. Leiden: Brill, 1985.

Williams, Michael A. *"Rethinking Gnosticism": An Argument for Dismantling a Dubious Category.* Princeton, N.J.: Princeton University Press, 1996.

Wilson, R. McL. "The New Testament and the Gnostic *Gospel of Mary.*" *New Testament Studies* 3 (1957): 236–43.

CHAPTER 6

The Two Poles of Parrhēsia
and Concluding Remarks

In concluding this book, I want to examine closely the last two hours of lectures that Foucault gave at the Collège de France shortly before he died. In these two hours, Foucault pointed out the direction he wanted to take up in a next year of study that was never to happen.[1] These two lectures help us fully unpack the way in which a specific practice of the care of the self, *parrhēsia*, is at the heart of differing views of the proper care of the self in early Christ movements as its meaning shifts over time. In tracing this evolution, it is possible to see that debates are centered on a difference regarding practice rather than doctrinal disputes per se. Foucault also shows that over subsequent centuries, this concept eventually comes to signify something totally opposite to its original meaning when used in the Christian tradition.

On this last day of his lectures, Foucault carefully qualified his remarks, saying that he did not have all the details worked out.[2] However, he pointed to a mixture of the Cynic care of the self and Platonic metaphysics, using a work of Epictetus to illustrate his points. Foucault said that for the Cynics, the care of the self was "a coupling" of two relationships. These

---

[1] These are the last two hours of lectures that are transcribed in Foucault, *Courage of Truth*, 307–342. I quote at length from them in this section because Foucault so carefully traces the way in which the practice of *parrhēsia*, an important part of taking care of oneself, undergoes several transmutations, and this discussion is crucial to my own thesis.

[2] Foucault, *Courage of Truth*, 317.

© The Author(s) 2017
D. Niederer Saxon, *The Care of the Self in Early Christian Texts*,
The Bible and Cultural Studies, DOI 10.1007/978-3-319-64750-0_6

two are (1) the constant vigilance one practices in relationship to oneself that focuses on adopting another way of living in this world combined with (2) the role of supervising others and pointing out to them how they must take care of themselves. The verb that Epictetus uses is *episkopein*, and Foucault says that "Cynics are the episcopes of others."[3] Graham Burchell, the translator of Foucault's work, provides this definition of an episcope:

> an instrument for projecting enlarged images of opaque objects onto a screen by means of reflection, or an optical instrument employing mirrors used for observation in armed vehicles. In English, episcope is also the pastoral supervision exercised by a bishop. Foucault seems here to be giving the word the meaning of inspector, supervisor, overseer.[4]

Foucault goes on to describe the way that the Cynics point others to transforming one's own self, altering the relation that one has with one's self as it were, in order to change this world. If this change occurs within individuals, the world can "get back to its truth."[5] In other words, it is not about hoping to get to another world beyond this one, a world that one goes to after dying, but rather, it is about those who inhabit this world here and now living in such a way that the world will return to functioning as it should.

Foucault points out, then, that although Cynicism has not contributed much to "philosophical doctrine," it has shaped the concept of how to *live* philosophically for centuries.[6] Of course, throughout the last three years of the lectures, he had pointed out the way in which philosophical doctrine evolved into the basis of support for Scholasticism. Later, this doctrine became completely separated from living life philosophically with the advent of the "Cartesian moment," but here he seems to be saying that the idea of living philosophically that one does find in Christianity at least in some respects comes from this coupling, this whole new way of thinking about the care of the self.

---

[3]Foucault, *Courage of Truth*, 311–312.

[4]Foucault, *Courage of Truth*, 312.

[5]Foucault, *Courage of Truth*, 315.

[6]Foucault, *Courage of Truth*, 315. This part is in the manuscript of his lecture rather than in the lecture he actually gave, a manuscript to which his translator fortunately had access.

However, there is one *other* important shift or major difference in the conception of self-care as it becomes intertwined with Christianity, or what will become its dominant form that is then anachronistically seen as *the* "Christianity" of the first three centuries. This shift is one of the "master strokes of Christianity"—linking the idea of living in a whole different way here on earth ("an other life" or *une vie autre*) as the "true life" with the idea that when one dies, one is able to have access to a world other than this one (*l'autre monde*). In addition, Christianity makes one other major adaptation—something that is not a part of either the Cynic or the Platonic notion of the care of the self. This change involves linking the care of the self to the concept of obedience. One thinks of God as the master and oneself as the slave, or servant, of God. This also includes obedience and complete submission to the authority of those who are said to be God's representatives here in this world. Participating in "an other life" here and now and, upon death, the "true life" of the other world both rest on this principle.[7] In other words, Foucault maintains that there is a "pinning together" of "a Platonic sense with a Christian sense that will play a crucial role in Christian asceticism and ideas of complete obedience."[8] This linking results in a whole new kind of way of relating to one's self, a new kind of power structure, and "a different regime of truth."[9] I cannot help but note here that obedience will eventually include the recitation of the creed—a creed that has an interpretation of *pistis* as "belief"—belief in certain propositions—built into it. The translation and understanding of *pistis* as "loyalty", "trust," or "confidence," which characterized the relationship of Jesus to God and of Jesus to others, will be overshadowed.

Here, we begin to think of the way in which the discourse of martyrdom—the idea that enduring the whole process of becoming a martyr as well as the final act of dying itself—assures one of entering another world (*l'autre monde*). We also begin to consider the way in which the renunciation of self is expressed in thinkers like Clement of Alexandria. In this view, one begins to conceive of the fleshly body as shameful, and one's care of the self involves working toward purification of one's body and soul through baptism and a life in the community of the church. This, too, involves the supervision of

---

[7]Foucault, *Courage of Truth*, 319–320.
[8]Foucault, *Courage of Truth*, 320.
[9]Foucault, *Courage of Truth*, 320–321.

one's care of the self through the bishops, who are episcopes as described above.[10] What will become important in order to truly go about the care of the self in coming centuries is the practice of *confession* in which the care of the self is arbitrated completely through ecclesiastical authority. Even in the first and second centuries in texts such as the *Letters of Ignatius*, Ignatius insists that one must do nothing without the bishop being present.[11] Most importantly, the idea that the care of the self is arbitrated through ecclesiastical authority—an authority granted only to men in the Church that will come to exist—will become unquestioned by most, and those who engage in a form of self-care outside the church's purview will often be deemed "heretics."

However, in several texts we have examined in this book, the *Gospel of Mary* being the most striking example, a Christian care of the self does not involve the renunciation of the flesh. In addition, the care of the self is *not* mediated by outside authority. In fact, in the *Gospel of Mary*, the Savior specifically says that there is no such thing as sin except in the form of acting in accord with a force contrary to nature (*GMary* 3.3–4). This could refer to the "nature" of Stoic monism in which all that comes forth is good, the nature of creation in Jewish thought in which God declares that all that has been created is good (Genesis 1:31), or both. At the time that the *Gospel of Mary* is written in the second century, Augustine's notion of

---

[10]Harry Maier discusses the care of the self as the renunciation of the flesh in his article about Clement of Alexandria's view of self-care mentioned earlier. See Maier, *Clement of Alexandria and the Care of the Self,* 719–745.

[11]For example, as mentioned in Chap. 3, Ignatius emphatically thunders: You must all follow the bishop as Jesus Christ followed the Father, and follow the council of presbyters as you would the apostles; respect the deacons as the commandment of God. Let no one do anything that has to do with the church without the bishop. Only that Eucharist which is under the authority of the bishop (or whomever he himself designates) is to be considered valid. Wherever the bishop appears, there let the congregation be; just as wherever Jesus Christ is, there is the catholic church. It is not permissible either to baptize or to hold a love feast without the bishop. But whatever he approves is also pleasing to God, in order that everything you do may be trustworthy and valid. Finally, it is reasonable for us to come to our senses while we still have time to repent and turn to God. It is good to acknowledge God and the bishop. The one who honors the bishop has been honored by God; the one who does anything without the bishop's knowledge serves the devil (*Eph.* 8.1–9.1); see Holmes, *Apostolic Fathers.*

original sin, a sin actually physically inherited by all due to the sin of Adam and Eve, is still in the distant future. Moreover, the Savior encourages the disciples to "acquire" his peace within themselves (*GMary* 4.1–6) and to remember that it is within their own selves that the "child of true humanity exists" (*GMary* 4.5). Most importantly, they are *not* to follow any other rules than those that he himself laid down (*GMary* 4.9–10).[12]

In examining a text such as the *Gospel of Mary* alongside those of the so-called apostolic fathers, there is support for the argument that what is at stake in the disagreements between those in various early Christ movements are *competing ideas about what constitutes the care of the self*, not some kind of doctrine that was inherent in "Christianity." Rather, authors who will later be deemed heretics appear to be contesting the glorification of martyrdom as the ultimate care of the self while simultaneously arguing for the kind of the care of the self that Mary so beautifully engages in as the practice of *parrhēsia*, or frank speech, when she tells the others that they must not be afraid to preach the gospel, that the Savior's grace will be with them and shelter them (*GMary* 5.6). This *parrhēsia* encapsulates the idea of the care of the self as being free from passions such as fear and anger. Mary is unwavering, in sync with the Savior's own teachings through her close relationship with him, and she exemplifies open-hearted confidence in speaking to the other disciples and sharing a vision that may well come from engaging in certain mental and spiritual exercises that involve "a view from above." This is not a repression of passions but a practice that allows one to develop a broader, more objective, more neutral point of view as a result of transcending the passions at least temporarily. This text alone provides us with an alternative perspective on the care of the self in the second century.

All of this is reaffirmed in the very last hour of lecture by Foucault in which he talks about the practice of *parrhēsia* in the New Testament and in the writing of early Christian leaders (those whom he calls the "Fathers"). Foucault turns to tracing the evolution of the meaning of *parrhēsia* in four sources: the Septuagint (the translation of the Hebrew Scriptures into Greek), the works of Philo of Alexandria, books eventually included in what would be the New Testament, and writings of Christian monastics. Foucault quickly lays out several different uses of *parrhēsia*. One use is

---

[12]All references are from the translation in King, *Gospel of Mary*, 13–18. Emphasis added.

simply to tell the truth bravely, a practice that comes out of one's own basic integrity—being willing to stand up and say what people need to hear.[13] This is the classic, traditional definition of *parrhēsia*, and it appears in Philo's works. However, Foucault also cites Job 22: 21–28 to explain that in this text, *parrhēsia* is not the *practice* of speaking the truth within the context of a situation where one is at risk, but rather an *attitude*: "openness of heart, the transparency of the soul which offers itself to God's sight."[14] It is also associated with a soul that ascends to God. Philo even associates the term with a certain form of prayer.[15] In Philo, there is also a third meaning: *parrhēsia* is a characteristic of God.[16] Foucault then points out that in the Septuagint, in Proverbs, "Wisdom cries out in the streets, She raises her voice in public squares: She cries out at the entrance of thoroughfares; at the gates, in the town, she makes her words heard (Proverbs 1:20–21)."[17] The verb translated as "cries out" is actually the verb corresponding to the noun *parrhēsia*. In addition, there is yet another way in which the term *parrhēsia* is used. It indicates the "presence of God," but of a God "who is hidden and withdrawn" and to whom one appeals when one is having problems or suffering injustice.[18] Increasingly, too, *parrhēsia* will come to describe the relationship (even if it is assymetrical) between God and God's creatures.[19]

Foucault then moves to the way that *parrhēsia* is used in the New Testament. There he explains that it has "the connotation of courage, of speaking boldly, but it is also an attitude of the heart, a way of being, which does not need to manifest itself in discourse and speech."[20] The meaning is simply "trust in God, that confidence which every Christian can and should have in God's love, in [God's] affection for [people], in the link that binds and ties God and [people]. It is that parrhesiastic trust which makes prayer

---

[13]Foucault, *Courage of Truth*, 326–327.
[14]Foucault, *Courage of Truth*, 326.
[15]Foucault, *Courage of Truth*, 327.
[16]Foucault, *Courage of Truth*, 328.
[17]Foucault, *Courage of Truth*, 328n8.
[18]Foucault, *Courage of Truth*, 328.
[19]Foucault, *Courage of Truth*, 328.
[20]Foucault, *Courage of Truth*, 329.

possible and by which [people] can enter into relationship with God."[21] Here Foucault cites 1 John 5:13, "I have written these things to you, who believe in the name of the Son of God, so that you may know that you have eternal life." . . . "We have in [God] this confidence (*parrhēsia*) that if we ask anything in accordance with [God's] will, [God] hears us."[22] In 1 John 5:13, the verb "believe" is used, but in 1 John 5:14, the word "confidence", or *parrhēsia*, is used. "Belief," however, as noted above, can also be translated as "confidence, trust in, or loyalty to." I note that through the centuries, "belief" has been associated with assent to a certain set of propositions about Jesus and what one must believe in order to obtain salvation. It is in this very conflation of *pistis* and *parrhēsia* that Foucault locates the turn to the association of *parrhēsia* with obedience.[23]

Foucault goes on to describe the use of *parrhēsia* in other books of the New Testament such as Acts. When Paul first makes contact with other disciples of Jesus in Jerusalem, they are suspicious of him, even afraid of him, because he had previously been an opponent of those who followed the Christ. However, in Acts 9:26–27, Barnabas vouches for Paul, personally taking him to meet with the other disciples and telling them that he himself had heard Paul courageously preaching in Damascus even to the point that Paul's own life was in danger, and the others accept Paul. Paul then engages in preaching the gospel with assurance (*meta parrhēsias*) with them in Jerusalem. Likewise, in Ephesians 6:19–20, Paul asks the Ephesians to pray that he will be able to speak with assurance (*meta parrhēsias*) even though he is imprisoned.[24]

However, Foucault points out that the meaning of *parrhēsia* becomes more ambiguous in the writings of early Christian ascetics. First, he explains that there is a positive connotation with respect both to one's relationship to God and one's relationship toward other people. Specifically, regarding the latter, Foucault defines *parrhēsia* as "the courage

---

[21]Foucault, *Courage of Truth*, 329. The language in brackets reflects my own changing of Foucault's words to be consistent with the inclusive language we use today.

[22]Foucault, *Courage of Truth*, 329.

[23]Foucault, *Courage of Truth*, 329.

[24]Foucault, *Courage of Truth*, 331.

to assert the truth one knows and to which one wishes to bear witness regardless of every danger."[25] Here, he provides an example from John Chrysostom's *On the Providence of God* in which Chrysostom talks about sheep functioning as shepherds and soldiers functioning as leaders because of their *parrhēsia* and their courage (*andreia*). Chrysostom then refers to "courageous boldness" in the face of martyrdom and how it helps others: "Think what profit watchful men have undoubtedly drawn from these examples, seeing an invincible soul, a wisdom which refuses to be enslaved, a tongue full of courageous boldness (*parrhēsia*).[26] Foucault actually says, "The martyr is the parrhesiast par excellence."[27] He explains that *parrhēsia* refers to one's courage in the face of persecutors, a courage one exercises for oneself, but also for others, and those one wishes to persuade, convince, or strengthen in their faith."[28] However, at the same time, *parrhēsia* "is also a virtue with regard to God," or "confidence in God" that "cannot be separated from one's courageous stance toward others" as it is "trust in God; confidence in salvation, in God's goodness, and also in [God's] listening."[29]

However, in the next few sentences, Foucault goes on to say that this meaning of *parrhēsia* will be "obscured," or "clouded over." Moreover, this theme of *parrhēsia* as confidence "will be replaced by the principle of a trembling obedience, in which the Christian will have to fear God and recognize the necessity of submitting to [God's] will, and to the will of those who represent [God]." When that happens, the "openness of heart, that relationship of confidence which brought man and God face-to-face, closest to each other, is increasingly in danger of appearing as a sort of arrogance and presumption."[30]

Foucault then discusses the fourth to sixth centuries when there is, on the one hand, the development of monasticism with its own set of hierarchical structures and on the other hand, the development of the clerical structure. This latter puts the souls of the laity into the keeping of the priests. As Foucault refers to the writing of Gregory of Nyssa, Foucault

---

[25]Foucault, *Courage of Truth*, 331.

[26]Foucault, *Courage of Truth*, 331–332.

[27]Foucault, *Courage of Truth*, 331–332.

[28]Foucault, *Courage of Truth*, 332.

[29]Foucault, *Courage of Truth*, 332.

[30]Foucault, *Courage of Truth*, 333.

explains that within these structures, the idea develops that one cannot save oneself or encounter God directly, "look[ing] on God's face with full assurance (*en parrhēsia*) as Adam did."[31] Foucault argues that "if he cannot have that relation to God on his own, through the impulse of his soul and the openness of his heart, if he can have it only through the intermediary of these structures of authority, then this is in fact the sign that he must mistrust himself."[32] In fact, *parrhēsia* comes to be associated with pride and arrogance in the writings of the monastics. Foucault cites several examples.[33] However, what is important for our purpose is that he maintains that *parrhēsia* actually becomes associated with *not* taking care of oneself in the classical tradition of Greece and Rome. In fact, the very definition of self-care has morphed into an obedience grounded in *mis*trust of self.

Foucault actually associates the positive meaning of *parrhēsia* with martyrs, apostles, and mystics who boldly speak the truth that they have been given and also with confidence in God and God's love. However, Foucault also talks about an "anti-parrhesiastic pole in Christianity" that establishes the ascetic tradition. It involves a lack of trust with regard to one's self as well as fear with respect to God: "Here the relationship to the truth can be established only in a relationship of fearful and reverential obedience to God, and in the form of a suspicious decipherment of self, through temptations and trials."[34] He says that this second pole is the one around which the "pastoral institutions" developed and that the first pole (characterized by confidence and trust in God) has survived only "in the margins against the great enterprise of anti-parrhesiastic suspicion that man is called upon to manifest and practice with regard to himself and others, through obedience to God, and in fear and trembling before this same God."[35] This attitude makes the care of the self in a positive way impossible. In fact, the value of *parrhēsia* is actually *reversed*.[36] In fact, any truth

---

[31]Foucault, *Courage of Truth*, 332.

[32]Foucault, *Courage of Truth*, 334.

[33]Foucault, *Courage of Truth*, 334–336. For more recent work on the care of the self in the sayings of the desert fathers, see Smith, "Asserting Authority".

[34]Foucault, *Courage of Truth*, 337.

[35]Foucault, *Courage of Truth*, 337.

[36]Foucault, *Courage of Truth*, 338.

with regard to the self comes only through "the sacrifice of the self" and submission to authority.[37]

I would argue that in a text like the *Gospel of Mary*, Mary engages in speaking the truth that she has come to know in relationship to the Savior, a relationship that gives her an open-hearted confidence in God. This, then, is *parrhēsia* in two senses. It is the *practice* of *parrhēsia* as bold, courageous speech in the face of Peter's and Andrew's suspicion and mistrust, and it is *parrhēsia* in the sense of an *attitude* characterized by a confident relationship with the Savior. As works such as this resurface, they help us to see that for some early groups identifying with the Christ, *parrhēsia* is represented in this way rather than as renunciation of an evil flesh, self-sacrifice, or obedience to those who establish new rules. It also helps us to see that Mary and Perpetua have much in common in this sense as Perpetua, too, speaks up courageously and embodies a confident sense of trust with regard to her future.

While Foucault eventually may have come to see martyrs as exemplars of *parrhēsia*, some of those in early Christ movements of the first to third centuries C.E. challenged any kind of discourse that even indirectly encouraged those in early Christ groups to *desire* to practice the care of the self as martyrdom with an accompanying *parrhēsia* that glorified it. However, at the same time, the very texts that disrupt discourse that exalts martyrdom do not in any way reflect the lack of courage or a failure to embrace martyrdom that writers such as Irenaeus and Tertullian attributed to "Gnostics." In the *Gospel of Mary*, the question is not whether or not one will suffer but whether or not one has the kind of *parrhēsia* in God that allows one to boldly engage in the *parrhēsia* of preaching the gospel. This is in no way a lack of boldness but *precisely the opposite*. Most importantly, this work and others that have been newly discovered help us to see that there is a whole spectrum of perspectives regarding the practice of the care of the self in the early Christian movements rather than a false binary opposition of "orthodoxy/heresy."

---

[37]Here, I use the phrasing Foucault himself used in another lecture that also helps to illuminate his thoughts about the way that the care of the self becomes transmuted throughout the centuries and acquires a meaning that is at odds with its original meaning in the Greco-Roman tradition. Foucault, "Christianity and Confession," 189–190.

In summary, then, the words of scholars James W. Bernauer and Jeremy Carrette ring true. They say that Foucault's work calls theologians to conceive of ideas in a completely new way that liberates theology from what it "silently thinks".[38] This book has explored one significant way in which we can do exactly this. The history of the early Christ movements can be reconceptualized by thinking not in terms of theological or doctrinal differences per se, but in terms of the ways that various groups identifying themselves with Christ were conceiving of the proper way to care for the self. Using this lens, it has been an inquiry into how our categorization of some groups as "proto-orthodox" and others as "heretical," particularly those deemed "Gnostic," might shift.

The second-century context of stories of persecution has proven fertile ground for exploring these questions in their representation of martyrdom as a process of identity-formation and practice in patiently enduring suffering and even sacrificing oneself. Foucault's argument that "Christian culture has developed the idea that if you want to take care of yourself in the right way you have to sacrifice yourself" is relevant here.[39] In this respect, my work has built on that of Judith Perkins, Daniel Boyarin, Elizabeth Castelli, and others who discuss the representation of martyrdom in these philosophical terms. These scholars articulate the way in which martyrdom became a discourse that emphasized the ideas mentioned above, representing the meaning of martyrdom in a quite particular way and glorifying it. In some cases, the writing by or about the martyrs themselves functioned as a "technology of the self." This process is a kind of care of the self that goes hand in hand with the idea of martyrdom as an imitation of Christ's sacrifice, a belief in a fleshly resurrection, and notions of apostolic authority. We have explored these ideas in the texts of *I Clement*, the *Letters of Ignatius*, and two texts associated with Polycarp.

However, juxtaposing newly discovered, extracanonical works with those mentioned just above has been important, too. Those in a variety of other groups identifying with the Christ (but all too often labeled "gnostic" or "heretical") disrupted the increasingly predominant discourse of the

---

[38]See page 5 of Bernauer and Carrette, *Michel Foucault and Theology*, 2004.

[39]See "The Power and Politics of *Michel Foucault*," an interview with Michel Foucault in the *Daily Californian* (April 22, 1983): 20, cited in Bernauer, *Michel Foucault's Force of Flight*, 180, n. 92, 230.

glorification of martyrdom while simultaneously arguing for the care of the self in terms more consonant with the traditional therapy of emotions. Specific texts—the *Apocalypse of Peter* and the *Testimony of Truth* (both among those found near Nag Hammadi), two fragments preserved only in the writings of Clement of Alexandria (one attributed to Basilides and one to Valentinus), and the *Gospel of Judas* (made accessible to the public by National Geographic only in 2006)—provide striking examples. These writings urge courage in the face of persecution, but they do not frame the meaning of martyrdom in the same way that the authors of the works attributed to Clement, Ignatius, and Polycarp do. In fact, they do not occupy a unified position regarding the significance and function of martyrdom, but rather, they represent multiple perspectives along a spectrum, providing a variety of responses regarding the issue of persecution. As Candida Moss says, "Where fissures appear, they do not, as Clement would have it, break down upon lines of orthodoxy and heresy, or even into tidy geographically bounded models. These texts intersect with one another to make, unmake, and remake early Christianity."[40]

Such an examination also leads us to see that the distinction between elite and popular forms of religion is itself a false binary opposition that close reading of the works reveals. The acts of the martyrs are not theological treatises, but they do contain insights about living philosophically (philosophy as a way of life) that involve the care of the self. At the same time, the texts of the so-called Gnostics show concern for "the little ones," an insistence that none be led astray through false interpretations or promises, and an interest in providing moral exhortation helpful to those wishing to utilize the example and the teachings of Christ for the care of the self. Thus, there is value in reading them in terms of the ways that they complement each other.

Finally, this book compares and contrasts the representations of two important women, Mary and Perpetua. The works associated with their names represent both figures in terms consonant with those who have successfully engaged in the therapy of emotions. The *Gospel of Mary* portrays its main character as the one who has successfully negotiated the path of freedom from the passions. Unwavering in her emotional and spiritual stability, she is able to encourage the other disciples to face any persecution boldly. Both her attitude of confidence and the way in which she speaks

---

[40]Moss, *Ancient Christian Martyrdom*, 165.

courageously are forms of *parrhēsia*. Moreover, she is able to share a vision of the ascent of the soul, a practice involving the care of the self. Likewise, the *Passion of Perpetua and Felicity* represents its central figure as one who is free from the passion of fear. She, too, engages in *parrhēsia* when she speaks frankly with her father. Moreover, she is an unperturbed leader for those imprisoned with her, demanding better food and speaking for all in refusing to wear the clothing of Roman priests and priestesses in the arena. She, too, shares visions, one of which involves an ascent to heaven, that serve to strengthen the fortitude of others. Her ability to remember and interpret her visions and dreams as she contemplates death reinforce her representation as one who is well along the way in the kind of transformation that comes with the practice of the care of the self. Throughout the text, she faces martyrdom courageously. In fact, the portrayal of her death shares much in common with the depictions of Greek heroines who died a "noble death" although these other cases serve to reinforce existing social norms, not to transgress them as Perpetua does by renouncing her family ties.

The work extolls Perpetua's bravery, however, only in the context of willingness, even a desire, to subject herself to violence. Indeed, in some early Christ movements, those in authority spoke against or prohibited women's leadership outside the context of martyrdom and thus effectively silenced women's voices. It is, therefore, crucial to complement the representation of Perpetua's engagement in the care of the self with that of Mary. The portrayal of the latter disrupts a discourse in which the heroines are often those who represent an ideal in which virtue and suffering must go hand in hand.

This book has focused on understanding the conflicts among various Christ movements and deconstructing a false binary opposition between orthodoxy and heresy primarily in the context of the second and third centuries C.E., a period in which the labeling of others as "Gnostics" or "heretics" became pronounced. For example, Irenaeus's lengthy *Adversus Haereses*, or *Against Heresies* (ca. 180 C.E.), dates from this period. However, the implications of the book are also relevant in the context of both intra- and interfaith conversations today. In the postmodern era, many readily acknowledge the limits of both idealism and empiricism, that is, the impossibility of achieving certainty regarding the metaphysical but also the limits of human reason. In addition, we understand the futility of the dry, dead ends of doctrinal debates and the tremendous suffering and injustice that has come by imposing, at times even forcing, certain theological interpretations arising out of these debates on others.

However, the need for a care of the self that will inform our ethical commitments and our collective solutions to the problems of the twenty-first century may be just as relevant for us as it was for the ancients. When we read newly discovered texts that supplement our understanding of the ways in which various groups identifying with Christ adapted the notion of the care of the self to meet the spiritual needs of their own times, both a better understanding of the history of these early groups and insights relevant for postmodern spirituality may emerge. Bernauer, one of Foucault's most insightful interpreters, explains that Foucault focused his work on helping human beings glimpse the prescribed, confining ways in which they had been thinking and break free of the restrictions that certain ways of thought had imposed. He helped us to see that being willing to engage in new ways of thinking could be "a powerful movement of escape."[41] Rethinking the history of early Christ-related movements by re-conceptualizing them as offering competing, sometimes complementary, perspectives on the care of the self rather than a history of doctrine characterized by a false binary opposition between orthodoxy and heresy can be a means of escaping the limitations of prescribed ways of thinking in a postmodern, pluralistic age. Continuing to accept a paradigm in which the history of the early groups identifying themselves with Christ as the history of a binary opposition between orthodoxy and heresy and in which the discrediting of "Gnostics" plays a major role seems, in this sense, to miss a major opportunity for the liberating kinds of thought that Foucault hoped his insights would help others to engage in. Bernauer sums up Foucault's revolt against enslavement to prevailing discourses this way: "This breath of life or force of resistance, this Foucaultian spirituality, bears witness to the capacity for an ecstatic transcendence of any history that asserts its necessity."[42] Such a statement exquisitely captures the potential that a juxtaposition of the voices of the apostolic fathers, the texts of Nag Hammadi, and others bring to our understanding of early groups of Christ followers. We no longer need to buy into a discourse in which "orthodoxy" and "heresy" are asserted as necessary components of the telling of Christian history. We are free to unravel the twisted threads of our past and knit them together in ways that allow for fuller collaboration among various groups in our own time and place.

---

[41]Bernauer, *Michel Foucault's Force of Flight*, 16.
[42]Bernauer, *Michel Foucault's Force of Flight*, 180–181.

REFERENCES

Ancient Works

Apostolic Fathers
Holmes, Michael W., ed. and trans. *The Apostolic Fathers: Greek Text and English Translations.* 3d ed.; Grand Rapids: Baker Academic, 2007.
Gospel of Mary
King, Karen. *The Gospel of Mary of Magdala: Jesus and the First Woman Apostle.* Santa Rosa: Polebridge, 2003.

Modern Works

Bernauer, James W. *Michel Foucault's Force of Flight: Toward an Ethics of Thought.* London: Humanities Press International, 1990.
Bernauer, James W. and Jeremy R. Carrette, eds. *Michel Foucault and Theology: The Politics of Religious Experience.* Aldershot, Hampshire: Ashgate, 2004.
Foucault, Michel. "The Power and Politics of Michel Foucault." *The Daily Californian* (April 22, 1983): 20. Repr. in James W. Bernauer, *Michel Foucault's Force of Flight: Toward an Ethics for Thought.* London: Humanities Press International, 1990.
Foucault, Michel. "Christianity and Confession" in *The Politics of Truth.* Edited by Sylvère Lotringer. Translated by Lysa Hochroth and Catherine Porter. South Pasadena, CA: Semiotext(e), 2007.
Foucault, Michel. *The Courage of Truth. Lectures at the Collège de France 1983–84.* Edited by Frédéric Gros. Translated by Graham Burchell. New York: Picador, 2011.
Maier, Harry O. "Clement of Alexandria and the Care of the Self." *Journal of the American Academy of Religion* 42.3 (1994): 719–45.
Moss, Candida R. *Ancient Christian Martyrdom: Diverse Practices, Theologies, and Traditions.* New Haven, Conn.: Yale University Press, 2012.
Smith, Zachary B. "Asserting Authority: Power Structures and Self-Care in the Apophthegmata Patrum." Ph.D. diss., Fordham University, 2015.

INDEX

© The Editor(s) (if applicable) and The Author(s) 2017   203
D. Niederer Saxon, *The Care of the Self in Early Christian Texts*,
The Bible and Cultural Studies, DOI 10.1007/978-3-319-64750-0

Spirit, 37, 42, 53, 63, 95, 96, 105, 120, 143, 148, 150, 166
Spiritual body, 119
Spiritual exercise(s), 17, 18, 41, 191
Stability, 51, 99, 138, 141, 142, 144, 145, 148, 151, 155, 198
Stable, 7, 99, 139–141, 147, 151
Steadfast, 33, 138, 139, 143, 144, 147, 148, 157, 174, 176
Steadfastness, 141, 155, 159
Stoic, 5, 13, 31, 32, 34, 36, 48, 54, 59, 60, 68, 83, 89, 90, 97, 104, 106, 120, 121, 133, 140, 150, 158, 160, 176
Stoicism, 34, 48, 119, 133, 140, 176
Stoic monism, 190
Stowers, Stanley, 44
Straw, Carole, 40, 48
Streete, Gail, 168, 169
Stromata (Miscellanies), 63, 86
Submission, 50, 52, 189, 196
substitutionary blood atonement, 79, 100
Submission to God, 189
Suffering, 6, 8, 21, 22, 31, 35–42, 47, 51, 54, 61, 67, 72, 76, 80, 84–87, 117, 118, 122, 123, 138, 144, 146, 151, 160, 161, 164, 171, 172, 174–177, 192, 197, 199
Suffering Self, The
discourse of, 22, 72, 121, 133
Supercessionist theology, 24
Surface structure, 49
Syriac, 156

T
Talmud, 24, 25
Taussig, Hal, 149
Tchacos Codex, 25, 94, 117, 118
Technologies of the Self
definition of, 21, 31

Technology
of self-writing, 6, 23, 41, 42, 133, 167
Tertullian, 53, 62, 63, 77, 90, 93, 112, 113, 119, 121, 136, 156, 163, 170, 171, 196
Testimony of Truth, 7, 65, 77, 81, 120
Thecla, 155, 156, 164, 169, 170
Theology
freeing it from what it silently thinks, 197
Therapeuein, 32
Therapy of emotions, 5, 32, 36, 37, 39, 54, 59, 65–67, 77, 78, 81, 82, 88, 90, 92, 100, 101, 118, 133, 137, 139, 140, 155, 157, 173, 198
2 Thessalonians, 143
Thomassen, Einar, 95, 104, 107, 109
Thought
as "a powerful movement of escape, 200
Tinker, George, 49
Tite, Philip, 63, 106
To bear witness, 21, 194
Transfiguration, 68
Transformation
of the self, 6, 20
True discipleship, 38
Tuckett, Christopher, 139, 141, 146
two-natures Christology, 70, 73, 74, 100, 122

U
Unwavering, 7, 98, 139, 140, 147, 191, 198

V
Valentinian myth of wisdom, 90
Valentinians, 62, 66, 89, 90, 121
Valentinus